The Calling of
Katie Makanya

A Memoir of South Africa

Margaret McCord

John Wiley & Sons, Inc.

New York • Chichester • Weinheim • Brisbane • Singapore • Toronto

ISBN 0-471-24691-3

For John and Margaret
with love

∇△∇

Among the many friends who kept encouraging me to write Katie's story, I particularly want to thank Ray and Maggie Bradbury and Bonnie Wolf. Dr. Veit Erlmann and Eileen Haddon were very helpful in identifying the English newspapers commenting on the performances of the Jubilee Choir in London during 1891; Naomi Ainslie made a number of pertinent suggestions; and Elizabeth Johnson spent long hours at the typewriter preparing the manuscript. I also want to express my gratitude to my agent, Julie Popkin, for her continued support.

Contents

Preface　*vii*

Part One

Durban 1954　*3*
1　Uitenhage 1877–1885　*5*
2　Port Elizabeth 1885–1889　*18*
3　Kimberley 1885–1889　*23*
Durban 1954　*31*
4　London 1891　*32*
5　England 1892–1893　*48*
Durban 1954　*58*
6　Kimberley 1893–1894　*59*
7　Soekmekaar 1893–1894　*73*
Durban 1954　*92*
8　Johannesburg 1894–1895　*93*
9　Johannesburg 1895–1897　*109*
10　Soekmekaar & Johannesburg 1897–1899　*128*

Part Two

Durban 1954　*141*
11　Durban 1899–1902　*142*
12　Amanzimtoti 1902–1904　*146*
13　Durban 1904–1906　*167*
14　Soekmekaar 1906　*183*
15　Durban 1904–1909　*191*
16　Johannesburg 1909–1910　*201*
17　Durban 1910–1917　*206*
Durban 1954　*209*
18　Durban 1917–1930　*210*
Durban 1954　*226*
19　Durban 1930–1939　*228*
20　Adams 1939–1954　*243*
California 1993　*253*

Preface

As a child, Katie was so nearsighted that she could barely see the blackboard at school, and the effort of learning to read gave her chronic headaches. To compensate for her poor eyesight, she trained herself at a very early age to listen to those around her and to remember what was said. This may explain her prodigious memory, for she seldom forgot a name, a face, an event, or the circumstances surrounding a particular individual.

She also had an instinctive sense of drama which enabled her to conjure up events long past and by the use of body language and dialogue give them a sense of immediacy, a quality which I inevitably picked up when working with the transcripts of taped recollections. This has led a number of African scholars to ask how much of Katie's life story is told in her own words and how much I may have embellished it.

Most of the dialogue is taken verbatim from conversations as she remembered them. There are a few exceptions. Under the stress of strong emotion (as, for instance, when she talked about the death of one of her children) she occasionally lapsed unconsciously into Zulu. At such times I hesitated to remind her of the language barrier between us for fear of interrupting her train of thought. Instead I waited until the end of the day's session and then asked one of the nurses at McCord Zulu Hospital to listen to the tape and tell me what she had said. Few of these younger women shared Katie's fluency in English, and their translations usually needed some paraphrasing to blend in with Katie's style of speech.

In general the physical descriptions of people and places are mine. Until Katie was eighteen, her vision of the world around her was one of blurred shapes and undefined patches of color. Up to the time she got her glasses, she described what she knew, not what she saw. For instance, when she first spoke of seeing Romohokpa's Location from across a valley, she mentioned that "the little courtyards around the huts were all connected and all the people lived close together." This was very different from the widely separated Zulu kraals in Natal, and only when I travelled to the Northwestern Transvaal and visited her relatives could I visualize the Location sixty years earlier and grasp the shock she and her mother must have felt in finding themselves in such an alien environment. Her comments about England were more pictorial, based, I suspect, on the comments of her fellow choir members rather than on what she herself actually observed.

All the events covered in this story were part of Katie's recollections, but they are only a fraction of the material she recorded on the tapes. In some ways Katie's mind was like a computer in that it dredged up a welter of memories and experiences without any forethought or attempt at organization. A remark about one incident might suddenly remind her of another which had occurred at a different time and in a different context. Consequently her narrative moved back and forth over the years and shifted without warning from place to place or from one group of people to another. The result was a rich, colorful, impressionistic collage of anecdotes. After transcribing the tapes (which took up two hundred pages of single-spaced, legal-sized pages) I wrote my first draft of Katie's life story. It ran to eleven hundred pages of typescript. It took several drafts to pare the material down to manageable size and still retain the essential ingredients of a black woman's life in South Africa from 1873 to 1954.

I am indebted to Lois Goodenough Petersen for the copy of a letter from Mr. Curzon which she found among the papers of the American Board of Missions in the Natal archives in Pietermaritzburg after the South African publication of *The Calling of Katie Makanya*. This letter supports the position taken by the Zulus in Johannesburg who formed the Zulu Congregation in 1897 at the beginning of what was known as the Ethiopian Movement. This was a trend inspired by a growing spirit of independence from the European missionaries which was sweeping through African churches of all denominations.

I am also indebted to Russell Martin, editor at David Philip, Publishers, Ltd. in Cape Town for the verification of the names of individuals whom Katie mentioned, particularly in the years before I was born. Although Russell was unable to trace two women in London in the 1890s, a Mrs. Keithley who supposedly lived in Bedford Square and a Miss Gosling "of the furniture-making family," I have accepted on faith their presence during those years. Russell was also kind enough to have the spelling and meaning of the few Zulu phrases I used checked by Zulu linguists, who seemed puzzled by the name of Katie's husband, Ndeya Makanya. According to Zulu custom, babies were named in accordance with some condition associated with their birth, but the word *Ndeya* called up no such association. However, Katie's grandson, Desmond Makanya, assured me that his grandfather's name was indeed Ndeya but avoided answering any further questions. The mystery of Ndeya's name was solved by a group of nurses and midwives at McCord Hospital in Durban who all agreed that it indicated a premature birth. This narrowed down but did not contradict Katie's loose definition of the name as meaning "a little one." She was always very careful about observing what she called "the courtesies," whether conforming to the polite conventions of an English tea party or adhering to the complicated structure of mentioning or addressing family members in traditional African society.

Margaret McCord
Los Angeles, 1996

▽△▽

Part One

Durban
1954

Katie sits enthroned on a straight-backed chair in my rented apartment. Her rounded cheeks gleam like polished ebony. Her head is crowned with a velvet cloche, frayed at the seams and pulled down over her ears. Her brown silk dress, probably bought at some church rummage sale, is thirty years out of date, and her leather shoes are scuffed. But her back is straight and she holds her head with regal dignity.

'He mentions me,' she taps at the book in her lap. 'But you know, Ntombikanina,' – she still calls me by my African name – 'there are some things he forgets.'

'Different people remember different things,' I reply.

She nods. 'You are very much educated so you know about these things. That's why you must write my story.'

'But Auntie, I can't do that,' I gasp.

'Why not?'

'Because—' (I search for the right words) '— we live in different worlds.'

She shakes her head impatiently. 'Now you talk foolish. God only created one world.'

'I mean we lead such different lives.'

'What does that matter? When you were little you slept in my bed, ate my food, played with my children. When I was too busy to answer your why-why-why, you tied my baby John to your back and pretended he was your own brother. You were like a daughter to me.' Katie's eyes, magnified by her small gold-rimmed spectacles, sparkle with amusement. 'When I used to speak of Margaret, my husband would laugh and ask me, "Which one? The black one or the white one?"'

'But things changed between us after I started school,' I say.

Katie shakes her head. 'They didn't change. You still came to me for comfort when you were hurt or frightened. You still came to show off your treasures or pester me for stories. Even when you were in high school you would come into the supply room when I was having my afternoon tea and ask, "What was it like when—?" And just before you went to America and I was having that trouble with Livingstone, you came to see me in my house and held my hands and cried the tears I could not shed.'

'That was a long time ago, Auntie.'

'Yes, a long time. Yet you didn't forget me. You wrote me letters. You sent me presents. Once you went to visit my brother John in Chicago.'

'Of course I didn't forget you.'

'Then you'll write my book.'

'No,' I say slowly. 'It's not enough to put down all the things you did. I'd need to know what you thought, how you felt. I'd need to understand you. But how can a white girl really know a black woman?'

'Your father knew me.'

'I'm not my father.'

'You are like him. That's why I can trust you. I can tell you anything, even those things you do not want to hear.'

'I still don't think—,' I begin, but at this moment my nine-year-old son Johnny bursts through the front door, tosses his school cap and satchel on a chair and skids across the wooden floor to drop down at Katie's feet.

'You promised—,' he says.

'Not until you've greeted your mother,' Katie tells him.

'Hi, Mom,' he calls back over his shoulder.

'Not like that! A gentleman stands when he addresses a lady.'

Obediently he clambers to his feet. 'Good afternoon, Mother.'

'Good afternoon, son,' I reply and glance over at Katie for her approval. But her attention is focused on Johnny.

'Very good. Now! You wanted to hear about my old ancestor?'

'Yes.' She waits until he adds quickly, 'Please.'

'It was a long, long time ago.'

'How long?'

'When I was four or five. Half as old as you are now. That must have been—' (she pauses, counting on her fingers) '—in 1878. I was standing with my sister Charlotte by the wagon tracks in front of our house.'

Lulled by the cadence of her voice, I lean back against the sofa, listening to a story I have heard so many times I can almost repeat it word for word. I close my eyes and the years drop away. I am a child again, an unseen presence on that African hilltop beside two little girls in blue cotton dresses. Their closely cropped hair frames their faces. Their bare feet scuff up the dust. They are watching a short black man cracking a whip over the heads of two oxen which are pulling a cart towards them. In the cart an old, old woman throws off her blankets.

1
Uitenhage
1877–1885

She looked like a witch.

Her skin was as wrinkled and black as a dried prune, and her little red eyes peered through layers of wrinkles, half-foolish, half-wise, as though she had once known but had long since forgotten the timeless secrets.

The two little girls waited. In spite of the African heat, the younger child felt a shiver run down her back. She pulled at her sister's dress. 'Come away, Charlotte,' she muttered.

But Charlotte grabbed her arm and held her firmly at the edge of the wagon tracks. 'Katie, you stay here,' she whispered fiercely in her big-sister voice. 'Grandfather's coming.'

'Yes,' Katie said uncertainly, gazing down the hill at the short black man with streaks of grey in his hair and beyond him to the old woman huddled in the ox cart. 'But who's she?'

'Our old ancestor,' Charlotte said, tightening her fingers on Katie's arm.

As the cart approached, Grandfather raised one arm in greeting. *'Weu!* I rejoice to see you.'

'We rejoice also,' Charlotte called back.

Grandfather laughed and nodded towards the old woman. 'She gave me no rest. She did not want to stop to eat or even to sleep.'

Still laughing, he lifted the old woman gently to the ground and reached back for her walking-stick. While he outspanned the oxen, she hobbled forward, her bones rattling under her shapeless black dress.

'Hawu, my little Anna!' she said, tapping Katie's shoulder. Her mouth gaped open, empty of teeth, and her voice echoed the faint screech of an owl. Katie clung in terror to Charlotte's hand and again she tried to pull away. But Charlotte stood still, her chin held high, and stared back at the Old One. Charlotte was six years old and she was not afraid of anything, neither witches nor ancestors.

'She's not Anna,' Charlotte said firmly. 'She's Katie, daughter of Anna.'

'Not Anna?' The old woman shook her head in confusion, and suddenly tears glistened in her little red eyes and she wailed aloud to Grandfather. 'My son, the Zulus have taken Anna.'

'Anna's still working her fields,' Grandfather said. 'These are Anna's girls. They'll take you to the house and make you tea.'

'Tea? Yes, I want tea,' she mumbled.

Did witches drink tea and cry real tears? Witches knew everything. A witch would have known her name. Katie's fears eased.

Together the two girls guided the old woman over the clean swept earth, and steadied her walking-stick as she pulled herself up the steps of the veranda and seated herself in Ma's rocking-chair. The evening wind was already touching the hilltop. Katie ran inside for one of Ma's shawls to tuck around the old woman's shoulders, then turned to follow Charlotte to the cooking hut. But those wrinkled hands clawed at her dress.

'Katie, daughter of Anna, stay with me. Let that other one go.'

Charlotte hesitated. She did not like being thus dismissed. But her duty was clear, and after a moment she ran off alone to make the tea. The old woman beckoned Katie closer and stroked her cheek. 'Yes, you are Anna's daughter,' she said. Her voice dropped slyly. 'But that other girl? Who is she?'

'She's my sister Charlotte.'

'No. She's not like us.'

'She *is*,' Katie cried out. Of course Charlotte was her sister. Yet as she looked down at her bare feet and twisting hands, she saw that indeed the old woman spoke true. Her own skin was as black as the old woman's, as black as Ma's. But Charlotte was different. Like Pa, her skin was the colour of mealie tassels just before harvest time.

'But she *is* my sister,' Katie said.

Already the old woman had forgotten her question. 'I want my tea.'

Katie ran off quickly before she could change her mind. When she and Charlotte returned with the tray, Grandfather was squatting on his heels beside the rocking-chair, looking out on the hills which rolled down and down from the house like a great pile of green and red and golden calabashes. He was speaking gently to the old woman, pointing across the hills to other African homesteads, each protected from snakes by a patch of bare swept earth, and down to the valley where the river ran full, and beyond to the red corrugated-iron roofs and green trees of the white people in Uitenhage five miles away.

'Yes, it's good land my son-in-law has chosen,' he was saying, 'and a good house he's built for my daughter.' He stood up, reaching for the two blanket rolls he had unpacked from the ox cart. 'Where do we sleep?'

'I'll show you, Grandfather,' Charlotte said eagerly, leading him through the door into the two-room wattle-and-daub farmhouse.

On the veranda Katie managed to lift the heavy teapot and pour tea into a cup without spilling. As she stirred in two spoonfuls of sugar, she could hear

Charlotte's voice inside the house: 'You'll sleep here in the room where we sit and study and work. The other room has Ma's bed, and the Old One will sleep with her.'

'My tea,' the old woman grumbled. Katie held out the cup but the old woman made no move to take it, just looked at it greedily until Katie raised it to her lips. She drank then, slowly at first, testing the heat, then gulped noisily. Suddenly she sat up straight and called out, 'Anna comes.'

Ma was moving up the hillside, a short, fat black woman with a basket of mealies on her head, and a hoe over one shoulder. 'Father! Grandmother!' she called out happily. 'I didn't think you'd come so soon.'

'Your grandmother was in a big hurry to see you,' Grandfather called back.

'Such a big hurry she even called me Anna,' Katie said, taking the hoe.

'Then she thought the Zulus had taken you away,' Charlotte added, helping Ma set down the basket of mealies. 'Ma, who are the Zulus?'

'We do not speak of them,' Ma said firmly.

'Our ancestor said—'

'Hush.'

But the old woman had already heard. 'The Zulus! They're coming back. Quick, my children, we must hide.' She tried to pull herself out of her rocking-chair but Grandfather held her down.

'We're safe here,' he said calmly. 'The Zulus are far away by the eastern sea.'

Still the old woman perched on the edge of the rocking-chair, wailing in despair. Knowing nothing, yet sensing her fear, Katie felt such a rush of pity that, without thinking, she patted her hand.

'Oy, my little one. You are with me. But I thought I buried you under the bushes.'

'I am here, Great-grandmother,' Katie said softly.

From that time forward until she went away with Grandfather in his ox cart, the old woman would not let Katie out of her sight. Sometimes the old woman thought Katie was Ma as a child. Sometimes she knew Katie as Ma's daughter. And sometimes she thought Katie was her own baby come back from the dead. But whoever she thought Katie was, she warned her constantly against those terrible Zulus. Time and time again she unwound the black scarf from her head to reveal the yellowed bone showing through the matted white hair.

Her thoughts were too mixed up to tell what had really happened. At last one evening after the old woman had been put to bed, and Ma, Grandfather, Charlotte and Katie were sitting on the veranda watching the purple shadows greying into night, Katie asked what the Zulus had done.

'We do not speak of the Zulus in this house,' Ma repeated.

'It's time, Anna,' Grandfather said. 'When the girls are old enough to ask their questions, they are old enough to hear.'

Ma sighed and reluctantly began to speak. 'It was long ago, when your ancestor was still a young woman. In those days our people were called the Mbo and they lived in Pondoland. They were happy there until they heard that Shaka the Zulu was eating up all the tribes around him and was still unsatisfied. And so the men sharpened their spears and made ready to defend themselves. But in that place there were too many trees and streams for the real sport of battle, so the warriors ran to look for a clear field in which to fight.'

Ma paused. From down on the hillside came the soft *hoo-hoo* of an owl, like the mournful echo of a child's cry.

'Go on,' Grandfather prompted.

'Before they left,' Ma continued, 'the warriors warned their women to flee, and leave the children behind so that their crying would not betray their whereabouts. Some did abandon their children. But your ancestor refused. She tied her baby on her back and took her little boy by the hand, and all three hid in the bushes.'

'You were that little boy?' Katie asked Grandfather.

'Yes,' he said. 'I remember very well. Those Zulus passed so close to our hiding place I could see the dirt under their toenails. But they did not see us. They were laughing too loud at a girl who was trying to hide in the river. This girl's head was under the water, but the current caught her skirt and her bare buttocks floated up in plain view. "That is a beautiful sight and we will return when the fighting is over," those Zulus called out as they kept running up the path.'

'So you escaped?' Charlotte said.

'Almost. We crept out of the bushes, but too late we saw one last Zulu straggling after his brothers. As he passed us his knobkerrie swung down, crushing the baby's skull, and swung down again on my mother's head. He ran on supposing her dead, and why she did not die, I cannot say.'

'What happened then?'

'That girl came out of the river and pulled my mother to her feet and helped her bury her poor dead baby.'

'That's why we do not speak the name of Zulu in this house,' Ma said flatly.

'Let me finish,' Grandfather said. He smiled at the two girls. 'We walked for many days until we reached Matatiele. There we found my father with the other men of the Mbo, still waiting to fight and laughing at the Zulus who hadn't the courage to follow them so far. But they were afraid to return to their own country. Instead, they separated, some going to work for the Boers, others going another way to become the dogs of the Xhosas. That's why we are now called Fingoes – because we wandered about in a land that was not our own.'

'Don't you own your land in Blinkwater?' Charlotte asked.

'Yes. But how I got it is another story.'

In the days that followed, Charlotte listened to their ancestor. But she did not wait patiently when the old woman's thoughts wandered away from her words, and bothered her with questions. The old woman thought her disrespectful and more than once told her angrily to go away.

'I don't care,' Charlotte told Katie. 'I'm tired of hearing only about the long-ago.'

For the old woman, however, the long-ago was more real than today and the Zulus were the evil spirits that haunted her dreams. On the last morning of her visit she woke up very excited.

'Katie!' she called out frantically. 'Don't go with him, Katie.'

'Go with who?' Katie asked sleepily.

'That Zulu. That heathen warrior.'

Charlotte sat up on her mat, yawning. 'What's she yelling about?'

'She thinks she sees a Zu—, a bad man.'

'Yes, I see him.' The wrinkled chin trembled. 'Run, Katie, or he'll eat you up.'

Katie slid across the floor and knelt by her bed, for she could see that the old woman was truly afraid. Her fear made Katie herself uneasy and she glanced over her shoulder half expecting to see some hideous, feathered warrior leaping through the door, but there was only Charlotte behind her giggling, and Ma and Grandfather crowding anxiously into the little bedroom.

'Don't worry yourself, Mother,' Grandfather called out. 'Katie is safe with Anna, and now you must rouse yourself. The porridge is hot and the ox cart is waiting.'

The old woman did not speak while Katie fed her the porridge, or when Grandfather carried her out to the ox cart and pulled the blankets over her shoulders to shield her from the cold morning air.

'Go well, Grandmother,' Ma said.

'Go well, Great-grandmother,' Charlotte repeated.

But Katie said nothing because of the tight sorrow in her throat. She could only nod when the old woman whispered, 'Remember what I told you, my little Anna.'

'But I'm Katie, daughter of Anna.'

'Yes, you too, Katie. You must remember.'

Grandfather cracked his whip and the oxen began to lumber slowly along the wagon tracks.

'Even now she doesn't always remember who I am,' Katie said, holding back her tears as the ox cart jolted down the hill.

'I know,' Ma replied. 'She's too old. No one knows how old she is. Only that she had already borne her children in the time of Shaka. You are more fortunate, Katie, because you know your birth date exactly.'

Yes, the girls were indeed more fortunate. Ma was not like the other mothers who told their children they were born in the time of this war or that war. Ma was an educated woman. She wrote everything down in the family Bible. First the record of Charlotte's birth, and then 'a second daughter, Katie, born on July 28, 1873 at Fort Beaufort in the Cape of Good Hope.'

Katie never knew why Ma called her Katie. First there was Charlotte, then Katie, Phillip, Henry, John and finally Mary Ann. Pa was a Christian too, but not in his early years, and he did not altogether put aside the customs of his people. He called Katie by her home name, Malubisi – which means 'Mother of Milk' – because she was born at milking time.

On Saturday afternoons Pa came home from his work in Port Elizabeth and did not leave again until after the church service on Sunday. All day Saturday Katie could feel her excitement building. When the sun threw the shadow of the peach tree to the edge of the chicken run in the backyard, she started listening for the train's whistle and began watching for Pa to round a bend in the road. Then together she and Charlotte raced down the hill to meet him. Katie always reached him first, throwing herself into his arms so that he could swing her up to sit on his shoulders, while Charlotte skipped along beside him, chattering all the while about what she had learned in school that week.

'What did you learn, Malubisi?' Pa asked Katie when he set her down on the veranda.

Katie thought for a moment. 'My seven times multiplication table.'

'You learned that last week.'

'I learned it again,' Katie said stubbornly.

'But you must remember what you are taught one day so you can learn something new the next, or else you will grow up ignorant – as ignorant as I was when I was young.'

'You? Ignorant?' Katie laughed, unbelieving.

'Yes, I knew nothing. I was already grown before I saw any white people. They came into our country and shot us down before we could get close enough to throw our spears.'

Charlotte stilled her chatter and Ma, too, was silent as Father spoke, his voice like a river, sometimes swift and deep, sometimes quiet and shining with laughter.

'So my father called to me and some of my brothers and said: "I've heard these men with straight hair come from the south. Go, therefore, and search out their homeplace and find me some guns."'

He crooked his arm so that Katie could lean back with her head against his shoulder.

'I journeyed many days. When the food I took with me was finished, I killed a rabbit or buck. Nevertheless, I was often hungry and in time I grew thin and weak. But a Boer farmer in the Orange Free State saw me and gave me some trousers and put me to work. One day he gave me a box of figs and told me to take it to the storekeeper in the village some miles away. He also gave me a piece of paper which, he said, would tell how many figs there were and what the cost would be.

'But on the way I wanted to eat a fig, so I took the paper and said to it: "My *baas* says you can talk. We will see how well you talk today." Then I covered the paper with a big stone so it could not watch me, and I ate ten figs. When I was finished I removed the stone and put the paper back in the box. Yet when I delivered the figs the storekeeper grumbled because ten figs were missing and he would not give me all the money that was wanted.'

'Was your *baas* very angry?' Katie asked.

Pa laughed. 'I don't know. I ran away. I was afraid of his paper. I thought it was magic, because I covered it with a stone so that it could not see, and yet it saw and told the storekeeper how many figs I had eaten.'

Katie laughed at Pa's foolishness, but Charlotte did not think it funny that his people beyond the mountains could not read or write. 'Some day we'll go there to teach them,' she said. 'I'll go beyond this place, beyond Port Elizabeth, beyond the sea. I'll go to England to study what the white people are taught. Then I'll come back to teach our people.'

'Ho, miss, and where will the money come from?' Ma interrupted.

'Wait,' Pa said, 'perhaps all this will come to pass.' Always he encouraged Charlotte's dreaming, for God works in mysterious ways and perhaps He would guide Charlotte's feet as He had guided Pa's out of the wilderness until he came to the Cape. There he saw Ma and loved her. Because she was a Christian schoolteacher, Pa went to night school and learned the magic of the papers and the wonders of the Bible. In time he rose to be a foreman on the road gangs in Port Elizabeth and a lay preacher for the Presbyterians on Sunday. Then he and Ma were married. He never found the guns for his father or returned to his people beyond the mountains.

'Why doesn't your father come to visit us?' Katie asked.

'He lives too far.'

'Then can we go to visit him?'

'Some day,' Pa said. 'When you have finished your schooling.'

'But I don't want to go to school.'

'Why not?'

'Because my books are too heavy in my hands. They make my head ache and my eyes all red and watery.'

In this way she was different from Charlotte. Charlotte was never content to listen to what others told her but had to know a thing for herself out of her own thoughts or else find it written down in a book.

But for Katie, words in books had no more meaning than chicken scratchings in the dust. What she learned, she learned by listening – to Charlotte and Ma reading aloud, to the teaching of Mr Joba, to snatches of conversation overheard on the road. In time her ears caught the rhythm and melody of each different voice, each different tongue – the high clear notes of the English walking the streets of Uitenhage, the soft throatiness of the Boers driving their wagons up to the shops, the rippling lilt of the Xhosa language, all so similar yet each as different as the notes of a song. Sometimes she heard the words of the Europeans spoken, heard them repeated by her own people and, in the repeating, coloured and changed until the original sound was lost and a new word created. By the end of her second year in school she could speak English, Dutch, Xhosa and Pa's Sotho.

On their way home from school soon after the Christmas holiday, Katie and Charlotte saw the Redcoats drilling behind the courthouse in Uitenhage. Later when they stopped to rest themselves at the river, Katie listened to the chatter of the women who were washing their clothes. One of them was speaking of the Zulu king, Cetshwayo, who was threatening to drive all the white men into the sea.

'Is there really going to be a war?' Katie asked Pa when he came home on Saturday afternoon. He nodded his head.

'I'm told the Zulus are buying guns from the Portuguese.'

'Those Zulus!' Ma exclaimed angrily. 'Those heathen!'

Pa chuckled. 'You must blame their women. I'm told they are angry because of two women who ran away from their husbands and found refuge with the English.'

'This is no time for jokes,' Ma said. 'Those Zulus are always fighting.'

Despite Pa's teasing, he was not happy about Cetshwayo's war. After church one Sunday he kept shaking his head over news of the British defeat at Isandlwana where the Zulus had wiped out a whole regiment of white soldiers.

Many of the people, however, were excited by Cetshwayo's victory. Among the women on the road there was the gossip of this man or that who had run away to join the Zulus. But within a few weeks there was much weeping among those women, for only a few of the men came back, all of them sick and wounded.

When the church bells tolled out the news of Cetshwayo's surrender, there was rejoicing in the white people's houses in Uitenhage. In the kraals and African farmsteads, however, the news was received in silence. Even Ma felt sorry for Cetshwayo, who was banished from Zululand and sent down to Cape Town to live as a prisoner of the Queen. 'It would have been better for him to have died in battle,' Ma said, 'for how can the spirits of his ancestors watch over him when he is gone so far from his homeplace?'

Pa, too, did not seem happy. He was strangely silent when an old man whose son had gone away and come back with a bullet hole in his chest spoke out in anger. 'The white soldiers were not fair,' he said. 'They made no sport of battle. It wasn't enough that they had rifles and Maxims and machine-guns against us. They used a mediciné also. This my son has told me. A terrible medicine which they sprinkled in a certain way so that when it touched the skin of a warrior it drove him to the river with a terrible thirst. Then, when he drank of that water, he died.'

'Yes, I have heard this too,' Pa said. 'In Port Elizabeth our people are saying "Basibulala ngetyhefu" – They are killing us with poison.'

'But I do not think it was the English who did this,' one of the deacons said. 'It was that Frenchman, Napoleon, because he was angry when his son was killed.'

'I have heard that also,' Pa said. 'But I do not know if it is true. In my daughter's history book it says that Napoleon is dead.'

'Perhaps that's why it is such a strong medicine,' someone suggested.

And so the talk went on and the rumours spread. Bitterness festered, especially among the Christians, for the Europeans had brought Christianity to the Africans and had preached against superstition and witchcraft, and yet they themselves had betrayed the Word by the use of magic potions. Katie found all the talk very confusing.

'Are some of the white people heathens also?' Katie asked.

'I have never heard a white man say he was not a Christian,' Pa said slowly. 'Yet I have seen some in Port Elizabeth whose wickedness would make our own heathen shudder. For among our own people evil comes out of ignorance and fear. But among the white people? Whence comes their evil I cannot say.'

But Charlotte knew. 'It comes from Satan. Those Europeans who are wicked are the messengers of Satan, sent to confuse us.'

'But how can you tell which of the white people are really Christians and which are Satan's messengers?' Katie asked.

'By prayer,' Ma said.

'By study,' Charlotte said.

Katie waited for Pa's answer, but he just shook his head and remained silent.

Suddenly Charlotte was gone away to school in Port Elizabeth – gone with her big-sister knowingness and deep thoughts and whispered stories in the dark. There was nothing left of her except her letters, which Pa brought home every Saturday night – flat words written down on paper about her new mistress and her new school and her clothes which were too tight and would Ma please make her a new dress.

Katie's brother Phillip was now going with her to the mission school in Uitenhage. Their younger brother, Henry, was herding Pa's cattle, and Ma was carrying a new baby, John, on her back.

The weeks passed into months and the months into a year, two years, three, until in time the shape of Charlotte's face was only a pale blur on the edge of knowing. Yet the sun throws long shadows. Charlotte was with Katie still – a vague creature fashioned out of Ma's proud words and Pa's dreams of her future. They talked about her all the time. On a hot Sunday afternoon when Grandfather came again from Blinkwater, they brought out all Charlotte's letters for him to read.

The heat pressed heavily against Katie's forehead as she sat on the edge of the veranda. Grandfather half dozed behind her. Ma's rocking-chair creaked placidly under her weight, and Pa's voice buzzed around Katie's ears like a persistent fly. All this talk about Charlotte made her head ache, and she thought wearily that if only this were another day, not Sunday, she could go swimming in her secret pool, float naked in the cool green water under the silken curtain of the weeping willows. But on this day Ma would never let her go. It was forbidden to swim on Sunday.

She poked her fingers idly through the dust, watching the particles rise shimmering in the still air until Ma's voice jerked at her, sharp with disapproval. She does nothing but scold me, Katie thought, yearning again for the secret pool.

'It's so hot,' she said slyly. 'Even the water for drinking is hot from standing so long. Shall I go down to the river and fill the pails again?'

Ma nodded, unthinking, her attention caught by some remark about Charlotte. She hardly noticed when Katie slipped around the house to the kitchen hut and picked up the water pail very carefully so the jangle of the tin would not be heard on the veranda. Even then Ma might still change her mind. She was very strict about needless work on Sunday.

The sun's glare scorched the hillside, but down by the river the light filtered softly through the trees and glistened on the still surface of the pool. The rich dark smell of decaying leaves mingled with the freshness of growing plants. Katie glanced just once through the drooping leaves to make sure that Phillip and Henry had not followed her, then she pulled off her sticky clothing and inched her naked body along the scratchy surface of a willow branch. She ventured out further than she ever had done before, swung on the branch for a moment in the cool air and then let go.

The water tingled her skin briefly before her knee struck against a jagged edge of rock. She felt a pain like a Zulu spear thrusting up her thigh, and waves of blackness blotted out her thoughts. She flailed wildly in the pool, which churned and gurgled around her. But just as Ma had promised long ago, God was watching over her and He put in her hands a branch to hold her up so that she could drag herself back onto the bank. A snake slithered away into the maidenhair ferns as she lay helpless, moaning with pain and terror, unable to keep from slipping off into a grey emptiness.

The steady throbbing of her knee pulled her slowly back to awareness and the blurred shadows steadied into the grotesque form of a willow tree. Apart from the drumbeats in her knee, her body felt numb. She was more surprised than frightened by the blood spurting out of a deep gash across her kneecap. This stopped when she straightened her leg and clamped the flesh together. The long stem of a vine worked almost as well as her fingers when she wound it tightly enough. She washed the mud off her hands and face and dried them in the air before pulling on her dress and filling the water pail so that Ma would ask no questions. Then slowly she hobbled up the hill.

She knew she had sinned on that Sunday afternoon. And she had been punished. Yet God was kind, for He had put out His willow branch to save her from death. To save her. Her! For the first time she felt God loved her, and this gave her the strength to walk straight when she entered the house, so that Ma noticed nothing.

But even He could not keep her from stumbling on the playground at school the next morning. Her knee began to bleed. When Mr Joba saw bloodstains on her dress, he looked at her so strangely that she was afraid and wanted to hide herself. But he said nothing, only motioned her silently outside, then called his wife away from the younger children. Katie cowered back from Mrs Joba, afraid she was going to scold; but instead she smiled and spoke softly.

'Don't be afraid, Katie. There's nothing wrong with you. The blood is natural. It only shows you are becoming a woman. Just go home and tell your mother. But you must not speak to any men on the way. You hear?'

'I hear,' Katie said, bewildered by something as mysterious in her smile as in the slippery look of Mr Joba's eyes.

She shivered in the hot sunlight and clamped her teeth together to keep from crying out as she walked. A thick stick was lying on the road beyond the school gate, and by leaning on this she could hop along, dragging her injured leg. Nevertheless she had to rest often. It was already afternoon by the time she reached the river, where she could wash her dress and dry it in the sun. She was easier in her mind when her dress was clean, for now perhaps Ma would ask no questions. But when she stood up, the pain was worse than before. After hopping only a few steps, she felt her strength going, and put out her arms to break her fall.

It was almost dark when Grandfather found her. He lifted her in his arms and carried her up the hill and into the house. Not until he laid her down on Ma's bed did he ask any questions.

'How did you hurt your leg?'

'At the river – yesterday,' Katie moaned.

Grandfather pulled up her dress and looked at the wound. 'Yesterday? You did this yesterday? But you said nothing.'

'I was afraid. Because I went swimming.'

'You foolish child. But I must find your mother. She was very worried when you didn't come home.'

Katie heard him calling from the veranda in that high sing-song which carries over the hills, then heard his footsteps returning, the cool touch of a wet rag on her forehead. Soon there was Ma's bustle and her anxious voice.

'What happened? Where did you find her?'

'Near the river. She hurt her leg yesterday.'

'Yesterday? And she didn't tell us?'

'She was afraid.'

'Why?'

Grandfather hesitated and then, his voice pleading, 'Anna, she's very sick.'

'Why was she afraid?'

'You mustn't punish her now.'

'What did she do?'

'She went swimming.' Grandfather sounded miserable.

'Swimming! On Sunday?' Ma was horrified. 'She knows that's forbidden. She needs a thrashing.'

'Not now.'

'What are you saying – "not now"? Do you place yourself against me? You, who would never let me go swimming on a holy day!'

'Please, Anna.'

Nevertheless, Ma was very strict. She brought out her bamboo stick. Katie hardly felt the sting of it across her shoulders. But she could not help crying when Ma washed out her wound with salted water. It was like fire on her flesh. She knew she was burning up. Savage faces leered at her out of the fire, and Charlotte smiled secretly from under her panama hat while she repeated the psalms that Ma had taught them.

'—though I walk through the valley of the shadow of death, I will fear no evil: for thou art with me; thy rod and thy staff comfort me—'

'It wasn't a rod. It was a big stiff branch of the willow tree,' Katie muttered.

Katie felt a soothing hand on her cheek and then Ma's voice. 'Father! Come quickly!'

Katie opened her eyes and there was Ma in her rocking-chair, but she was not on the veranda. She was next to the bed.

'Your chair looks funny in here.'

'Ah, Katie, my child!' Ma began to cry, and still crying, she called again to Grandfather to bring some strong tea. 'And put plenty of sugar in it,' she added.

Grandfather came and knelt on the floor, slipping his arm behind Katie's shoulders and holding the cup to her lips. His face was wise and full of love.

'Drink this,' he said, 'and after a while you can have some porridge.'

After a few sips of the tea Katie was very tired, but there was something she had to tell them though she could not remember what it was. As her eyes closed again, she could hear Grandfather speaking.

'Anna, it is two days now you've sat here. You must get some sleep. I'll watch over her.'

That was what she wanted to tell him. About God. 'For thou art watching over me and I will praise thee all the days of my life.'

It was a long time before Katie was strong enough to walk the five miles to school. In the evenings, Ma talked to her about becoming a woman. One afternoon she took Katie out into the hills in search of special grasses and showed her how to twist them into pads to place inside herself when she was old enough for the blood to come. 'And during that time you must be careful not to speak to any boys,' she warned, 'or else you will grow up to be a loose woman.'

'So that's what Mrs Joba thought when she saw the blood on my dress,' Katie said.

'Yes,' Ma said.

In time Phillip brought back her slate and reader from school and Ma taught her at home. It was easier there. Katie did not have to stare helplessly at the blackboard and guess at the numbers when she tried to copy her sums. Ma wrote the numbers on her slate, and if she made mistakes, Ma explained her errors. And her book was not so heavy in her hands, because if her head ached after reading a few sentences, Ma let her rest before continuing.

At the end of the year she went back to school to take her Standard Four examinations; and, to Mr Joba's surprise, she passed without difficulty.

Katie could not wait to show her certificate to Pa. He was pleased. For the first time he seemed as proud of her as he was of Charlotte.

'Now you too can go to the upper school in Port Elizabeth,' he said.

'Oh no!' she cried out. She did not want to go to Port Elizabeth, because in all the years since Charlotte had gone away she had never had any holidays or come back home to visit. 'I don't want any more schooling,' Katie said.

But Pa did not hear. Nor did he notice the tears rolling down her cheeks. 'Now that Charlotte has won a place in her boarding school, I think her Missis will want you. If you please her, she will give you time off from your work to go to school.'

When Pa came home a week later, he had everything arranged. On Sunday afternoon Katie walked down the hill for the last time. She was eleven and a half years old.

2

Port Elizabeth

1885–1889

Katie dreaded the Edwards' Memorial School in Port Elizabeth, but she did not worry about the job Pa had arranged. When she was very young she had thought the white missionary ladies who gave out the prizes at the annual Sunday school picnics were angels come down out of heaven.

Mrs Hutchinson was, however, altogether different. There was no softness in her. In her house it was 'Katie, do this' and 'Katie, do that' and nothing but work, work, work. At dawn Katie carried heavy pails of water into the kitchen. While the water was heating on the iron stove, she dropped to her knees to wax the floors. As soon as the baby started to fuss, she rushed into the nursery to dress him and take him to his mother before starting the laundry. After she hung out the washing to dry, she left for school. In the afternoons she watched over the baby again until his bedtime. After that, the ironing and mending. She had no rest until Mr and Mrs Hutchinson finished their dinner and the servants sat down together to their evening meal.

Katie was bewildered by the other servants.

She shared a room over the stables with the housemaid, Clara, a scrawny woman who boasted of the pennies given her by the men she entertained in the hayloft at night. Even when Katie pulled her blanket up over her head, she could still hear the wrestling and grunting on the other side of the thin partition which divided their room. Those sounds and the stench of horse dung rising up through cracks in the flooring and the wind rattling the panes in the one small window kept her awake.

The cook was kinder than Clara. He always held back some of those little frosted cakes he made for Mrs Hutchinson's tea parties, and when no one was looking he would drop one into the pocket of Katie's apron. But the cook not only stole the cakes, he also stole extra rations from the pantry to feed the stream of relatives who came to visit him. And when he baked bread he put aside a cupful of yeast to give to the gardener.

Katie was curious about that yeast. 'Do you like to eat it?' she asked the gardener one night. He looked at her and nodded. He seldom spoke. But Clara laughed so loud that rice spattered out of her mouth.

'You had better take our little schoolgirl out behind the carriage house and give her some,' she managed to gasp out.

'Some what?' Katie said.

'Some—,' Clara began, but the cook told her to hush.

After they had eaten and were climbing up the ladder to their room, Katie asked Clara again what it was the gardener would give her behind the carriage house.

'Mealie beer,' Clara said. 'He brews it secretly in the bushes at the top of the garden. The yeast makes it bubble until it is very strong, then he sells it to his friends.'

Katie looked up at Clara in alarm, wondering if she and the cook and the gardener were those messengers of Satan that Charlotte had told her about so long ago. Terrified, Katie crawled into her blankets and prayed silently to God to protect her against such drunkenness, thievery and fornication!

She was as lonely in school as she was in Mrs Hutchinson's house. She did not do well in her studies. She came late and left early. Sometimes she fell asleep over her books. During recess she stood alone on the playground.' The other children knew each other from playing together before the first bell, and never asked her to join in their games. Only on Monday nights when Pa came to see her did she feel herself come alive. He brought news of Ma, Phillip, Henry, John and a new sister Mary Ann. Always he asked what she was learning in school, his eyes so eager and expectant that she told him what he wanted to hear — she was learning something new every day. She had no chance to complain about the other servants because the cook always seated her father at the kitchen table, and stood there listening. If they walked outside, the gardener began clipping the grass at the edge of the driveway where he could hear everything they said.

It was like this for three years. But then Katie's life suddenly changed.

At church one Sunday afternoon, Mr and Mrs Xiniwe sat down on the bench beside her. Mr Xiniwe was headmaster of her school and director of the choir. She knew he was very strict and felt a little frightened in his presence. But he did not seem to notice her, and she was so relieved that during the singing of the second hymn her voice rang out in praise of the Lord. Suddenly Mr Xiniwe turned and looked down at her, his eyes intent.

'What is your name?' he whispered fiercely.

'I'm Katie, daughter of Lange Jan Manye,' she stammered.

'I know Manye. His daughter Charlotte was a very good student and my best singer. Are you her sister?'

Katie nodded.

'Then why aren't you in the school choir?'

'I'm not asked,' Katie said.

'Then report to me tomorrow. We rehearse every day at recess for the big competition between the school choirs.'

From that day forward Katie felt herself among the chosen. All the choir members were eager for their school to win the competition, and when they heard she was Charlotte's sister they were very excited.

'Before Charlotte went away we always won,' an older boy told her.

Katie had friends at last, especially a clever girl in her class who sat in the row behind her. Sometimes they had the chance to talk after choir practice was over. To her, Katie confessed that reading her books and peering at the blackboard made her head ache so, that when she was called upon in class she did not know the answers.

'Don't worry,' her friend replied. 'Just stand up and pretend to cough and listen to my whisper. I'll tell you what to say.'

The competition was to be held in the Methodist mission church on the first Saturday night in May. But when Katie asked for time off, Mrs Hutchinson glared at her suspiciously.

'Don't be ridiculous,' Mrs Hutchinson said. 'I'll not have you running about in the streets after dark.'

'But the headmaster will take me and bring me back,' Katie cried out in desperation.

'No,' Mrs Hutchinson said.

It was not until Pa persuaded her that Mrs Hutchinson finally gave her permission, and then only on condition that Pa himself went with her.

Pa did not go home to Uitenhage that week. He came to the competition instead. The Methodist, Presbyterian and Anglican missionaries who were to judge the choirs sat on chairs behind a table in front of the pulpit. In the pews behind them were the parents and friends and teachers from all the other schools. To Katie's surprise she saw the housemaid, Clara, and the gardener sitting in the middle of the hall. They waved to Pa and pointed to a seat beside them. Halfway through the programme the cook came in and stood near the door.

They were still sinners, Katie thought, but they had left off their wickedness on this night to come and hear the singing, and she felt a sudden wave of affection sweep through her. Their presence gave her confidence when she walked up to the platform with the other choir members. She waited quietly while Mr Xiniwe lifted his hands and the others started their humming, and when he nodded to her to carry the melody, her voice came out loud and clear.

'Like a church bell,' Mr Xiniwe said when Pa went up to congratulate him on winning first place.

'Like Charlotte,' Pa said, looking down proudly at Katie.

'No, not like Charlotte. Not like anyone. Never have I had in any of my choirs a singer like Katie,' Mr Xiniwe replied. It was the first time anyone had ever put her ahead of Charlotte.

Clara was waiting outside on the road with the cook and the gardener when Pa and Katie came out of the hall. As Pa bent down to light his lantern, Clara patted Katie's shoulder.

'You sang well,' she said.

'Very well,' the cook added.

'Everyone sang well, but you were best,' the gardener said. Katie looked at him with amazement. Never before had she heard him say so many words all at once.

She felt a bubble of happiness in her stomach which seemed to lift her off her feet, until it seemed as if she would float up over the trees unless Pa held her firmly by the hand.

A few weeks later Pa arrived unexpectedly one Friday night. 'I'm going to my homeplace,' he announced. 'My father sent a messenger to tell me he is very old and he wants to see his grandchildren before he dies.'

'What about me?' Katie cried out anxiously.

Pa laughed happily. 'You too. We're all going. To Kimberley first. I'll need to earn some money first and I'm told the pay up there is very good. Charlotte already has a job as teacher there. As soon as I sell my cattle, we will go.'

'When you go home tomorrow, can I come also?'

'No,' Pa said. 'There's no time. I've come to tell your Missis that she must find another nurse-girl. At the end of the month you will get on the train and come to us in Kimberley.'

Never go back to the little house on top of the hill? Tears gathered in Katie's eyes. Pa's grew impatient. 'Didn't you hear me, Katie? I said you must tell your Missis I need to speak with her.'

'I'll tell her,' the cook said.

When Mrs Hutchinson came to the back door and heard Pa's news, she was very displeased.

'I can't let Katie go. Not until my son is ready for school.'

'In one month my daughter will take the train to Kimberley,' Pa said, lifting up his chin in that way he had.

'Absolutely not! I won't hear of it.' Mrs Hutchinson turned abruptly and left the kitchen, her footsteps tapping quickly down the hall. Her voice echoed from the dining-room. 'Katie wants to leave. After I've spent three years training her. But she's just like all the other kaffirs. No sense of responsibility. Her father just turns up without any warning and says she has to leave at the end of the month.'

'She won't let me go,' Katie told Pa.

Over at the table the cook began to laugh. 'Don't worry,' he said softly. 'She's just like any other Missis. If we don't do exactly what she tells us, she'll say we have no sense of responsibility.'

'Or call us ungrateful,' Clara said.

'Or stupid,' the gardener said.

Pa nodded. 'She can't hold you here.' He reached into his pocket and brought out some coins. 'Here is the money for your ticket. In one month you will take the train.'

In the end Mrs Hutchinson relented. On the day of her departure she gave Katie a bundle of second-hand clothes to take to Ma. 'Now hurry. Cook is waiting to take you to the station.'

As they stepped out the back door, Clara came running from the stables to hand Katie a bright-red crocheted bag. 'This is to keep your money in,' she said.

Katie held out both hands politely to show that what she gave was not a little thing.

At the bottom of the driveway the gardener was cutting the bushes. As Katie and the cook approached, he reached into his pocket and pulled out two bright new pennies. 'If you get hungry—,' he began.

'I've already cooked her food for the train,' the cook interrupted.

'Then you can buy some sweeties,' the gardener said. Katie was so surprised that she just stared at him. He began to laugh. 'You don't have to be afraid of this money. It didn't come from selling my beer. It's good Christian money. I saved it from my pay.'

Katie smiled and held out her hands.

3
Kimberley
1890–1891

Katie waved to Phillip and Henry as her train pulled into the Kimberley station. At first she did not recognise the dignified young woman standing next to them until she saw her suddenly lift up her long black skirt and run wildly beside the slowing train, more like a crazy schoolgirl than a dignified teacher.

'Charlotte!' Katie screamed, leaning out the window. Charlotte kept running, her steps slowing as the train slowed. As soon as Katie jumped onto the platform, Charlotte flung her arms around her, upsetting her basket of possessions so that the bundle of second-hand clothing toppled out of her arms and broke open on the platform.

'Katie!' Charlotte said, hands clutching her shoulders. 'How glad I am to see you. But you've grown so big, so pretty.'

'You too. You look like a very important lady.'

'I am,' Charlotte said. 'I'm a teacher now and you must treat me with proper respect.' She took several mincing steps forward, pushed out her chin and sniffed haughtily as she beckoned Phillip and Henry.

'Come, children. Pick up these clothes. They look very untidy.' The boys paid no attention to her play-acting but hung back uncertainly. Charlotte laughed. 'You see how important I am, how everyone obeys me!'

She picked up the basket and handed it to Henry, piling the scattered clothing into Phillip's arms. Then she grabbed Katie's hand and pushed through the crowd to the roadway. 'Come on! There's nothing to see here. Kimberley's an ugly place.'

Indeed it was ugly. There were no trees, no grass, no wide avenues, no large brick houses, only row upon row of corrugated-iron buildings. Sweat darkened the khaki shirts of Boers shouting orders to black men unloading the train. Englishmen in dark coats mopped their faces. Crumpled paper skittered along the ground. The sun glinted on the bright-blue flies flashing over wrinkled orange peels, horse dung and broken bottles. Wagons rolled by, fluffing up the dust which settled like an incurable disease on the white, black, brown and yellow skins.

'Yes, it's an ugly place,' Katie said, her feet quickening with Charlotte's. Past the watering trough, past the post office, the butcher shop with its fly-speckled meat, and the general store, and into the African location.

The town around the railroad station was ugly but the location was worse than any place Katie had ever known. Here the iron houses, streaked with rust, seemed to push their way into the road. Broken windows were patched with scraps of wood and stuffed with rags. Few people wandered about in the heat of the day, though Katie heard a mumble of voices behind the walls, the whimpering of children, a quick burst of laughter. Occasionally from an open door a shrill voice called out a greeting to Charlotte, who waved and hurried on as if she did not notice the stink of urine, garbage, and stale smoke.

'Is this where we live?' Katie gasped. 'Everything's so— I want to vomit.'

Charlotte stopped suddenly, turning to face her. 'Who do you think you are, to come here and criticise? Are you too big for the rest of us? Ma doesn't complain. She says we're lucky to find a house with a real chimney and an inside stove. Are you better than Ma?'

'Oh, Charlotte!' The heat and the dry air and Charlotte's anger and the sickening smells brought tears to Katie's eyes. Charlotte suddenly squeezed her hand.

'We mustn't quarrel so soon. And this place is not so bad when you get used to it. At night the stars are very bright. As Ma says, we can lift up our eyes to the Lord and see that He is watching over us.'

They ran on past a bend in the road and, without Charlotte's telling her, Katie knew at once which was their house. It was cleaner than most. Bright curtains hung in the windows, and although the tiny veranda sagged in the middle, Ma had found a place for her rocking-chair. The gate creaked as Charlotte pushed it open, and then Ma was in the doorway, tears streaming down her face.

Katie began to cry also as she felt the strength of Ma's arms around her, the sweet, safe, musty smell of her breasts, the sound of her heartbeat, and the steady rhythm of her love drawing her back into the family, back from the loneliness of Port Elizabeth.

'Is this a time for sorrow?' Charlotte teased. Ma laughed and wiped her face.

'Come, Katie. You've seen Phillip and Henry. Now we'll find John. Don't worry if he tries to hide. He's very shy. Like you were as a child.'

'And Mary Ann?'

'Sleeping.'

'Can I see her?'

'When she wakes up to nurse. After dinner.'

She followed Ma down the dark hallway into the dining-room but Charlotte gave her no time to look around. 'You put the spoons on the table. The dishes are in the kitchen. I'll go find John.'

Katie giggled silently inside herself: Charlotte was still ordering her about even though they were no longer children and the farm at Uitenhage was far away. Yet Katie did as she was told, and the spoons and dishes were all laid out by the time Charlotte returned, carrying John on one hip.

'There. See Katie?' she said.

John stared, solemn-eyed, clinging still to Charlotte's neck. He did not let go of her until the front door banged open against the wall and Pa rushed in and everything was all commotion, with the boys searching through the bundle of second-hand clothes for shirts to fit them, and Ma calling the girls to help carry in the food, and in another room the crying of the baby and Charlotte running to fetch her, jouncing her on a shoulder until Ma was able to sit down and put her to the breast. When Pa had thanked the Lord for what He had provided, they all picked up their spoons.

In their manner of eating, Ma's family were different from most. They followed the Boer customs Ma had learned as a child in Blinkwater. Thus it was that Ma in her own home never fed her menfolk first and separately but sat everyone around the table together. On that first night Pa was speaking about the new gold mines opening up in Johannesburg. 'Even Mr Rhodes is sending his servants up there—,' he began, when suddenly there was a great rushing of wind outside, and a creaking of metal; the walls of the little house began to shake and the tea in Katie's cup spilled onto the table. She jumped up in alarm, but Pa told her to sit down. 'It's nothing,' he said.

'What do you mean – nothing!' But even as she spoke the noise faded, and the house settled.

'It's only the train,' Ma said calmly.

'It goes past at the bottom of the land at the back,' Phillip said. 'It always shakes the house.'

'Two times every day,' Henry added proudly. 'Sometimes I go out and wave to the people. Some always wave back.'

Katie laughed. 'I thought I'd come to live by the walls of Jericho. I was listening for Joshua playing his trumpet.'

'I'm learning to play the trumpet,' Phillip interrupted. 'Our teacher has one. Yesterday he let me blow on it.'

'Just one blow and you think you can play?' Charlotte teased. 'You'd better practise on your whistle.'

'You want to see our whistles, Katie?' Henry asked eagerly, his earlier shyness forgotten. 'Pa made them.'

He pushed back his chair and stumbled around the table to a box against the wall. 'See?' Henry held up a bamboo stick with holes cut in it and sounded different notes. He pulled out two more whistles of different lengths, and passed one to Phillip and one to Pa.

'Let's have a concert, Pa. We can play our whistles and Charlotte can sing and—' He looked at Katie uncertainly.

'I will also sing,' Katie said.

Pa began humming in his deep bass, nodding to each in turn to catch the harmony, and when they were all ready he nodded again and together they began singing, 'O Lord, our help in ages past, our hope for years to come . . .'

As Katie felt her own voice coming in an octave higher than Charlotte's, she glanced at Ma, saw the love reflected in her eyes, saw the candlelight glowing on Phillip's face and Henry's, looked at little John staring up at her while he still fingered his food, at Pa and Charlotte, so alike in their manner, their heads thrust proudly upward, their teeth showing white against their lips. And in the singing together, she forgot the filth and the smells outside and the shaking walls and the ugliness of this Kimberley. At last she was home again.

Perhaps she had worked too long for Mrs Hutchinson, for after the first happiness of seeing Ma and Charlotte, Katie began to miss some of the luxuries she had taken for granted in Port Elizabeth – the long bars of yellow soap, the soft sea mist, the endless supply of water.

It was the dry season in Kimberley when she arrived. The water tank was empty. There were rivers in the distance, but it was a long way for the girls to carry water and Ma doled it out sparingly – so much set aside for tea and coffee, a cupful each morning for their body-washing, and all the rest saved for the laundry. There was never enough water to grow vegetables except during the rainy season when the tank overflowed and the roads became rivers of slippery clay.

Ma never complained. One afternoon a boy fell on the road and cut his leg on some broken glass. Ma hurried out to him with bandages and a pan of salt water. Soon the neighbours were calling on her whenever anyone was sick or wounded. Once, when Mrs Cele fell sick with the fever, Ma sent Katie over to her house several times a day to wipe her body down with a wet towel until her fever broke.

'You're a very good nurse,' Mrs Cele told Katie.

'That's what I want to be – a nurse,' Katie told Ma when she got home.

Ma hesitated and then spoke slowly. 'It takes much study to be a proper nurse. You have to know all about medicines—'

'You can teach me.'

Mama shook her head. 'All I know is how to wash out wounds and bandage them up. This I learned when I was a girl and watched your grandfather caring for his workers on the farm in Blinkwater. But I know nothing about sickness or medicine—'

'You can't be a proper nurse,' Charlotte interrupted scornfully. 'The nursing schools here are only for white girls. If you go to work in a hospital, you will just be a servant, mopping floors and cleaning up after the Europeans. If you really want to do important work, then you must study hard and become a teacher.'

'I don't want to be a teacher,' Katie said, feeling discouraged. She too wanted to make Pa proud, but she was having as much difficulty at her school in Kimberley as she had had in Port Elizabeth. Her headaches were more frequent now, and by afternoon her eyes were red and swollen.

Ma took her to see a white doctor who gave her some medicine – it cost seven and sixpence – and told her not to use her eyes so much. But how could she stop using her eyes when she had to read her books?

With Charlotte's help Katie managed to pass her Standard Six examination but she did not win a scholarship to any high school. Although Pa could not hide his disappointment, Katie was secretly relieved. She knew she was not clever in the head like Charlotte. All her cleverness was in her hands. Already Ma had taught her how to use the sewing machine, and she was making Charlotte's clothes as well as her own.

'How is it you don't get headaches when you sew, only when you read?' Charlotte asked. When Katie did not answer, she added, 'I think you're just lazy.'

To make matters worse, Pa would not allow her to go anywhere without Charlotte. And Charlotte gave her no peace. If Katie wanted to stay at home and sleep, Charlotte called her a know-nothing. If she wanted to visit her friend Martha, Charlotte would not leave them alone but listened to everything they said.

'Am I a baby to be carried around on my sister's back?' Katie grumbled.

'No,' Pa said. 'But you are the junior sister. Among my people the eldest girl is always in charge of the younger ones. That is the custom.'

'But we don't live among your people. We live here in Kimberley.'

'Nevertheless, until Charlotte marries, she will be in charge of you,' Pa said firmly.

So the girls did everything together. They went to concerts or meetings at the church. On Saturday afternoons before choir practice they stopped to watch a football game or cricket match, and every Saturday night there was a party somewhere, sometimes to honour a visiting soccer team, more often to greet a returning traveller or to say goodbye to another.

In Kimberley there were always people coming and going, and at these parties there was much talk of what was happening in this place or that, of famine in one part of the country or floods in another, of disease killing off the horses in the coastal regions or smallpox troubling some tribe to the north. There was talk, too, of Dinuzulu, the son of Cetshwayo, who was still laughing at the Boers because they could not stop him from milking the English cow, of Oom Paul Kruger who had his own Republic across the Vaal, and of Mr Rhodes who was sending his friends beyond the Limpopo to visit that great chief, Lobengula. Lobengula's daughter was married and living in Kimberley, and his granddaughter Martha was Katie's best friend.

Mr Simon Sinamela, the director of their church choir, gathered together the best singers from all the local churches and formed a group to sing at Christmas in front of white people's houses. With Katie and Charlotte, there was David, a postman; then Neli, a thin man, not much older than Charlotte, who came from Fort Beaufort and sometimes visited Ma because she knew his homeplace; Wellington, who had gone to school at Fort Hare and was now a clerk on the diamond mines; Liza, whose father was working on the railroad; and Nettie, who was also a teacher in Charlotte's school; and a few others Katie did not know. There were bass voices, tenors, altos, contraltos and sopranos, and almost every night the group practised together.

Before long the choir was being invited to sing at garden parties almost every Saturday afternoon, and sometimes one or two nights a week as well. Ma began to complain because Charlotte and Katie were never home. Nevertheless she was pleased that the two girls did not argue so much, Katie wanting to do one thing and Charlotte another. They both seemed quite content to spend all their free time practising new songs.

One Saturday night in March the choir sang at a very big party in honour of a Mr Howell from England, who afterwards beckoned Mr Sinamela aside. As Mr Howell talked, sometimes shaking his finger, Katie watched Mr Sinamela's eyes grow big as though he could not comprehend what he was hearing. Then he stroked his face, scratched his ear, and stroked his face again. Mr Howell kept talking, stopping now and then to ask a question, then talking some more until at last the members of the choir grew tired of waiting and decided to go home.

The very next day when Katie came home, Charlotte called out in great excitement: 'We've got to hurry to Mr Sinamela's. He's got some news. He sent a message to Nettie and me at school telling us not to fail him.'

'Maybe he just wants to give us what he owes.'

'That's not what he said. He said it was important news.'

Maybe! Maybe! The two girls kept talking about their maybes as they ran through the location, but even their wildest thoughts were nothing compared with what he told them.

'That Mr Howell from England,' Mr Sinamela paused and looked around at his singers, 'he wants us to go to England and give concerts there.'

'To England!' Katie gasped. She glanced over at Charlotte with a mixture of respect and apprehension, remembering that time long ago when they were children and Charlotte had said that one day she would go to England. Now she would go! It seemed almost like magic the way everything Charlotte wanted somehow came about.

Suddenly Martha giggled and then everyone began to talk at once. Mr Sinamela was laughing like a mad thing and the men were pounding each other on their backs. But Charlotte was strangely silent, as though she knew but did not believe what she heard.

A tingle of excitement swept through Katie as she caught the full meaning of Mr Sinamela's announcement. It was not only Charlotte who was invited. All the members of that special choir, herself included, were going to England.

'How soon?' she asked, and when no one heard her in all the confusion, she leapt up on a chair and shouted out, 'When do we go?'

'In two months or three,' Mr Sinamela said. 'Mr Howell wants to hire an Englishman from the Royal Academy in London to be our musical director. He will be looking for other singers also.'

Katie jumped down from her chair. 'Come on, Charlotte, let's go tell Pa.' For the first time and without thinking, Katie was telling Charlotte what to do.

The two girls ran through the darkened streets of the location, carelessly in the rain, not thinking about the potholes in the road or worrying about the shadows. Why they did not fall, they could not say. They crashed through the gate in front of their house and rushed into the dining-room, both of them gasping and laughing and trying to talk at once.

'Stop this crazy shouting and tell us what happened,' Ma said.

'We're going to England!' Charlotte sang.

'It's our chorus,' Katie added. 'An Englishman, Mr Howell, wants to send us—'

'We're going to England!' Charlotte kept singing. And right there, in the tiny space between the table and the wall, she began to stamp and shake her body in a dance of triumph, acting not at all like a proper Christian schoolteacher.

'Charlotte, behave yourself,' Ma said sharply.

'We're going to England!' Charlotte sang.

'To England?' Pa whispered, awestruck. 'My daughters are going to England?'

In spite of Ma, Charlotte's feet moved faster, her arms swinging in her own rhythm, and Pa, without thinking, began to clap his hands until at last even Ma began to laugh and tap her feet on the wooden floor.

Phillip and Henry, roused from sleep, scrambled up from their sleeping mats and stared at Charlotte.

'Why's she dancing?' Phillip mumbled.

She and Katie are going to England!' Ma told him.

'Why?'

'To learn about the world, silly,' Charlotte sang out.

'To see the great white Queen in her purple robes and jewelled crown,' Pa said.

His words touched lightly at Katie's mind. She remembered a picture in one of her schoolbooks showing a royal coach and six white horses and soldiers marching. Her own heartbeat quickened, the blood drummed in her knees, her ankles, her toes. Her feet began to move, slowly at first, then faster and faster, until she too was leaping and whirling with Charlotte while the walls quivered and the windows rattled and the floor shook.

'To England!' Charlotte shouted again, locking her arms in Katie's as they both leapt upwards in one last burst of energy before falling exhausted to the floor.

Durban
1954

'*How old were you when you went to England?*' *I ask.*

Katie lifts the microphone towards her mouth. After two weeks of sitting next to my rented tape recorder, she has lost her awe of this new machine.

'*I was seventeen.*'

'*How many were there in the choir?*'

'*Only six of us from Kimberley,*' *she says.* '*Charlotte, Martha and me, and also Wellington, David and Neli. Of those others who were chosen, some feared the voyage over the ocean, one man died, and Charlotte's friend Nettie got married instead. Even Mr Sinamela was missing. His wife was jealous when she was not invited and would not let him come.*'

'*Only six?*'

'*There were more. Mr Balmer, our director, took us on a tour of the Cape to find other singers to make the choir strong. I told him of Mr and Mrs Xiniwe in Port Elizabeth, and they joined us with their two little nephews, Albert Jonas and John Xiniwe. Wellington told of Frances Gqoba, whose brother had been to school with him at Lovedale, and also about another classmate, John Hadebe, who was studying to be a teacher.*'

Kaltie counts off the names on her fingers. '*Then Mr Balmer found John Mbongwe from Burghersdorp, and also Josiah Semouse who had fought against the English in the Basotho War and afterwards walked four hundred miles to Lovedale to learn how to be a telegraph operator, and George McClellan, a teacher in Graaff-Reinet. And one missionary told him of Johanna Jonkers, and another of Sannie Koopman and Anna Gentle.*'

'*That made sixteen. Then there was Miss Clark, a middle-aged music teacher from Cape Town, who was hired to be our chaperone.*'

Katie's eyes twinkle with amusement. '*Charlotte liked her very much, but she bothered me. Instead of calling me by my proper name, she always called me Kitty. And that silly name was what got me into so much trouble.*'

4

London

1891

In London great stone buildings all covered with smoke-moss towered up into the sky, blocking out the sun. The streets below were as dim and shadowed as paths through a forest. But there was no silence here. Voices, footsteps, whistles, fog horns, clattering hoofs, creaking wheels, somewhere a hand organ. Day and night, the busy hum of the city never stopped.

Katie had heard so much about the wonderful things she would see in London that she was not surprised by the trains running along the tops of houses or the great buildings with roads underneath them or the double-decker horse-drawn buses lumbering down the streets. But when she stepped down from the train at the railway station she was amazed to see white men carrying heavy trunks on their backs.

'Look, Charlotte, these Englishmen are their own kaffirs,' she giggled. For the first time in her life she used the word 'kaffir' with malicious glee. At home the Europeans called the black people kaffirs. The blacks did not like this. 'Kaffir', although an Arab word meaning 'infidel', was too much like the Xhosa word *kafula,* which means 'to spit upon'.

All the singers had objected when Mr Howell changed the name of the group from the Jubilee Chorus to the Kaffir Choir.

'We don't like to be called kaffirs,' Mr Xiniwe had told him.

'But that's what you are. You come from Kaffraria.'

'We come from the land of the Xhosa.'

'It's the same thing,' Mr Howell said. 'The English know about kaffirs and will be curious to hear you sing.'

Now, as Katie looked about the station and saw all those Englishmen running up to the singers and wanting to carry their suitcases, she could not stop laughing. But she did not see anything funny about the streets outside. In the hansom cab she wrinkled her nose in disgust at the piles of manure left in the middle of Piccadilly and the bird droppings encrusting a statue in Trafalgar Square. The white people were a puzzle, she thought. Here in England they did not seem to notice the dirt and grime, yet in Port Elizabeth Mrs Hutchinson was always asking, 'Won't you kaffirs ever learn to keep things properly clean?'

The inside of the McCready House Hotel in Henrietta Street, however, was very different. Fresh sheets were turned down in the room Katie was to share with Charlotte and Martha, and there were no stains in the wash-basin or dust on the floor.

At dinner on the first night at the hotel they were all asking when they would see the wonderful things Mr Balmer had described.

'You'll have to be patient,' Mr Balmer warned. 'You haven't come over here on a holiday. We'll have to rehearse every day. We'll only go sightseeing one afternoon a week.'

'Tomorrow?' Wellington asked.

'No. Tomorrow we go to see our theatrical agent, Mr Vert. He's the man who arranges all our concerts.'

When they reached his office at 6 Cork Street, Mr Vert stood up behind his desk and held out his hand to Mr Balmer. He hardly looked at anyone else. He spoke very quickly as though in a hurry. Even at that first meeting, he took only a few minutes to listen to their singing before holding up his hands for silence.

'They're better than I expected,' he told Mr Balmer. 'As the first kaffir choir to visit England, they're something of a novelty, but you have your work cut out. In four days the last public celebration of Queen Victoria's Jubilee will take place in the Crystal Palace with a tonic sol-fa competition. I understand these kaffirs are used to sight-singing?'

'Yes, but competing with some of the best choirs in England?'

'Don't worry, no one expects them to win. But after the one obligatory piece they will have time to present some of their own numbers.'

'But only four days. That's hardly enough time—'

'Just do the best you can. This is, after all, the best possible opportunity for them to perform in front of thousands of people. If they do well, requests will come pouring in.'

A great crowd was assembled in the enormous hall in the Crystal Palace – the newspapers said there were over twenty-eight thousand visitors and singers. Mr Balmer and Miss Clark were both very nervous, but the Africans were too amazed to feel any fear when they saw the strange machines on the stage turning out sheets of music, words and all, for a five-hundred-man choir from Europe. Later, when the leading soprano from the Nottingham Tonic Sol-fa Choral Society did not seem always sure of her notes, Mr Balmer stopped his fidgeting and looked over at Katie and smiled as if he knew she was a better singer.

The Africans' turn came that evening. They had no trouble sight-singing from the music sheets, and afterwards when they sang 'Does Anyone Here Know the Big Baboon?' the audience laughed and shouted for an encore.

Mr Vert seemed very excited when he came to the hotel the next afternoon

to congratulate Mr Balmer. 'Even the Queen is interested. A command per-
formance has been arranged for the 24th of July.'

Mr Balmer looked startled. 'I didn't expect—'

'You'd better spend the night of the 23rd at the South Palace Hotel in
Portsmouth. We'll take the early morning ferry. Her Majesty is at her summer
palace down at Osborne on the Isle of Wight.'

In Portsmouth, the five girls were crowded into one bedroom, and they lay
awake for a long time telling one other all they had heard or read about
Queen Victoria. Katie could hardly sleep in her excitement at the thought of
seeing the Queen in her jewelled crown and purple robes.

During the night a light wind came up, ruffling the waves on the Solent. By
the time the singers reached Osborne, they were all exhausted by lack of
sleep and the rough ferry-ride. As soon as the girls were ushered upstairs into
one of the two dressing-rooms set aside for the choir, they curled up in the
deep armchairs and fell asleep. Two hours later a maid came in with a tray of
sandwiches and tea, followed by Miss Clark who fussed over them until they
started dressing.

Their programme was divided into two parts. For the first, the singers
dressed in the old way, according to their tribe, with beaded robes covering
their breasts, carved wooden combs in their hair, and anklets of seed pods
which rattled as they stamped their bare feet on the floor. Dressed thus, they
sang as their people used to sing when they hunted or danced or gathered
together for some celebration. For the second part of the programme, they
dressed in Christian clothes, the men in dark suits and the girls in white
dresses with long white gloves, and they sang the English songs Mr Balmer
had taught them.

As soon as the girls were ready, a lady-in-waiting led them through the cor-
ridors and down a wide staircase to the empty Indian Room. It was bigger
than any room Katie had ever seen. Sunlight streaming through tall uncur-
tained windows shone on a huge carved peacock over the fireplace, thick
Persian rugs covered the floor, and there were enough armchairs to seat a
hundred people.

Slowly at first, and then more rapidly, groups of people drifted into the
room – ladies in silken gowns, soldiers in uniform, Scots in green and yellow
kilts, Indians wearing turbans, a West African boy in a scarlet tunic, and
twenty or thirty Englishmen in black frock coats and grey trousers.

Mr Vert leaned down to speak to Miss Clark. 'There's the Duke and
Duchess of Connaught with Prince Arthur. Princess Margaret and Princess
Victoria Patricia are over by the window. I think that's the Count and
Countess of Hohenau talking to the Crown Prince of Italy—' He went on
whispering while Miss Clark's cheeks grew pink with excitement. All at once
his words were lost in a hissing of breath as the door behind the choir
opened. Katie, trembling, turned her head, expecting to see at last the tall and

stately figure of the Queen in her purple robes and jewelled crown.

But she did not see her.

There was only a little old woman standing there in the doorway, as short and fat and round as Ma, wearing a simple black dress and a white lace bonnet and no jewellery at all except for rings on her fingers. Beside her and holding on to her hand was a small girl with yellow hair.

Katie was disappointed. The little one must be one of the royal princesses coming in with her nanny, she thought. Nevertheless there was a strange dignity about that old woman, and all the men, even the Crown Prince of Italy, were bowing as she approached. Miss Clark stood up and motioned to the choir to rise to their feet, and Mr Balmer gave the signal for 'God Save the Queen'.

Still Katie could not believe. Nevertheless, when the anthem was over, Katie threw back her head and shouted out with the others, *A! Umhlekazi,* which means 'Hail, your Majesty!', until the old woman was comfortably seated with the little princess on a footstool beside her. Katie knew then that this old woman must be Queen Victoria. She was very disappointed. Pa had been wrong. She wore no crown, no purple robes. She had no page-boys or soldier-guards or even advisers proclaiming her power. She was just like any old widow-woman listening politely as Mr Xiniwe stepped forward to thank her for summoning the choir to Osborne and tell her about the various parts of their costume.

The Queen nodded. Then, as Mr Balmer came forward and Miss Clark struck the first notes on the piano, she leaned back to listen intently, her head tilted a little to one side as she tried to understand the words of the hymns 'Lizalis' idinga Lakho' and 'Vuka Deborah'. She laughed heartily when the two young nephews of Mr Xiniwe stepped forward and began to dance during the singing of 'Singamewele', a traditional Xhosa song and dance about twins. The choir sang a wedding song, a travelling song, a work song, with different members taking turns with the solo parts, and finally a goodbye song, before they left to change into their Christian clothes for the second part of the programme.

In the dressing-room, one of the Queen's ladies-in-waiting asked Miss Clark if there was anything she needed.

'Thank you, no. We have everything,' Miss Clark said, turning back to pull the strings of Mrs Xiniwe's corset tighter.

The lady turned to Katie. 'Here, let me help you.'

Katie shook her head. 'I can dress myself.'

'But perhaps a little powder—' The lady pulled a powder-puff out of a box on the dresser and dabbed at Katie's face. Katie peered into the mirror and began to giggle as she wiped the powder off.

'In my country it is only the rickshaw boys who whitewash themselves, and they only paint their legs.'

'But you want to look stylish,' the lady said, and began to pull the neck of her dress down over her shoulders.

Katie stepped back, hiding her irritation with a burst of laughter. 'At home it is only the heathen women who expose their breasts.'

Miss Clark rescued her with a quick 'We're ready to go down now'.

The buzz of conversation stopped as the choir re-entered the Indian Room. This time the old woman patted the arm of her chair with the flat of her hand in time to 'The Merry Peasant', 'The Dawn of Day', and 'On the Mountain', but when the programme ended with the Lord's Prayer, she bent her head and closed her eyes. At last, after Mr Balmer turned and bowed before her, she tapped lightly with her fan on a little table, and immediately everyone in that huge room began to applaud. Then, in the midst of their noise, she rose to her feet and pulled the little princess up by the hand.

'I'm pleased to see you here and I admire your singing very much,' she said to the choir, before stepping towards the younger of the two boys whose dancing had so amused her and asking his name.

'Albert, Ma'am.'

'Albert? That's a good name. My husband's name was Albert. And your brother?'

'He's John, Ma'am.'

'That, too, is a good name. I once had a very loyal servant whose name was John.'

She took one step back and looked around at each of the men. 'I'm told that there is one of you who fought against my soldiers.'

Josiah stood very straight, but when he answered her his voice squeaked with fear. 'It was me, Ma'am. When I was still young and not yet civilised.'

'And now?' she smiled.

'Now I'm educated, Ma'am.' His nervous squeak slowly disappeared as he gained in confidence. 'Now I understand these things. And like me, my people are grateful because you have pardoned them for their ignorance.'

Nodding, she turned to the rest of the choir and smiled again. Before she could speak, however, the little princess pulled at her hand and cried out, 'Granny, Granny, come away. I don't like these darkies.'

'Hush, Alice, you mustn't be afraid. These are Granny's people.' As she spoke those words, it seemed to Katie that Queen Victoria was smiling directly at her as if sure the child would be forgiven for her ignorance.

In that moment, Katie knew that this little old woman in the black dress and lace cap was indeed the great Queen–Empress of Africa as well as of England. So great was Katie's pride in knowing that she was one of Granny's people that, until she felt Martha's nudge, she almost forgot to dip into the low curtsy which Miss Clark had taught her. Even then, out of the corner of her eye, she watched Queen Victoria walk out of the room, her little round body seeming to grow tall and stately and that white lace bonnet to glimmer like a jewelled crown.

From that day on, Mr Vert kept them very busy. He arranged concerts in public halls, at private receptions, in schools and in churches. Afterwards there were always photographers and people who crowded around asking questions. Newspapers printed stories, some of which were very funny. One said Katie was an African princess. Perhaps the man who wrote it mistook her for Martha, who was Lobengula's granddaughter. But it made everybody laugh, and from then on Wellington, that big clown, always addressed her as 'your Highness' and bowed down very low whenever she appeared.

Music critics also came to hear them. In August an article appeared in the *Musical Times*:

> A quartet, or rather a solo accompanied by three voices, bore so close a resemblance to Rossini's 'Cujus animam' that it is difficult to accept it as a specimen of native music at all.

But Mr Vert was quick to have another writer publish an article stating:

> This quartet, 'Africa', is the composition of a Kaffir who had never heard of Rossini or his *Stabat Mater*, and did not dream that such a selection as 'Cujus animam' was in existence. It is descriptive of how the natives hum some portions of their songs.

Another critic wrote:

> The musical capabilities of the Kaffir Choir which during the last month has claimed attention in London must have been a surprise to many. Hitherto the African has been deemed so undeveloped as to be thought scarcely worthy of association with music, but, as in many other instances, this supposition has apparently arisen from ignorance rather than knowledge.

Katie did not understand the rest of the article with its mention of diatonic chants, consecutive fifths and augmented fourths, but Mr Balmer told her it was a very important analysis of their native songs.

People also came to visit them at the hotel. Dr Joseph Parker, the minister of the City Temple, Holborn, where the choir had given a Service of Song, often brought retired missionaries or ladies from his church to drink tea with Miss Clark and the girls. It was these ladies who started the trouble in the choir by asking Mrs Xiniwe if she would like to earn some extra money by giving a speech about her life in Africa.

As soon as she stood up, the ladies in the missionary society began asking her questions – foolish questions about everyday matters that Mrs Xiniwe could answer without thinking. And for this she was paid a guinea. If it was that easy, Charlotte also wanted to earn some extra money. So when Miss Forbes, who was the principal of a girls' school, suggested that one of the choir tell her students about Africa, Miss Clark suggested Charlotte. She, too, came back to the hotel with an extra pound in her purse.

'Very good,' Mrs Xiniwe said. 'Of course, I always get a guinea, but you're still young.'

However, when Miss Clark sent Charlotte to another school, Mrs Xiniwe complained. 'It isn't fair for her to earn twice when I've only had one chance.'

'Charlotte is a teacher, so it's more fitting for her to talk to schoolgirls,' Miss Clark replied. But although Mrs Xiniwe had never passed Standard Six, she kept grumbling. She even went to Katie.

'It isn't proper for Charlotte to be running to this place and that place and leaving you behind. Your mother would not like it.'

Katie looked at Mrs Xiniwe in astonishment, for when she spoke of Charlotte her voice came thin and rasping and her eyes glittered like those of a cobra which had once reared up on the path in Uitenhage. Charlotte had killed the snake with a stick but Katie was so terrified her mouth had dried up.

That night as they were undressing, she told Charlotte what Mrs Xiniwe had said.

'I know,' Charlotte said, 'but don't worry about it, she's just jealous.'

'And greedy too,' Martha added.

'But always before, she's been so kind. Today she was not like herself at all. She frightened me.'

Katie could not forget those days in Port Elizabeth when Mrs Xiniwe beckoned her over to sit beside her in church, or the times at school when Mr Xiniwe said she was his best singer. She tried to please both Charlotte and Mrs Xiniwe, but it was no use. At the dinner table or during rehearsals, Mrs Xiniwe would stare at her and then whisper to Frances or Johanna, who would glance at Katie and laugh.

One day Katie asked Frances what Mrs Xiniwe was saying.

'Nothing,' Frances muttered.

'Yes, it is. It's something. I want to know.' Frances shrugged and tried to move away, but Katie caught her arm and held it tight. 'Tell me.'

'She says your eyes are very big when you look at her husband. She says it isn't right.'

Katie gasped. 'But he's an old man. You don't believe her, do you?'

But Frances looked away and would not answer.

Charlotte just laughed when Katie told her. 'Mr Xiniwe still thinks of you as a schoolgirl,' she said. 'Moreover, he gets tired of his wife's complaining. He doesn't pay any attention to what she says.'

When Mr Xiniwe's manner towards her did not change, Katie felt more at ease. Soon she was too busy to think about anything except singing, washing and mending her clothes and writing her letters to Ma and Pa.

The choir was giving concerts five days a week. Mr Balmer was now keeping one girl behind in the dressing-room during the first part of the programme; while the others were changing for the second part, she would be ready to come out and sing a solo. Katie's turn came in the first week in August, and she was chosen again a week later. The choir was scheduled to sing at a garden party which the Baroness Burdett-Coutts was giving for the International Congress of Hygiene and Demography. Her husband, who was at the earlier concert, wrote a letter to Mr Vert requesting that Katie be the one to sing the solo at his wife's party.

When Mrs Xiniwe heard this she complained to Mr Balmer. 'Katie! Sing again? But you always take us by turns, and on that day—' (she counted on her fingers) '—on that day it's Johanna's turn.'

Mr Balmer shook his head. 'If the Baroness wants Katie, then she shall have Katie.'

'But it isn't fair. The one who sings alone always gets the best presents. It's not right for Katie to get more than her share.'

'If that's what's worrying you, I'll tell everyone that presents are not permitted.'

'No, no,' Mrs Xiniwe answered quickly. 'That's not fair. We'd all lose, but—'

'Then I don't want to hear anything more from you.'

Mrs Xiniwe stopped her grumbling to Mr Balmer, but she was still dissatisfied and kept talking against 'those girls from Kimberley'. One morning Johanna cornered Katie in the little writing-room off the lobby of the hotel.

'I want the magic charm you wear. Mrs Xiniwe says that's why you were chosen in my place.'

'Magic charm?' Katie looked at her in disbelief. 'Don't be silly. We're all Christians. We don't believe in such things.'

'Then how is it you girls from Kimberley always get the best presents?'

'You get presents also.'

'I only get stockings and shawls. I want a bracelet all made of silver like the one you have.'

'But I don't wear any—'

'Yes, you do. Mrs Xiniwe knows.' Johanna sounded very fierce as she pushed her face up close to Katie's and fumbled at the buttons of her blouse. 'Where do you carry it?'

Katie tried to jerk away but Johanna's thick fingers pinched her neck. When Katie tried to push her hand away, Johanna bobbed her head so that Katie's fingernails grazed her cheek, drawing little spots of blood.

'*Ow!*' Johanna screamed, putting her hand to her face. When she saw the blood, her eyes widened in fear and she shrank back. '*Hawu!* You have claws like a cat, just like Miss Clark says. Yes, you do carry a magic charm if you can change yourself into a cat.' She reached behind her for the doorknob, backed out of the door and banged it behind her.

Katie sank down on the chair and rubbed at her neck. She felt shaken and confused by all the silly talk of a magic charm, and only then did she catch the meaning of Johanna's last foolish words. She really thought Katie could turn herself into a cat, and all because Miss Clark, instead of using her real name, always called her Kitty. Laughter bubbled up from her stomach into her chest and brought tears to her eyes. She was laughing so hard she did not hear Miss Clark.

'Kitty, stop it. What's the matter with you? Why did you scratch Johanna?'

'She thinks I'm a cat.' Laughter caught her again and she almost fell off the chair. Suddenly she felt the sharp slap of Miss Clark's hand on her cheek.

'Stop laughing! Tell me why you hit Johanna.'

'Because she thinks I carry a magic charm.'

'What absolutely idiotic nonsense!'

'But she does. And she grabbed me. I was only trying to get away. I didn't mean to scratch her.'

'I won't have this fighting. You'll both have to shake hands.'

Miss Clark, being English, thought this would settle their quarrel. But Johanna's voice was sullen and she looked over Katie's head at the wall behind. Katie stared at the welts on Johanna's cheek and laughed silently inside herself, sensing the power within her – a power not of her own choosing but growing out of Johanna's own thoughts put in her head by Mrs Xiniwe.

'What will she say next?' Katie asked Charlotte that evening.

'Don't worry,' Charlotte said firmly, 'Miss Clark and Mr Balmer already know she's a troublemaker, and everyone else will just laugh at her talk of magic charms.' Charlotte stayed by Katie's side every minute.

On the afternoon before the concert for the Baroness, Sannie was sleeping in her room and the others had all gone out with Miss Clark. Charlotte went upstairs to iron her dress and left Katie behind to finish her letter to Ma.

Katie was re-reading what she had written, when she heard Miss Clark's voice in the lobby calling out to Johanna to bring in the rest of the parcels. She did not hear Mrs Xiniwe come into the writing-room. She only sensed her presence. As she looked up into those black shiny eyes it seemed to her that Mrs Xiniwe's head was swaying from side to side like a cobra about to strike.

'OLorddelivermefromallevil,' Katie muttered frantically. She felt snake poison spreading through her blood; her bones seemed to melt and her head grew heavy. How long she slept she did not know. Perhaps only a minute, for she was still praying to the Lord to deliver her from evil when she woke up and found herself alone. She felt too tired to go down to dinner, too tired to get out of bed in the morning. Charlotte took up hot tea and toast. Martha ironed her dress. Miss Clark came to take her temperature. Mr Balmer stood at the door and asked her how she felt.

'She's all right,' Miss Clark said. 'We'll just let her rest for a while. You go on ahead with the others. We'll follow in a few minutes.'

Katie could hear the muffled voices of Frances and Johanna, Wellington's burst of laughter down the hall, Mr Balmer's heavy tread, a board creaking. And then, from outside, the triumphant sound of Mrs Xiniwe's voice: 'If Katie's too sick to get up, Johanna will have to sing.'

Charlotte squeezed Katie's fingers. 'That isn't true. Now that troublemaker has gone out of the house, don't you feel better?'

'Yes,' Katie said, 'I feel better already.' She stretched out her legs and arms and rolled her shoulders back against the pillow. It was good to feel the catch of muscle beneath her knees, the air filling her lungs. She was up and dressed by the time Miss Clark knocked on the door to say their carriage was waiting.

The air was soft and warm with late summer, and flower vendors were pushing their carts down the Strand between the Lyceum and Gaiety theatres. It was a long ride to Hampstead Heath. The houses were fewer in number in that part of London, set further back from the road and half-hidden behind great iron fences and trees. As they turned into the driveway of Holly Lodge, Katie caught her breath at the great clumps of yellow and purple chrysanthemums and, beyond them, the grass stretching away into the trees. Near the house, which rose up as high as the summer palace at Osborne, a few early guests stood about on the lawn, the ladies with parasols to match their gowns and the men in tall grey hats and frock coats. A brass band was already playing on a small stage decorated with rose blossoms twined around the supports. On either side of the stage, long tables were set up and covered with meats, jellies, sandwiches, hard-boiled eggs, cakes, cheeses, trifles, nuts, sweets and huge platters of fruit. Katie had never seen so much food.

Mr Balmer stepped forward to help Miss Clark down, and then held out his hand to Katie. 'How do you feel?'

'Hungry. Is it all right if I take a peach?'

'Of course not,' Miss Clark said sharply. 'It's not time. Anyway, you mustn't eat before you sing, you know that.'

'She forgets everything.' Mrs Xiniwe was standing behind Mr Balmer with the other members of the choir. Her eyes were glittering, growing larger, shutting out Mr Balmer and Miss Clark and Charlotte and closing down on Katie like a black fog. She felt Charlotte's arm around her, sensed others moving, so her feet moved with them. But she did not remember entering the tent behind the stage which was to be used as a dressing-room. Charlotte told her later that she fell down on the grass inside and began to moan that her voice was finished. It was Charlotte who sent Miss Clark to ask for a bottle of ammonia and Charlotte who held it under Katie's nose as she tried blindly to push the burning, choking smell away.

'Wake up and behave yourself,' Charlotte told her.

She opened her eyes. But behind Charlotte and a little to one side Mrs

Xiniwe was staring down at her, and the black fog closed in again. Charlotte's voice cut through it. 'Wake up or I'll make you smell this medicine again.'

Katie choked and sputtered and tried to sit up but she would not open her eyes, not until Martha ran to the other tent and called Mr Xiniwe.

'Katie!' he said in his headmaster's voice. 'Katie, look at me!' Her eyelids fluttered, opened enough for her to see his light-skinned, bony face. 'What's all this foolishness? Your voice is not finished. You will sing well today.'

'No—'

'She's too sick,' his wife said.

'You shut your mouth, woman,' Mr Xiniwe shouted harshly, and then, gently, he whispered to Katie. 'I've said you're going to sing. Didn't I teach you well in school? Remember the competition. You were frightened then, but it was easy once we started. Remember?'

'I remember.'

'Then you'll sing today.'

'I can't.'

'Do you want these English people to say I failed with you?'

'No, sir.'

'Then you will sing. We'll show all those white people outside how well we Africans can sing their English songs. You hear?'

'Yes, sir.'

'That's good.' He lifted her up onto a couch in the middle of the tent, and she heard him telling Mr Balmer that today he must be the one to lead her in her singing.

'Can she sing?' Mr Balmer asked anxiously.

'Oh yes. She's better now. It was just a little *ufufunyane*, a kind of hysteria our girls get sometimes when they're afraid of bewitchment. Katie will sing very well. But no piano.'

'No piano?' Mr Balmer sounded surprised.

'In my school at Port Elizabeth we had no piano. It's easier . . .'

Their voices faded into the rustle of clothes, the movement of bodies, and bare feet padding over the grass. Quietness crept into Katie's bones as she lay there, repeating to herself the song Mr Balmer had taught her.

Too soon Miss Clark's arms lifted her shoulders. 'Time to get dressed.' She pulled Katie's green street dress over her head, tossed it behind her, held the white voile for Katie to step into, and buttoned it down the back. Then she dabbed at Katie's eyes with a wet cloth and stood back, tilting her head to one side. 'You look lovely,' she said as she handed her the long white gloves.

Katie kept her eyes on the grass as she followed Miss Clark out of the tent, and walked up the steps of the stage. The brass band was gone, only their empty chairs remained. Mr Balmer came up after her. Mr Xiniwe followed, still fingering his collar. There were many more people out on the lawn than when she'd arrived, hundreds and hundreds of people it seemed.

'Now I present Miss Katie Manye, the youngest of our girls. And Mr Xiniwe, her first music teacher. Miss Manye is a Xhosa from the Cape of Good Hope—'

'I'm not Xhosa. I'm Sotho,' Katie said.

'Never mind—,' Mr Balmer hissed, his lips scarcely moving; and then to the people below, 'and although English is not her native tongue, she will now give you "Drink to Me Only with Thine Eyes."' He stepped back, and Mr Xiniwe moved over to a corner of the stage where Katie could see him clearly and still half-face the people on the lawn below.

'Ready?' he called out. As Katie nodded, his hands moved gently, gathering the rhythm out of the air, and the song rose up in her throat without her thinking of it.

''Tis the last rose of summer left blooming alone,' she sang while the sun-light glinted on Mr Xiniwe's cheeks and nose and little curly beard, giving a brightness to his face. He smiled proudly at her and she knew she was singing well. '—So soon may I follow, when friendships decay—' Suddenly, briefly, she knew the sadness in this song. Her voice trembled and broke, then rose up strong again until Mr Xiniwe's hands twisted in the air, catching the rhythm back to himself, holding the silence for a moment before the clapping began, then grew louder and louder.

Somewhere a man shouted, then others called out again and again for an encore. Katie laughed because she knew that, together, she and Mr Xiniwe had done well and now everyone would say he was a good teacher. Mr Balmer stepped forward and held up his hand for silence. But the people down on the lawn paid no attention. They just kept on clapping and shouting. One young man ran forward and pulled a rose from among the decorations and held it up to Katie. She had to lean way over the railing to reach it, and when she straightened up, the clapping and shouting came louder than ever. Mr Balmer raised both his arms to quiet the crowd, but those English people went on shouting as if they were mad.

As she stood there in the warm summer air, Katie felt as though she were divided in two. One part was just herself, Katie, waiting obediently for a white man to tell her what to do. The other part of her was altogether differ-ent, no longer waiting for instructions but knowing that she, and only she, could quiet this crowd with her singing. She moved forward then, resting one hand on the railing, and with the other brushed that rose the young man had given her across her mouth. The clapping died away. Mr Balmer sat down beside Miss Clark on the piano bench. Katie half-turned to face Mr Xiniwe, and as she did so, she saw from the corner of her eye the other members of the choir coming across the lawn towards the stage. She waited, while they filed up the steps and moved over to sit·on the empty chairs. She smiled at Charlotte and Martha and then, still smiling, she looked over at Mrs Xiniwe whose eyes were flat and empty.

This time it was Katie who chose her song. 'Remember the hymn we sang at the school competition?' she called out softly to Mr Xiniwe.

'"Abide with Me"?'

Katie nodded and paused while he hummed the opening notes. Then her voice rang out, high and clear.

The Baroness was very old. And like many old people she liked to give advice. She disapproved of the singers walking barefoot during the first part of the programme for fear they would catch cold and die of pneumonia. She promised to have her shoemaker measure them for slippers the next day – brown ones for their programme and fancy ones for them to wear at other times.

When she finished speaking, her guests crowded around the singers to ask questions about Africa. Katie's heels sank into the grass until the muscles in her legs ached, before she was free to follow Charlotte and Martha over to the refreshment tables. As they filled their plates with sandwiches and cakes, she hovered over the fruit, choosing one peach, then putting it back and choosing another. Suddenly the young man who had handed her a rose was standing beside her.

'You have a beautiful voice,' he said.

Katie smiled, reaching for a bunch of grapes to set on her plate beside the peach, wondering if Miss Clark would call her greedy if she ate a pear as well.

'How do you like England?' the young man said.

'Very much,' she answered, ready to be friendly, until she saw the expression in his eyes. She did not like the way he looked at her. He reminded her of the times in Kimberley when she and Charlotte had gone to the football games, and young men had leered at them and called out cheeky remarks. Charlotte had told her never to pay any attention to such advances. She did not want to pay any attention to this young Englishman either, but he was very persistent and kept crowding her, so she had to keep stepping backward, all the time looking for Charlotte or Martha or Miss Clark to come and rescue her. She did not want to quarrel with him for fear Miss Clark would call her rude. But when he asked her if she had come to England to look for a husband, her anger overcame her fear.

'You're talking foolishness,' she said, more loudly than she realised. 'It isn't right for blacks and whites to mix. God made the white people here and the black people in Africa, and he divided these countries by a very, very wide river. So why are you talking to me this way? When I want a husband, there are plenty of pretty black boys in Africa.'

At that moment an old man with grey hair and a big grey moustache left the group of people he was talking to and came towards her with his hand outstretched.

'Miss Manye, may I tell you how much I enjoyed your songs?'

'Thank you, sir,' she said gratefully.

'Perhaps you would like some punch?' He offered her his arm, and as they walked back to the refreshment tables, he whispered, 'Don't let him worry you. He was just flirting with you as he would with any young girl. I don't think he meant any disrespect.'

'No, sir,' she said.

'Whereabouts in South Africa do you live?'

'In Kimberley, sir.'

'Ah, Kimberley! Then you should be wearing diamonds around your neck.'

'Me?' Katie giggled. 'We black people don't wear diamonds, otherwise the police would come and put us in jail.'

'I won't let any policeman arrest you.'

'Nevertheless, I don't like diamonds. If I choose a necklace, then I'll choose—' She looked around at the rich ladies standing on the lawn and pointed to one who was fingering a strand of white beads: '—some like those.'

He followed her eyes and then glanced down at her and smiled. 'Then you have very good taste. I, too, like pearls better than diamonds. But don't tell my friends in Kimberley. They'd think I was trying to ruin their business.'

On their way back to the hotel, Miss Clark asked her what she had been talking about with Lord Knutsford.

'Lord Knutsford? Who's he?'

'I saw you walking with him.'

'You mean that old man? He's very nice.'

'But what were you talking about?'

'Pearls. I told him I didn't want a diamond necklace, only pearls.'

'You told him what?' Miss Clark was so shocked that a red blush crept up her neck and into her face. 'Kitty, you didn't!'

'I did. Was that wrong?'

'Heaven help us! You mustn't ask the Colonial Secretary to give you a pearl necklace. Do you know how much pearls cost? Enough to feed you for twenty years back home. And even if they didn't cost anything at all, you must never, never ask anyone to give you presents.'

'But I didn't ask. He was asking me—'

But Miss Clark would not listen, and after they got back to the hotel she complained to Mr Balmer, and he, too, seemed very upset.

'After this, Katie, I want you to stay close to Miss Clark so that she can correct you if, in your ignorance, you say something to bring discredit on the choir.'

Katie no longer had time to worry about Mrs Xiniwe. Although she was not clever enough to give speeches, she was now earning a little extra money by singing at weddings in Dr Parker's church.

At the first wedding, Katie thought she would never forget the beauty of the English bride in her white satin gown and the wreath of orange blossoms holding down her veil. Some day she would make a dress like that and wear it when she found herself a husband. She wondered who that husband would be. No one here in England! She liked Wellington, but he was always clowning. John Hadebe talked only of books. Neli treated her like a child. None of the men in the choir would make a suitable husband. She would have to wait until she went home and could look for him in Kimberley.

Already Katie was homesick. She was almost as lonely in London as she had been during that first year in Port Elizabeth, because Charlotte was always going out with Miss Forbes during their free time and even Martha had found a friend in Miss Gosnell. Katie had no one to take her anywhere, except Miss Clark.

Then one day Mrs Keithley came with Dr Parker to drink tea with the members of the choir. She was wearing a grey silk dress, grey feathered hat, and small gold-rimmed spectacles. Behind them her large grey eyes looked out with the serene promise of a cloudless sky just before sunrise. Instead of asking questions like the other ladies Dr Parker brought, she just sat back and listened. Once she looked over at Katie and smiled, patting the empty space beside her on the sofa. When Katie moved shyly over to sit down next to her, Mrs Keithley whispered, 'You haven't said a word all afternoon.'

'No one's asked me.'

'Is something the matter? Are you unhappy here?'

'Oh no,' Katie said. 'I like England very much.'

'Your eyes are bloodshot. I thought you'd been crying.'

'No,' Katie said. 'I was mending my clothes, and my eyes always get red and watery when I read or sew.'

Mrs Keithley gazed at her intently. 'Does your head ache too?'

'How did you know?'

'I used to have that same trouble. Until I got these spectacles. I'd like to take you to my eye doctor.'

'I saw a doctor in Kimberley. But all he did was give me some yellow ointment, which didn't do any good. And he charged me seven and sixpence.'

'It won't cost you anything to see my doctor.'

Mrs Keithley came in her carriage the next afternoon. The doctor's rooms were in a tall building overlooking Hyde Park. Katie's hands felt clammy when he sat her down in front of a strange machine which he called a stereoscope, but it did not hurt her when she looked through the eye-pieces. Then he shone a bright light into each eye before sitting down to write in a book.

'Myopia,' he said when he had finished writing, 'and astigmatism. Two years ago I couldn't have done much about the astigmatism but recent developments—'

Although she did not understand the long words he was using, she realised he was promising to help her see as well as anyone else.

'You mean you can give me spectacles like Mrs Keithley's?'

'Yes. I'll have them ready for you in two weeks.'

Katie was breathless with excitement when she and Mrs Keithley went out into the street. 'But how can I wait for two whole weeks?'

Twice before her glasses were ready, Mrs Keithley came to take her out on afternoons when no concerts were scheduled.

Once they went to the big shops to look at coats. Mrs Keithley kept shaking her head. 'Shoddy material! Too tight across the shoulders. We'll do much better having my dressmaker cut down one of my coats to fit you.'

They went to Westminster Abbey, where Mrs Keithley showed Katie a plain black stone marking the grave of David Livingstone.

'Do you know who he was?' Mrs Keithley asked.

Katie shook her head.

'He was a missionary doctor in Africa and also a great explorer. He loved Africa very much. It is said that when he died, his servants cut out his heart and buried it under a tree in the jungle before bringing his body back to the coast to be shipped to England.'

At last Mrs Keithley took her back to the eye doctor, who fitted small, round gold-rimmed spectacles to her nose and led her to the window. Katie gasped with amazement. The tops of the trees, always before a blur of green, separated out into distinct leaves. The faces of people in the street below were clearly visible. The whole world looked different. Colours were brighter, outlines of buildings sharper. When she reached the hotel, she picked up a newspaper Charlotte had left on her bed. For the first time in her life, the printed words no longer looked like chicken scratchings in the dust.

5

England

1891–1893

In October Mr Balmer took the choir on a tour of northern England, Scotland and Ireland. For five months they travelled constantly, seldom staying in one place for more than two or three days, and sometimes only for a night, before catching another train and riding on to another town. The girls unpacked, washed their clothes, ironed, rehearsed, sang, ate, slept and packed.

In the tedium of their days, they grew increasingly peevish. Anna Gentle was tired of sleeping in so many strange beds. Sannie Koopman held herself aloof and talked to no one. Frances and Johanna jealously guarded their presents while craning to see what Katie, Charlotte and Martha were given. Mrs Xiniwe was the most difficult, ceaselessly complaining about 'those girls from Kimberley'. Charlotte tried her best to ignore her, but one Sunday in a hotel in Manchester she lost her temper.

Mrs Xiniwe was saying that as soon as they returned to London, she and her husband were going back to South Africa, 'because we are not getting the money we were promised, and it's all her fault.' She pointed at Charlotte.

It was true that in Africa they had each been promised two pounds a week for spending money but were given only ten shillings when they arrived in England. Mr Balmer promised to make it up to them from the proceeds of their concerts once they became better known. Charlotte understood this and tried to explain it to the other members, but Mrs Xiniwe insisted that Mr Balmer and Miss Clark were trying to cheat them.

'And Charlotte is helping them by spreading lies,' she added.

Charlotte's self-control shattered. She jumped up, rushed over to Mrs Xiniwe and yanked at her collar.

'Do you call me a liar?' she hissed. Her fist slammed into Mrs Xiniwe's eye.

In the police court the next day, Charlotte was charged with assault. She did not try to defend herself but said she was willing to apologise and ask forgiveness. Nevertheless, she was ordered to put up five pounds to ensure the peace and ordered to pay the court costs. Fortunately, Katie still had the seven pounds she had saved up and was able to give Charlotte whatever extra money was needed.

But in Chesterfield, a more serious problem forced Charlotte and Mrs Xiniwe to forget their quarrelling for a little time. Two hours before the choir was scheduled to leave for Sheffield, Anna Gentle came rushing downstairs to say that Sannie was very sick. Mr Xiniwe sent Anna to call Mr Thompson, a retired missionary from Africa who had attended one of their concerts and had offered his help if they ever needed it. He came to take Sannie to see a doctor in the workhouse hospital, but she did not want to go. She said someone would steal her trunk if she left it behind. To ease her mind, Mr Thompson promised to take care of it.

'Of course you must see a doctor,' Miss Clark said firmly. 'And if he says you should stay in the hospital, then you will stay. Mr Thompson will look after your things, and when you are better, he and his wife will help you get on the right train so you can join us on the tour.'

Everyone talked and worried about Sannie. They waited anxiously for news in Sheffield. When a letter finally came to Miss Clark, they stood around her while she opened it.

Miss Clark gasped. Her hands began to tremble. She stumbled to a chair and called for Mr Balmer; when he came, she did not speak, just handed him the letter. Stunned and frightened, the choir members waited in silence to be told that Sannie was dead.

But it was worse than that. Sannie had disgraced them all.

After the choir left Sheffield, Mr Thompson had thought he should notify Sannie's family that she was sick and opened her trunk to search for an address. Inside was the dead body of a newborn baby. Apparently, Sannie had given birth during the night. Too frightened to cry out to Anna for help, she had suffered the pain silently and tried to tend herself.

No one in the choir had known that Sannie was pregnant. They simply thought she was getting fat from eating so many sweets and apples. Even Anna Gentle, who shared her room, suspected nothing.

'How is she now?' Mrs Xiniwe asked.

'She's all right.'

'Then she'll soon be joining us?'

Miss Clark looked indignant. 'Of course not. She's going to prison for three months, and she's lucky she wasn't charged with murder. At the inquest the coroner concluded that the child died during childbirth, so she was only charged with concealment of birth.'

After this, Miss Clark kept all the singers busy visiting castles and factories between their concerts. And after rehearsals Mr Balmer read aloud any newspaper articles about them. In Bradford someone described them as

> Black as black could be, but the men splendid in physique, of gentle manners and charming address; the girls also 'black but comely', with a charming modesty and conscious dignity about them that attracted and won immediate sympathy.

Charlotte laughed scornfully. 'What do these English people expect? To see a lot of savages?'

'That's what they expect,' Katie said uncomfortably, remembering the children in London who stopped to stare and point their fingers and cry out 'Look at the darkies'. In the provinces, even people already grown up stopped to stare at them.

In Leeds, the Reverend Mr Pringle met them at the railway station. He was a tall, lean man with bushy black eyebrows and stern eyes. He shook his head impatiently when Miss Clark suggested that with all their luggage they would need hansom cabs.

'No need to waste your money. God gave us two good legs to walk on.' Even Miss Clark was cowed by his manner. She looked uncertainly at her suitcase but finally picked it up herself and started walking while Mr Pringle, his empty hands dangling at his sides, strode rapidly ahead with Mr Balmer. At first Miss Clark tried to keep up with them. But she soon started lagging behind and at last put down her suitcase and paused to rest. As the other singers passed, Katie dropped back to wait with her.

'Are you tired too, Kitty?' Miss Clark said.

'Not yet. When I was little I walked to school every day, five miles there and five miles back.'

'But not with a heavy suitcase?'

'Sometimes with baskets of fruit. We carried them on our heads. If I was at home I'd be carrying my suitcase on my head, but here in England people would just stare at me and think me strange.'

Miss Clark sighed and started to bend down, but before she could grab the handle of her suitcase, brown fingers curled around it and Wellington's voice mimicked Mr Pringle's. 'God gave me two good arms to carry with.'

For once Miss Clark did not scold Wellington for being cheeky. Her lips twitched, but all she said was 'thank you', and then added, 'You're a real gentleman.'

It was a long walk to the hotel. Mr Pringle led them up a busy street lined on both sides with greengrocers, meat markets, pubs and barbers' shops. People crowded the doorways to gawk at them.

'I don't even have to carry my suitcase on my head to make people think me strange,' Katie said. 'I don't like it here.'

'Neither do I,' Miss Clark replied. She sounded tired, and her breath came in little gasps. 'I don't suppose these people have ever before seen anyone from Africa. They're just curious because we're different.'

Katie was surprised. Miss Clark had said 'we', although she wasn't black. Always before, she had seemed more like a know-everything white missionary teacher with her curtsies and her speech lessons and her proper manners. Now she was so tired that she did not notice that her hat had slipped to one side, dislodging a hairpin. Wisps of grey hair hung down on one side of her face, and she was beginning to limp. In her concern, Katie forgot about the staring eyes.

'Perhaps if we see a tearoom you can rest.'

'And have that oaf come looking for us?' Miss Clark said fretfully.

A few minutes later Mr Balmer and Mr Pringle disappeared through the door of a small hotel. Outside the entrance Katie reached up to straighten Miss Clark's hat and tuck away the wisps of hair.

'Thank you, my dear,' Miss Clark said. She straightened her shoulders, gritted her teeth and marched into the hotel without limping.

The other members of the choir were seated in the lounge. Mr Pringle was saying, 'Prayer meeting will be at eight o'clock tonight. And tomorrow morning our missionary society will meet to hear about your life in Africa—'

Mr Balmer interrupted: 'We were only booked for one concert—'

Mr Pringle ignored him, continuing: 'In the afternoon I have excused the children from their Bible studies to let you tell them how Christianity has changed your lives.'

'That's quite impossible,' Mr Balmer said. 'The choir needs time to rehearse and rest before tomorrow night.'

'Our Lord laboured for six days and on the seventh day He rested.' Mr Pringle glowered at the choir, his eyes under his bushy eyebrows as probing and curious as the eyes of the people outside. 'You, too, have work to do. Although your skins are black—'

'Why did God make some of us black and some of us white?' Katie blurted out.

For a moment Mr Pringle frowned at her until his eyebrows came together. 'Because you come from the seed of Ham. When Noah lay drunk and naked in his vineyard, Ham laughed out loud and passed him by. The Lord God was angry and cursed him and decreed that he and his children would be hewers of wood and drawers of water for generation after generation. So it is written in the Bible.'

'But we are not hewers of wood or drawers of water,' Miss Clark answered. 'We are musicians.'

She used the word 'we' again, and her calm voice was like cool water putting the fire out. Yet Mr Pringle's words worried Katie. She did not want to think she came from the seed of Ham, though it was true that among her own people there was much laughter. They laughed when they were happy. They laughed to hide their fears. Sometimes only they knew why they laughed.

She was still pondering Mr Pringle's words in York, where she and Charlotte met an American vaudeville troupe called the Bohee Brothers. The two girls had never known any Americans until they met these black and white men who danced and sang in the music halls and treated each other like equals. Charlotte could not leave them alone. She kept asking them questions about America, and no sooner had they answered one than she asked another, and at last one big black man held out his hands in pretended despair.

'How can we tell you everything in one day? America is God's own country. You must come and see for yourself.'

'We're coming, my sister and I,' Charlotte told him recklessly.

'No, we're not,' Katie interrupted sharply, looking up at the American. 'And anyway, if you like America so much, why don't you stay there?'

'Please, Katie, don't start a big argument,' Charlotte said.

'I didn't start it, you did.'

'Never mind,' Charlotte whispered; 'just go and talk to someone else.' Her big-sister tone warned of a quarrel if Katie did not do as she said. But even from across the room Katie kept watching her, wondering how she could fight against the crazy ideas that man was putting in her head.

In Newcastle the choir was taken to visit a coal mine, where they climbed into a tram without any roof and rode down through a large black hole until they were deep, deep under the ground. A miner helped the girls step out into the tunnel to touch the veins of coal. The light from his lamp showed the coal dust covering his face and hands.

'You're as black as I am,' Katie said, smiling shyly.

'Yes, miss.' He laughed and his teeth showed very white against the blackness. 'But I'm smarter than you because when I go up above I can be either black or white, whichever I choose.'

Katie laughed with him. She never knew his name but she thought of him in Edinburgh and in Glasgow, because in their laughing together he had not set her apart or treated her as a hewer of wood and drawer of water.

After their first concert in Dublin, a West African woman from the university, with skin as black as Katie's, came up to speak to them. Her name was Miss Steele and she invited the girls to drink tea with her on Sunday afternoon.

She lived in a small room above a greengrocer's store not far from the university. There was a stove in one corner of the room, a table and two straight chairs, and behind her bed a skeleton hanging from the ceiling.

'*Hawu!*' Anna Gentle gasped, 'What's that?'

'Only a skeleton,' Miss Steele said. 'Don't worry, it won't bite you.'

'But who was it when it was alive? Was it your brother?'

'I don't know who he was. But now he's my friend.' Miss Steele touched one bone and then another and another, rattling off strange words that Katie had never heard before. 'He's teaching me about our bones. I must know this if I'm going to be a doctor.'

Katie knelt down on the floor as far from the skeleton as she could get, staring up at Miss Steele with awe. She must be very clever to be studying in this school for white doctors, yet her manner was easy and her face was kind.

And as she knelt there, sipping her tea and listening to the others talk, it came to her that perhaps Miss Steele, with all her learning, could tell if what Mr Pringle had said was true.

But she did not like to ask her question in front of the others.

When Miss Clark stood up and beckoned the other girls, Katie pretended to lose her handkerchief. As Miss Steele bent down to help her look under the bed, Katie whispered, 'I too have a question to ask you. Can I see you again? Some place where we can talk privately.'

'I'm only free on Sundays. We'll have to talk now.' She called out to Miss Clark, 'The rest of you go on. I'll bring Katie in a few minutes and walk with her until she catches you up.' As their footsteps clattered down the stairs, she turned back to Katie and asked abruptly, 'Has some man got you into trouble?'

'Oh no, not that.' Katie was embarrassed. 'It's just that I want to know why God made some of us black and some white.'

'Is that all?'

'I need to know. I don't want to believe that I come from the seed of Ham—'

'You haven't.'

'But a minister in Leeds told me—'

'I know, I've heard that too. It's a silly story and only the ignorant believe it. In my medical school we have learned about pigmentation, the blackness in our skins which God has given us to protect us from the sun. Where I come from, it is even hotter than in the south where you live. White people cannot stay too long in my country or else they shrivel up and die. Poor things, they don't have this special blackness to protect them from the sun.'

Poor things! This clever black woman thought that Mr Pringle was a poor thing!

Katie laughed loudly, gleefully. She was still laughing when she caught up with Charlotte and Martha; and if people turned to stare at her, she did not mind. She just felt very lucky she was not one of those poor things who would shrivel up and die if left too long in the sun.

Katie and Charlotte remained in England for two years and three months. All the other members of the original choir returned to Africa by the end of the first year. But Charlotte was not willing to leave London, until she had found some way to continue her education. She could not forget what those Bohee Brothers had told her about the colleges for black people in America.

'There's one called Wilberforce University and that's where we'll go,' she told Katie. 'Now you've got your spectacles, it won't be so hard for you to study to be a nurse.'

Sometimes, in that half-dream state between waking and sleeping, Katie saw herself returning to Kimberley in a white uniform with a sister's cap pinned to her hair. But in the daylight she was not so sure. She wanted to be a nurse, but she also wanted to find a husband before she grew too old. One afternoon when Charlotte spoke again of going to America, Katie noticed with dismay that she was now saying 'when' instead of 'if', as though she had some secret plan to get them there.

'I'm not going,' she replied, so fiercely that it seemed as if, without her knowing it, she had already made up her mind. 'If you go, you'll have to go alone. Don't talk to me any more about such foolishness.'

'Very well,' Charlotte said, but there was a flatness in her voice as she lifted up her chin and stared straight at Katie. After that, there was an emptiness between them not altogether covered by their chatter, not quite forgotten by either girl when new singers arrived from Africa to take the places of those who had left.

Much to Katie's delight, Mr Balmer moved them all out of McCready House Hotel into a small boarding house in Seven Sisters Road, Finsbury Park. The girls were freer there. In the privacy of the boarding house they could leave off their stiff English corsets, and when the weather was warm they could run barefoot in the narrow rear garden. They could sleep later in the mornings because Mr Balmer held rehearsals in the lounge instead of marching them to some rented hall. Best of all, they could walk around the corner by themselves to buy newspapers or thread at the local shops.

With newcomers to look after, Miss Clark did not ask Katie and Charlotte where they were going when the ladies from Dr Parker's City Temple came to take them out. Katie was glad. She was sure that Miss Clark would be very displeased if she found out that Mrs Keithley had taken her to visit Mrs Emmeline Pankhurst in Russell Square. She would be shocked at the way Mrs Pankhurst spoke out her deep thoughts without any pretence of courtesy.

Mrs Pankhurst was a small woman whose hairpins were constantly falling out of her thick black hair and whose purple eyes glowed with enthusiasm when she told of some lady who had just been elected to the London County Council. 'She's opened the door,' she said, 'but one small victory is not enough. We have to keep on fighting for our rights.' She urged Mrs Keithley to march in a forthcoming parade and wear a special sash and hand out printed pieces of paper to passers-by.

'Who are you going to fight when you march in that parade?' Katie asked Mrs Keithley on their way back to her house in Bedford Square.

Mrs Keithley smiled. 'We're not really going to fight. We're just trying to educate the public and persuade Mr Gladstone that we women want the vote.'

'Oh.' Katie still felt very confused, but even with Mrs Keithley she thought herself too young and ignorant to ask more questions. It just seemed very strange to her that English women had no rights, yet they lived in a country that was ruled by a woman.

The summer of 1892 was warm and sunny. Almost every afternoon or early evening the choir sang at garden parties at the great houses around London. Katie started keeping a scrapbook to show Ma, cutting out pictures from the social columns of newspapers and magazines and writing down the names of people she met.

In mid-September, Mr Balmer called her aside and told her she was to sing 'Drink to Me Only with Thine Eyes', when the choir went down to Lord Knutsford's house in Surrey.

'But it's not my turn,' she said.

'I know that.' His face was smooth, unworried. 'But there's no jealousy now in this new choir, and Lord Knutsford has asked specially that you sing this song.'

Lord Knutsford did not have time on that day to speak to Katie by herself, but now and then when she caught his eyes across the lawn he nodded and smiled. Among the guests were English people she had met before, and one of them led her over to be presented to the Prime Minister. Katie was very surprised to find him such an old man and almost blind. If she was Mrs Pankhurst or Mrs Keithley, she thought, she would just go and ask Mr Gladstone to give her the vote.

At last, when Mr Balmer called the choir together to start back on their long journey to Seven Sisters Road, Lord and Lady Knutsford came forward to thank them for their programme, and handed out warm scarves to the men and fur muffs to all the girls, except Katie.

Katie was a little disappointed when he handed her a special gift in a box too small to hold a muff. But when she opened up the black velvet case inside her package, she gasped with delight. Gleaming against the satin lining was a single strand of pearls.

'So you won't forget these English summers,' Lord Knutsford said.

'I'll never forget you,' she answered shyly.

Sometimes in her bedroom Katie would hold the beautiful pearls around her neck, but Miss Clark would never let her wear them in public. 'What if you lost them? What if they were stolen? I don't think you appreciate their value,' she kept saying. But some day she would wear them, Katie promised herself. Some day when Miss Clark was not around to tell her what to do.

At the end of their third summer in England, Mr Vert called a meeting in his office. He shook hands with Mr Balmer and Miss Clark and greeted Charlotte by name. Charlotte seemed very pleased with herself. Katie wondered why, and in her wondering, she did not listen to Mr Vert until the surprised exclamations of the other singers caught her attention.

'You will all want to visit your families,' Mr Vert went on after a pause. 'But after a month in Africa, Mr Balmer and Miss Clark will take you on tour to America. That is, all of you except Katie. I have other plans for Katie.'

'I want to go home also,' Katie said loudly.

She could hardly hear his answer over the noisy arguments amongst the others. Some, like Charlotte, were excited at the thought of America. Others, like Katie, were tired of travelling. At last Mr Vert held up his hands. 'All right. I can see we won't settle this now. You can talk further amongst yourselves and then Mr Balmer can tell me what each of you decides. But you, Katie, I want to talk to you privately.'

'With Charlotte,' Katie said.

'This has nothing to do with Charlotte.'

'Nevertheless, she's my senior sister. If any man wants to talk to me privately, then he should ask permission of my sister. That is the custom among our people.'

Mr Vert laughed. 'Then Charlotte will have to stay, and Mr Balmer as well.' He waited until all the others had filed out of his office, then pulled three chairs up closer to his desk and motioned for them to sit down.

'The choir has done very well in England. Reviews on the whole have been excellent. Mr Balmer has gathered together a group of excellent singers, but you, Katie, are the best of the sopranos. In fact,' he paused a moment and looked at her intently, 'you're the best natural singer I have ever heard.'

'Me?' Katie said uncomfortably.

'Yes, you. With the right teachers and the proper training, you can become one of the great singers of our time. So after your holiday, I want you to come back here to study.'

'But—'

'Let me explain. I myself will raise the money to pay for everything, your passage back, your fees, clothes, everything. I just ask one thing: when you are ready, I want to be the only one to manage your concerts.'

Katie shook her head. 'I'm tired of studying. I don't want to be a great singer. I just want to go home.'

Mr Vert looked at her as though she were an ignorant child. 'I don't think you understand. I'll make you rich and famous – so rich you will be able to buy anything you want, go anywhere. You'll sing in the great concert halls of Europe, and even kings and queens will pay you homage.'

Katie laughed. 'A black girl like me? Whoever heard of such a thing?'

'They will,' he promised. 'When they hear your voice, they won't wonder who you are or where you come from. They won't see you. They'll just listen to you sing.'

Katie's laughter stopped abruptly. She thought of the children in London pointing their fingers and calling out, 'Come look at the darkies.' She thought of Mr Pringle, who told her she came from the seed of Ham. She thought of a white South African whose words had echoed across the dining-room in a big hotel, 'They may look civilised in their Christian clothes, but underneath, the blacks are all savages.' At least those people had seen her, and perhaps it was better to be seen and set apart than to be a nobody who is not seen at all.

Charlotte touched her arm and whispered for her to answer Mr Vert. Only then did she realise that he was no longer talking but waiting for her to answer some question she had not heard.

'I don't sing for people who do not see me,' she said abruptly.

'No, you misunderstand. I mean that when you sing, nothing matters except your songs.' When Katie did not answer, he turned impatiently to Charlotte. 'You explain. I don't think she understands what a wonderful opportunity this is.'

Charlotte reached out and squeezed Katie's hand as though there had never been any quarrelling between them and, speaking softly in Xhosa, she said, 'I too am tired of living only among the white people. But after we've had a nice long holiday at home, I'm going to America. Perhaps Mr Vert will let you come with me.'

'No,' Katie said. 'Already I've been too long away from Ma and Pa, and I want to find a husband among our own people. I don't want to marry in a foreign country.'

Charlotte squeezed her hand again and looked across the desk at Mr Vert and spoke slowly, each word clear and distinct: 'My sister understands and she is grateful, but she is no longer a child. If she wants to stay at home, then she can stay at home.'

'But I'll make her rich and famous,' Mr Vert kept saying.

'I don't want to be rich and famous,' Katie said stubbornly.

Mr Vert and Mr Balmer just stared at her, astonished into silence. Then suddenly they were both talking at once, explaining, pleading, scolding; but Katie paid no attention, just kept repeating that she was finished singing in front of people who did not see her.

On the way home in the hansom cab, Katie wondered if Mr Balmer was angry. He was silent, seeming to close up his thoughts around him. But that evening and all the next morning Miss Clark kept talking. She did not speak of fame or riches. She argued that Katie's voice was not hers to throw away but a sacred gift from God to bring happiness to the world.

'Then I will sing His praises in my church and perhaps in choirs also. But I will not sing alone.'

Dr Parker came and tried to persuade her, as did Mrs Keithley and Miss Forbes and many others. Indeed, it seemed to Katie that Mr Vert had called on everyone she knew to come and tell her that it was her duty to be a famous singer.

But Katie never sang again in England.

Durban

1954

'And so we came home,' Katie tells me. 'From the train we could see Ma and Pa on their back stoep waving a white sheet, and Phillip was waiting at the station with a big crowd come to greet us.'

'Were you ever sorry?' I ask.

'Sorry about what?'

'About not going back to England and becoming a famous singer?'

'No,' she says abruptly. 'I'd already been too long in England.' Her hand drops to her lap and she gazes out of the window. 'I was very happy until—' Her voice drops so low I can no longer hear what she is saying. I wait, not wanting to break her chain of thought, but when the silence continues I grow restless.

'Until what, Auntie?'

She turns back to me and raises the microphone to her mouth. 'Our house looked just the same except for hundreds of birds fluttering around the roof. When Phillip saw me looking at them, he told me he was now a pigeon-breeder. "I have all kinds," he said. "Blue ones, white ones, even some with red around their necks. And you will eat well tonight. For you I have killed some of my birds, and since yesterday they have been stewing on the stove."

'"What tough old birds they must be," I said. "It's the young ones with the feathers just beginning to grow that are the most tender."'

She laughs, but I notice she has not yet answered my question.

6

Kimberley
1893–1894

It was good to be home again, to hear the easy flow of Xhosa or Sotho as more and more of their friends crowded into the little house, their bodies spicing the air with the pungent smell of oil and sweat – that honest, human smell of people close together, a smell she had almost forgotten after so long in England where the white people, for all their washing and perfume, could never quite disguise the odour of their skins. Everyone came: Mr Sinamela and his jealous wife, members of their church, some of the teachers from the school where Charlotte used to teach, even a white man who wanted to write a story for the newspaper. The head deacon of the Presbyterian church arrived with his wife and his two younger daughters, but Katie was disappointed that Elizabeth, his eldest daughter, did not come. When she asked after her, the deacon's voice grew harsh and his eyes grew cold. 'I have no daughter Elizabeth,' he said, and turned away.

Katie was too shocked to ask questions, but even as she spoke to the others in the room, she kept wondering about Elizabeth.

At last when her legs were cramped from sitting too long and her head throbbed from all the excitement, Pa raised his hands for silence. 'We are honoured that you have come to greet my daughters. Now it is late; but before we separate, let us pray together and thank the Lord for bringing them safely home.'

As soon as the family was alone, Katie asked about Elizabeth. Pa shook his head in warning and motioned towards the younger children. 'We do not speak of Elizabeth.'

But Henry and John knew what Katie did not know, and they looked at each other and snickered behind their hands while Ma carried in the pigeon stew. After dinner the girls opened up their biggest suitcase and brought out shirts for Pa, a coat for Ma, suits for Phillip and Henry, a football for John, and a doll with eyes that closed for Mary Ann. Later Pa and Ma had to see all the treasures the girls had been given in England. Yet as Katie held up each present she'd been given, she kept thinking of Elizabeth; and as soon as Henry and John had rolled out their mats and gone to sleep, she asked again what had happened to her.

'She disgraced herself with a white man,' Pa said sternly. 'When her father found out, he chased her away and told her never to come back with her shame.'

'How could he be so cruel?' Katie gasped.

'He'd brought up his girls as Christians. How could he forgive her when he is the deacon? And what of her younger sisters? Would they learn from her to forget his teachings?'

'But it's not fair,' Katie said in despair. 'Elizabeth was a good girl. She must have been deceived by that man. Her father should have made him marry her.'

Phillip laughed derisively. 'White men spoil our girls and get them into trouble but they don't marry them.'

'Then her father should have made him pay.'

Phillip laughed again. 'Listen to her, Pa.' He mimicked her words. 'She talks like a white woman.'

'I do not,' Katie cried out, turning around and glaring at Phillip. 'I don't talk like a white woman. I talk like myself, you hear.'

'I hear.' But his laughter mocked her, and even Pa and Ma were grinning as though the words she spoke were childish nonsense. Charlotte too was silent, hesitating, her eyes troubled.

Katie ran into the bedroom and flung herself down on the iron bed. Poor Elizabeth, she wept, what had become of her? And what will become of me, she wondered, now that she had come home to find her own family setting her apart?

The door opened on a faint glow of candlelight and closed again. Charlotte's dress rustled across the room, and the bed creaked as she sat down and patted Katie's shoulder.

'I wish I'd never come home,' Katie sobbed.

'Hush! You're tired. Me also. I think I can sleep for a whole week. Come, unlace my corset.'

'Yes,' Katie said dully, sitting up, swinging her feet over the edge of the bed, fumbling with the laces of Charlotte's corset and then gradually drawing in a deep breath as her own corset was eased.

'Tomorrow we can leave these off,' Charlotte said happily, 'and be easy again.' She yawned and crawled into the narrow bed and curled her body to make room for Katie.

'How long before you go to America? Perhaps—,' Katie whispered, but already Charlotte was asleep. She was like that. Whatever she wanted to do, she did without hesitation. If she thought it was time to sleep, she slept. But sometimes, no matter how tired she was, Katie lay awake, thinking and worrying and listening to the different sounds of the night. The little house in Kimberley was full of noises: the heavy breathing of Phillip on his mat in the dining-room, the slither of mice and snakes above the canvas ceiling, the mumble of her parents' voices as they readied themselves for bed. The walls were too thin for privacy, and as she lay awake she heard Pa's words distinctly.

'I do not understand that one,' he was saying. 'Charlotte is sometimes troublesome because there is no turning her aside from what she wants; but she is easy compared with Katie.'

Ma sighed. 'She was too young when we let her go to England. Her thoughts and her manners were not yet altogether shaped. Now they are shaped, but not by us. She has returned black–English. Poor Katie.'

Pa sounded impatient. 'Charlotte's not like that.'

'No,' Mama replied slowly, 'Charlotte's a chameleon. She was already of an age to marry when she went away, and she knew our ways. Now she can put them on or take them off. But Katie doesn't know them.'

'Then Charlotte must teach her,' Pa said.

It was not easy to be a chameleon. Katie watched Charlotte walking down the street full of life and intelligence until a European approached, then suddenly drooping her shoulders as she moved aside to let him pass. More than once she had to pull Katie with her.

'Don't forget to look stupid,' she warned, 'or else some European will call you cheeky.' It was Charlotte that nudged her into silence before an older woman, that taught her to forget about sitting on the ground but to kneel instead with her legs close together for the sake of modesty and her weight resting on her heels.

There was so much to remember. Customs differed from one household to the next, depending on whether the family was Sotho or Xhosa or Swazi or Fingo, whether they were African or Coloured, Christian or heathen. But Charlotte moved easily among the different peoples, correcting Katie in a whisper and afterwards explaining their customs, until in time Katie began to lose the stiffness of her English habits.

The two girls went everywhere together. If Charlotte stayed at home, then Katie had to stay at home also. Even if Katie just wanted to visit Martha, Ma would not permit her to go alone.

'But in England I was allowed—'

'Not in Africa. You're grown and of an age to marry, so your senior sister must protect you,' Ma said firmly.

'Why doesn't she trust me?' Katie complained to Charlotte. 'I only wanted to gossip a while with Martha.'

'She trusts you,' Charlotte said. 'It's just the custom. It is for me to see that you don't disgrace yourself.'

'Like Elizabeth? Just because I took her side, they think I need a policeman.'

Charlotte shook her head. 'No, but if some man wants to make love with you, he must ask me first. If you like him, then I can tell him that although you are grown, you are still ignorant, so he must be careful with you and protect your name. And I will warn Pa so he will be prepared if this man's father comes to talk of marriage.'

'But what about you? You haven't any senior sister. What if some man wants to make love with you?'

For once Charlotte did not know the answer. 'In the country it's easy. Everyone there knows the leader of the girls. But here in town everything is all mixed up, and our customs become mixed up as well.' She frowned uncertainly and then began to laugh. 'But you don't have to worry about me. When Mr Balmer calls me, I'm going to America. I wish you'd come too. There's still time to change your mind.'

But Katie could not be persuaded. Instead, she and Charlotte walked the three miles beyond the railway station to Kenilworth, a village the De Beers mining company had built for the white people who worked on the diamond mines. Pepper trees shaded the wide main street. Red brick houses were set back in pleasant gardens, and there was plenty of grass.

Charlotte waited in the road while Katie went to the back door to ask for work. At the third house she got a job as a domestic – washing, ironing and helping the cook with the housework. She was to report every morning at six o'clock and stay until dinner was served at night. Only on Sundays could she leave early. She was paid seven shillings a week and provided with food. Best of all, she could still live at home.

After her work was over, she and Charlotte went to choir practice or visited their friends. Each day Katie kept hoping she would meet some man who would make her a good husband. It did not matter to her if he was tall or short, handsome or ugly. She just wanted to marry a true Christian and have many children. Sometimes, lying in their bed at night, Katie would speak to Charlotte of some man they had met, but always Charlotte found some reason why he was not to be trusted. He was not properly educated or she'd heard he was a gambler or he must have a sickness in his chest because he coughed too much.

Once at a party at Martha's house, they met a theological student from the Cape, and all evening long Charlotte kept pushing Katie towards him.

'But he's too old for me,' Katie told her on the way home. 'I think he must already have a wife.'

'But you didn't even find out. If he isn't married, he'd be a good husband.'

'Then why don't you marry him yourself?'

'I'm not ready to get married yet,' Charlotte said.

Katie could not understand why Charlotte was so slow about men. There was something in her manner which kept young men from seeking her out. Katie sometimes wondered whether any man who might want to make love with her would have the courage to ask Charlotte's permission.

It was at a concert on a Saturday night that Katie first saw Gershom.

He was tall, like Pa, with skin the colour of honey, and there was something about the way he strode towards them with his head thrown back and his eyes bold which wiped away Katie's weariness.

'Martha,' she whispered and nodded in his direction, 'who's that?'

'I think he's Gershom. Didn't you see him at Mrs Njapa's party?'

'No.'

'He came early, before me. But after a little while I didn't see him.'

He paid Martha no attention as he approached, and did not look at Katie. He was too busy pushing his way into the group clustered around Charlotte.

Katie put her hand on Charlotte's elbow. 'It's time to go.'

Charlotte nodded, finished one last story and then shook her head at further questions. But Gershom was not to be dismissed so easily. 'Miss Manye,' he said to Charlotte, 'I hear your father comes from Ramokgopa's village in the Soekmekaar district. My brother married a woman from that place.'

'Indeed?'

'Yes.' He looked down at her expectantly.

'Then your brother is very lucky,' Charlotte said abruptly and, linking her arm in Katie's, asked, 'Are you coming, Martha?'

Katie was shocked by her discourtesy. As she was pulled forward, she glanced back over her shoulder to smile an apology. Gershom's face was angry until she caught his eyes and then, hunching up his shoulders in mock despair, he grinned back at her as though they shared some secret joke.

'How could you be so rude?' she asked Charlotte on the way home. 'That man's a stranger here and he was only trying to be friendly.'

'A stranger? Him? Don't be silly. He was half drunk when he came to Mrs Njapa's last week.'

Yet in spite of what she said, Katie could not forget the shape of Gershom's face or the tone of his voice. He was more beautiful than any other man she had ever seen. He did not look like a drunkard to her. Long after Charlotte had gone to sleep, Katie lay awake on their narrow bed with the warm rhythm of Charlotte's breath on her neck, wondering if and when she would see him again.

The next day was Sunday. As she walked to Kenilworth in the first light of morning and came home in the heat of the afternoon, she looked eagerly around each corner, half expecting to see him on the street. But he was never there. Yet she felt his presence nearby, and when she saw him in church, sitting in the back row with Martha's brother, she was not surprised. All during the service she watched him out of the corner of her eye. He bowed his head reverently during the prayers and listened solemnly to every word the pastor spoke, nodding his head in agreement like a proper Christian. After the service was over, he half-smiled at Katie as she and Charlotte came out into the sunlight but did not approach her directly until Charlotte turned away to speak to Mr Sinamela. Then suddenly Katie found him standing beside her.

'Everyone at your house, are they well?' he asked softly.

'Very well,' Katie said. He was so tall that she had to bend her head back to look up into his face, and the uncertainty in his eyes made her want to laugh with happiness. Such shyness in a man so handsome was like magic that made her grow tall until she felt bigger and more clever than even Charlotte.

'Yes, even my brother Phillip is well,' she added slyly. 'Of course, he is crazy in the head about his pigeons. I think if a lion came out of the veld and stopped him on the street to ask about his pigeons, he would consider that lion a friend and bring him home.'

Gershom looked around the churchyard. 'Which one is Phillip?'

'That one in the new suit.' Katie nodded at a group of young men standing together.

Gershom smiled knowingly and then, as Charlotte came back, he turned carelessly away as if the words between them were nothing.

'What was he saying to you?' Charlotte eyed Katie suspiciously.

'Nothing much. Just asked if everyone in our family was well.'

'Why you? If his brother married a woman from Soekmekaar, he should have spoken to Pa.'

'I don't know why,' Katie said uneasily.

A few days later when Katie returned from work, Phillip and Gershom were both sitting in the dining-room with Pa. As always when he met some-one from Soekmekaar, Pa wanted to know about the rains and the crops and the changes which had taken place since he had left there so long ago. 'And your brother?' Pa asked. 'He has not yet come to visit us.'

'He works too hard,' Gershom replied. 'He only gets two Sundays off a month. Then he is very busy in his own church. He's Dutch Reformed, because of his wife. Before that he was Lutheran.'

'Then why aren't you Lutheran also?' Charlotte interrupted.

'I like the Presbyterians better.'

'But the Lutherans permit the drinking of beer, and we Presbyterians forbid any drinking.'

'Myself also, I don't like to drink,' Gershom said.

'Gershom's not a drinker,' Katie protested later as she and Charlotte undressed for bed. 'He told us that himself.'

'Katie,' Charlotte hesitated, and then in a rush of words, 'don't believe any-thing he tells you. No matter what he says, he smelled of beer when he came to Mrs Njapa's party.'

'You only say that, because you know I like him. You always find fault with any man I like,' Katie retorted, climbing into bed after Charlotte. But instead of fitting herself comfortably into the curves of her sister's body, she held her-self stiff and straight on the mattress, clutching the edge of the iron bedstead to brace herself into separateness.

Always in the past, she had told Charlotte everything, but in the days that followed there were some things she could not tell: how her chest almost burst with happiness at the sight of Gershom, how easily her laughter came whenever she heard him speak.

On Friday he was helping Phillip with his pigeons when Katie came home from work. On Saturday night he was already at Martha's house when Katie and Charlotte arrived. On Sunday he was sitting again in the back of the church. He even made friends with Mr Sinamela and joined the choir. But although they saw him often, Charlotte never left Katie's side or forgot for one moment that she was the senior sister. Nevertheless, it did not matter, for Katie and Gershom had much they could tell each other with their eyes, their hands, or the tilt of their heads. Katie knew he wanted to become her lover. Soon, she thought, he would ask her sister's permission. Others thought so too.

'Has he spoken yet?' Martha asked one Wednesday night.

'No,' Charlotte said.

'Perhaps he will speak tonight?'

'Perhaps.'

But Gershom said nothing to Charlotte before or during or after the choir practice.

'Martha's not the only one who's asked if he has spoken,' Charlotte told Katie. 'Nettie's sister also asked, and some of the other girls. Even Mrs Njapa. I tell you, Katie, he's making a fool of you.'

'He is not. It's you who are making a fool of me. You're so rude you don't give him a chance to speak.'

Gershom never did ask Charlotte's permission. He wrote a letter instead. Katie found it slipped under the cover of her hymn book on Sunday morning and waited, trembling, until Charlotte turned her head and she was able to slip it down the neck of her blouse. After church she kept urging Charlotte to hurry.

'Let's get home. We can set out the food and have it ready when the others come.'

'What a busy worker you are today,' Charlotte said flatly, calling to John and Mary Ann and stopping to tell Ma that she would take the younger children with her. 'Perhaps you think I didn't see, but I saw.'

She did not speak to Katie again until they entered the house; and then wearily, as though already an old woman, she told her to go and read her letter.

Katie hesitated. 'Please Charlotte, don't be angry.'

'I'm not angry, only ashamed.' She pushed the younger children ahead of her into the kitchen, leaving Katie alone. Her great rattling of dishes and the heavy stamp of her feet were worse than any quarrelling.

Katie pulled the letter out of her blouse. The large uneven writing on the envelope was smudged by the sweat from between her breasts, and the flap had come unstuck, but the words on the single sheet of paper inside were clear and black. 'Dear Miss Katie, In the greenness of your dress and with your interwoven eyelashes, you are more beautiful than the water grasses.'

Katie read his letter over and over, repeating the words out loud until it seemed as if Gershom were there in the room with her. No matter what Charlotte said, she thought, he would make her a good husband and give her plenty of children. She folded up the letter at last and pushed it down again between her breasts, waiting a moment while she thought up what to tell Charlotte. But she waited too long.

The front door banged. Phillip and Henry tramped through the dining-room into the kitchen, and Charlotte began asking Phillip what he knew of Gershom.

'Nothing much,' Phillip said. 'Just that he says he wants to be a pigeon-breeder.'

'Then you'd better find out all you can. If we're not careful he will get your sister into trouble.'

It wasn't fair for her to tell Phillip so soon. Katie rushed out to tell her to mind her own business, but at that moment Ma and Pa returned from church. Katie clamped her lips together as Pa sat down and began spooning the mutton stew over his rice. Ma held little Mary Ann in her lap, feeding her special pieces of meat and at the same time restraining John from sprinkling sugar on his stew. Across the table Phillip and Henry watched Katie slyly as they gobbled their food. No one spoke except Charlotte, and she talked too much and too fast about nothing. Then Phillip scraped his chair back from the table and stood up.

'I have to go out. Can I take the lantern?'

'Where are you going so late that you need a lantern?' Pa asked.

'The lantern's on the back stoep,' Charlotte interrupted quickly, and then, 'Pa, in all this time since we've been home, you haven't yet spoken of going back to Soekmekaar. Is the old man still calling you?'

'He calls,' Pa said, forgetting Phillip, 'but my girls give me no chance to speak of him. With you it is talk, talk, talk of America.'

'Now you are making fun,' Charlotte said. 'All our lives we have waited for you to take us back to that land beyond the mountains.'

'How can I take you if you go to America?'

'You can take the others, and when Katie and I come back we'll join you there.'

'I'm not going to America,' Katie said.

'But you must. Pa, tell Katie she must come with me.'

Pa shook his head. 'She went with you once; now she may stay at home if she chooses.'

While Charlotte was talking, Phillip left the house to go where he wanted to go and see whom he wanted to see. He would come back with news about Gershom, Katie thought nervously. She moved restlessly in her chair, and Gershom's letter inside her blouse brushed against her breasts like the quick touch of his hand, making her ache for the sight of his face.

All afternoon she waited quietly for Phillip's return, telling herself that he would bring good news to wipe away Charlotte's suspicions. Then Phillip and Charlotte would warn Pa so that he could think on the matter of *lobola* before Gershom came – came with whom? The brother who had married a woman from Soekemaar?

And what would Pa ask in return for his daughter? Ten head of cattle for himself and one for Ma, as the white people were saying was the proper *lobola*? Perhaps, being a Christian, Pa would not ask for anything at all. The missionaries preached against the system of *lobola*. They called it brideprice and scolded the people for 'selling' their daughters in marriage. But they did not understand. To the Xhosa and Sotho, Swazi and Zulu, and indeed among all the tribes, *lobola* was like a rope binding two families together when their children married. If a man gave so much for a woman, he would not want to ill-treat her, and she herself would try to be a good wife, knowing that her own father would have to give up those cattle if her husband said she was no good and sent her back to her homeplace. Thus *lobola* was one custom which even the Christians did not want to throw away. Nevertheless, it was not an easy matter. Pa would not ask what Gershom could not give, yet if he asked too little, people would think his daughter worthless.

The daylight faded. Ma's rocking-chair creaked on the front porch. Charlotte lit a candle and pulled it next to the book she was reading. Katie smeared jam on a slice of bread and gave it to Mary Ann, then lay down on her bed to rest while she waited for Phillip's return. She did not think she would sleep, yet before she knew it she was waking up in the darkness to the sound of Pa's voice.

'Where's Phillip? He should be home by now.'

'He's all right, Pa,' Charlotte said calmly. 'He'll come soon.'

'He should be sleeping. We should all be sleeping,' Ma said.

'Then you and Pa go to bed. I'm not finished reading, and when he comes, I'll lock the door.'

Charlotte was still sleeping when Katie left for work the next morning but Phillip followed her out to the gate. 'Katie,' he said heavily, 'you made much running about for me last night. I went to see Gershom's brother. First I went to the Dutch Reformed church, but this was not his Sunday. Someone told me where he worked. It was a long way to that place and I saw him for only a few minutes. He says it is true what Charlotte says. Gershom is not a true Christian. You must not marry him – his own brother says so.'

'You put those words in his mouth. Just because Charlotte has turned against me, you've turned against me also.'

He shook his head. 'Just listen to—'

'I won't listen.' Katie backed away, ready to run if he tried to grab her, but he just stood there, silent, staring at her as though he thought she was a wicked, headstrong girl. She cried out angrily, 'Why don't you mind your own business?'

'This *is* my business.' There was a quiet dignity in his manner which frightened her, because he no longer acted like a younger brother, to be teased and spoiled and ordered about.

'No, it isn't,' she said and turned and ran from him, all the way to Kenilworth. There, hardly pausing to greet the cook, she grabbed her brick, wrapped clean rags around it, and flung herself down on her knees to rub wax into the cement floor as if in this way she could rub out the memory of Phillip's words. By the time she was finished waxing all the inside floors, the cook called. Her cousin, he told her, was waiting at the back door.

Her cousin? She had no relatives in Kimberley. Her heart thumped with excitement. Perhaps Gershom had dared to seek her out. But the man who waited was altogether a stranger. He was tall like Gershom and his skin was the colour of honey, but he was older, heavier, and stern of face.

'Miss Katie,' he said in halting Dutch, 'I've come to warn you because you are the daughter of my wife's cousin. I don't like this business between you and my brother. I've heard you are a Christian girl, and I tell you this: my father is a drinker, my mother is a drinker, all my brothers and sisters are drinkers. I am the only one who does not drink. All the rest are no good and I've thrown them away. You must also throw them away. Forget this heathen brother of mine and open your eyes on someone else.'

'No, you're mistaken. Gershom is a good Christian. He comes to my church.'

'He's telling you lies.'

'It's you who are telling me lies,' Katie cried out in despair. 'You've thrown your family away and made yourself a stranger to them, so you are a stranger to me also.'

Yet all that day she worried about Gershom. One minute she half believed his brother, but in the next she remembered Gershom's face, the special way he smiled, and, thinking of him, she felt herself beautiful like the water grasses and loved him for making her beautiful.

She had no chance to mention Gershom's brother to Charlotte. When she came home that night the house was full of excitement. Martha was cutting out a dress on the dining-room table, Ma was busy running up seams on her sewing machine, and Charlotte was writing down lists and figures on a sheet of paper.

'I'm really going,' she called out to Katie. 'Mr Balmer and Miss Clark are waiting in Cape Town. Come with me, Katie. There's still time. Please. We can send a telegraph.' Her face was as loving and as bright as before the time of Gershom.

'When do you leave?'

'As soon as I can. As soon as Ma finishes sewing my new clothes. I need two dresses and bloomers and some flannel petticoats. It's going to be cold in New York.'

'You can have my coat with the fur collar, the one Mrs Keithley gave me.'

'You'll need that yourself.'

'I'm not going, Charlotte.'

'Ma, tell Katie she must come with me.'

Ma looked up from her sewing machine. 'Don't press her. Remember what Pa said. If she wants to stay, then she can stay.'

Two days later, after choir practice, Gershom stepped forward to greet them. Charlotte, with a slight shrug of her shoulders, turned away, leaving Katie and Gershom standing alone a little distance from everyone else.

'I see you found my letter,' he said softly. 'What do you say?'

'There's nothing for me to say. This is a matter for my father.'

'No, you must tell me yourself.'

Katie laughed at his impatience, shaking her head to tease him as he demanded an answer again and again.

'If you don't like me, you'd show me.' He stepped forward confidently. She backed away until she felt the cold air from the open door on her back, then quickly darted around him so he could no longer trick her into moving outside. Perhaps Charlotte was watching, for at this moment she reached out to touch Katie's arm.

'Come, Martha and I are ready to go.'

'Myself also,' Gershom said, escorting the three girls out of church and down the familiar streets. Halfway home, his fingers brushed Katie's elbow, and at his touch her whole body trembled, and involuntarily her steps slowed until his hand curled possessively around her arm and began pulling her gently out of the swinging light of Charlotte's lantern into the darker shadows of some bushes.

Charlotte suddenly swung her lantern in a wider arc and called Katie's name.

'I'm here,' Katie said, and yanked her arm from Gershom's clutch. 'I tripped over a stone in the road.'

'Oh,' Charlotte said.

Gershom walked on with them as far as their gate. Katie paused there, hoping that Charlotte would give them one more moment together, but she paused also.

'Goodnight,' Katie said at last.

'Rest well,' Gershom answered, and was still standing there when she glanced back at him from the door.

The next night Charlotte and Phillip talked to Pa. Mary Ann and John were both asleep by the time Katie returned from work, but the others were all sitting around the table in the dining-room. The light from their candles flickered in the draught.

'Go to your room and shut the door,' Pa said sternly. His hands were clasped together in front of him and his eyebrows were wrinkled together in thought. Ma sat across the table, her eyes worried. Phillip was biting his lips. Charlotte was crying. And Henry, little fourteen-year-old Henry, was looking at Katie as if she was not of the family.

'Go to your room,' Pa repeated with heavy authority.

'But I—'

'Did you hear?'

'Yes, Pa.'

Katie undressed in the darkness and lay down on the bed, trying to catch their words, but they kept their voices low and the wall between distorted the sounds so that she could not understand what they said. Nevertheless she heard the uncertainty in Ma's voice, the quaver in Charlotte's, and the sadness in Pa's. It was a terrible thing to disappoint those you love, and her head throbbed and her chest ached with the pain of hurting them. Yet she could not bring herself to ask their forgiveness or promise to give up the thought of Gershom.

It was a long time before Charlotte came to bed. Katie heard the rustle of her clothes dropping to the floor and the warmth of her body as she lay on her side of their bed.

'Katie,' she whispered, but Katie did not answer. There was nothing for them to say to each other.

In the morning Katie left for Kenilworth at first light. When she came home after her work, Martha was handing pins to Ma, who was busily fitting Charlotte's dresses. Mrs Njapa was out in the kitchen, ironing. While Katie filled a pot with water to heat on the stove, Henry came bursting through the front door.

'I saw Gershom with another man. I think they're coming here.'

Ma gasped. 'Go tell your father. He's over next door. And girls, pick up the dresses. Charlotte, I'll unpin you in the kitchen.'

She pushed the others through the door and shut it behind her. A few minutes later, they heard Pa enter and after him other footsteps and Gershom's voice, introducing another brother, not the one who had married Pa's cousin.

Katie moved closer to the door but Charlotte began talking loud nonsense. Martha laughed nervously. Mrs Njapa kept slamming the iron down on the stove. With all that noise Katie could not hear what the men were saying until Gershom began shouting in anger.

'You refuse everything. What is it you want?'

Charlotte stopped in the middle of a sentence; Mrs Njapa paused, her iron in mid-air; Martha, Katie and Ma stood silent, listening.

'Nothing,' Pa was saying. 'My daughters do not marry into the families of drunkards.'

'But I'm not a drinker,' Gershom shouted again.

'You lie,' Pa said bluntly. 'Do you think I'm an old fool who knows nothing?'

Gershom swore at Pa and threatened him with disaster through the magic powers of some sorcerer. But Pa said nothing, and at last Gershom and his brother stamped angrily out of the house.

Katie could not look at anyone because of the shame she felt. She stumbled past Pa into the bedroom and fell down on the floor with her head against the wall, shuddering with grief. Vaguely she heard a flurry of footsteps and Pa's firm voice, 'No, Charlotte, leave her alone.'

At last, when her tears were finished and she had dragged herself over to the bed, he came into the room and stood there looking down at her, a sad smile on his face.

'Ah, Malubisi, my heart is pierced to see you weep. But the tears you shed now are only puddles that will dry up under the sun. Yet the tears that women weep after marriage are like the rivers that grow wider and deeper until they are lost in the sea. Some day you will remember my words and say your father was wise.'

Katie's throat was too swollen for speech. Pa sat down and laid his roughened hand gently on her shoulder while the daylight faded and the spasms of her sobs eased. Not until Ma called him for his evening meal did he rise to his feet.

'Do you want food?'

Katie shook her head.

'Then rest well,' he said and left her alone.

She closed her eyes and tried to sleep, but although she was too weary to lift her hand, her thoughts moved swiftly as leaf shadows on a windy day. If only Gershom had promised to reform himself, she might have rebelled. But instead he had cursed and threatened, thus showing himself to be what Charlotte and Phillip and that other brother had said – a no-good heathen who must be thrown away. But what was there left for her in Kimberley without any dreams of a husband and children? Should she go to America with Charlotte? No, she thought, she did not want to leave her family again. She could hear them all in the dining-room, keeping their voices low. Only Henry was loud and curious.

'What do we do now, Pa? Will Katie run away? Or do Phillip and I walk with her to work each morning and bring her home?'

'Shame on you,' Pa said. 'You can trust your sister. Tonight her heart is troubled because she knows this business is finished. But tomorrow she won't be tempted by that man again.'

What made him so sure? Katie wondered. Perhaps because when she was little he himself had made her repeat after him the Ten Commandments:

'Honour thy father. . .' So it was said in the Bible, but so it was also said among those of their people who had never heard the Word. Wasn't that why Pa had brought his family away from the happy life on the farm in Uitenhage – because his own father had summoned him home, was waiting even now for them to save their money and continue their journey northwards?

For the first time in her life, Katie thought of that old heathen grandfather as a real person, not just an imaginary figure in the stories Pa told. What was he like, this old man with his several wives, his herds of cattle, and his many children – who still loved the one son that had left him so many years ago?

7

Soekmekaar

1894

As the wagon jolted over the rutted tracks leading northwards from Pietersburg, Katie pulled her blankets closer about her shoulders. Ma stirred, sat up, peered out through the canvas flaps.

'Ah, Katie,' she said, 'it's a cruel land.'

'Yes, Ma.' The wind tore at the canvas over their heads and whipped away between the strange forms of cactus which reared up in the grey morning like fragments of a nightmare. Clumps of grass drooped wearily over the yellow earth, and in the near-distance the pale grey-green trunks of the fever trees stood out along a dry river bed, like ghosts left over from the darkness. Yes, it was a cruel land – cruel as Gershom who had once come from some place hereabouts. Last night they had passed by the Lutheran mission where he had gone to school. Rasiaga, the wagon-driver, had pointed it out, had even admitted that some of the young men from Ramokgopa's village were students there.

'But Ramokgopa doesn't like it,' he had said. 'He says those missionaries are trying to break up our people.'

'Why does he say that?' Ma asked quickly.

'Because those of our boys who go there come back thinking they're bigger than the rest of us. They laugh at the old ways and want to wear European clothes. Soon they run away and lose themselves on the gold mines.'

'But that's not the fault of the missionaries.'

'Yes, it's their fault. They turn our boys into Christians and teach them to rebel. They go after our girls too, telling them not to marry the husbands chosen for them.'

'But—,' Katie began until Ma shook her head in quick warning. It was no use arguing with Rasiaga, a thick-chested, spindly-legged man with decaying teeth and putrid breath.

The day after their train arrived in Johannesburg, Rasiaga had arrived at the home of Ma's sister in Doornfontein with a message from Pa's father for them to continue their journey immediately.

'Not yet,' Ma said. 'Next week is time enough.'

'Today. The old man grows impatient.' Ma turned to Pa, but suddenly he too was in a great hurry, calling to Phillip and Henry to help load their many boxes into the wagon.

'What's Pa's father like?' Katie asked Rasiaga on the second day of their journey.

'He's old. No one knows how old. His legs are weak and his eyes are dim but he does not die. There are some who think he will never die.'

'But that's not possible.'

Rasiaga nodded. 'It is not possible.'

'Then why do some people think such things?'

'Because of a special medicine he drank in the days when your father and I were still young boys.'

'What kind of medicine?'

'A special medicine. The Old Man – he was old even then – was very sick in his stomach. So our chief – the other one who was father to Ramokgopa – sent for a very important *inyanga* who was known all over the land for his magic potions. He came and made this medicine, which was stronger than the spell cast upon the Old Man, and so he was cured. Since that day he has never been sick. All the others of his age group are finished – the old chief, the *inyanga* himself, and even many who were younger. But the Old Man lives on.'

'If that medicine was so strong, why didn't the others drink it?'

'There wasn't enough.'

'Why didn't the *inyanga* make more?'

'Because he needed many things, including the blood of a leopard which was still breathing. And there was only the one that we captured alive.'

'A leopard? Captured alive?'

Rasiaga laughed. 'Yes, and your Pa did it. He found a young leopard on the path. When it crouched to leap upon him, he caught it by the front legs and wrestled and wrestled with it. Even when it clawed his shoulder he did not stop his wrestling. After a long time it got tired and tried to run away. Then your Pa jumped under its belly and caught it by the tail. The leopard did not know what had it, and twisted round and round until it fell down exhausted. Then he took the back legs in one hand and the front legs in the other and put it round his neck. The rest of us saw him when he was coming back. From that time on we called him Musilingwe. No one now remembers his other name.'

Rasiaga told Katie many things she did not believe, but if she tried to argue he just laughed as though she knew nothing. Often she wished that Charlotte were with her and by her cleverness prove that what he said was just foolish nonsense. But it was three months ago that Charlotte had gone to America.

The wagon lurched suddenly as one of the wheels dipped into a hole. Behind her the pigeons began squawking. Those pigeons! Phillip had wanted to bring every one of his hundreds of birds, but Ma had threatened to give them all away unless, like Noah, he chose one male and one female of each kind.

As Pa and the boys righted the wagon and Rasiaga cracked his whip over the oxen, Katie reached into a sack of grain and tossed a handful into the pigeons' cage. But their noise had already woken the younger children. They were climbing down to chase after Pa, who was running across the veld, leaping over stones and clumps of grass while his dogs raced along beside him.

Ever since they left Pietersburg the day before, Pa had changed. He no longer sat with Rasiaga on the high box in front of the wagon, but kept leaping down and calling to John and Mary Ann to come and see one thing after another. One time he picked a monstrous scarlet blossom off a cactus plant and tossed it into Ma's lap. 'Didn't I tell you?' he shouted. 'We have bigger and more beautiful flowers here than any that grew in Uitenhage.' A moment later he jumped up to crouch beside Katie.

'See that koppie there? The one with the crooked thorn tree growing on the top? That's where I killed my first buck.'

'And there,' he pulled at Katie's arm until she leaned over the side of the wagon to look into the distance at the bare side of a mountain, 'there is Letlapa – the Rock – where we filled our water bags when I was a boy. And when a new chief was anointed, the people went there to get water for the ceremony.'

'I don't see any water.'

'Not now. But see the green streaks? That's where the waterfall used to be. There was a magic snake who lived there and called forth the water when it was needed.'

'Did you ever see the magic snake?'

'No, but others saw it. It's head was like a diamond, always shining very bright.'

'But any snake's head shines when it comes out of the water.'

'Not like this one.' Pa hesitated, frowned, and then went on. 'Anyway, who can tell if it was magic or not magic? It's finished now.' He waved his hand towards an avenue of trees leading up to a Boer farmhouse at the base of the mountain. 'Rasiaga has been telling me, that farmer there dug a hole on the other side of Letlapa to see where the water came from. When he did not find the source, he called another man from Johannesburg who drilled holes in the rock as they do in the mines, and he caused a big explosion. But when he did this, he killed the snake and closed the water up.' He shook his head angrily and muttered something under his breath.

'What's that you say?' Mama asked.

'I say it's a shame what the Boers have done to this land. When I was young the grass grew high and our cattle fat. Now nothing grows except the cactus and the thorn trees, and it is no use planting the grass any more.

Rasiaga says it is all the fault of the white men, who have angered the spirits of our ancestors.'

Katie looked quickly at Pa to see if he was joking, but when he saw her staring at him, he just repeated, 'That's what Rasiaga says', and ran off into the veld with his gun and his hunting dogs. She watched him go, still puzzled. 'Does he believe what the people say about the spirits of our ancestors?' she asked Ma.

'He believes in our Christian God,' Ma said loudly. Then more softly, 'But he is also remembering what he was taught as a child, and it is good for him to explain these things.'

'But does he believe?'

'Who can say what another believes or doesn't believe? I think it worries him to see all the changes and to hear what Rasiaga tells him, yet still he is happy to be coming home.' Ma hesitated, uncertain, until with a sudden rush of words she caught at Katie's hand. 'But I? Oh, Katie, to me this land is like the wilderness in which John the Baptist wandered for forty days. Remember how he lived on locusts and honey? Pa tells me that here the people eat locusts also. The women catch them and dry them in salt and save them for the time when food is scarce.'

'We won't catch any,' Katie said. 'And if some are given you, then you can be a very good wife and save them all so that Pa can have a big feast.'

The wind died down. The sun grew warm. Katie tried to sleep again. Suddenly Rasiaga jumped down off his high box and shouted out that they were almost at the river. As Ma and Katie clambered down to the ground, Phillip pulled at the leader rope, turning the heads of the two front oxen, and Rasiaga ran alongside the other animals, calling to each by name and cracking his long whip in the air over their heads, until they, too, turned down the river bank. The wagon lurched and clattered behind them. The team of oxen having splashed across the shallow stream, Rasiaga's whip cracked in the air again and they strained against their yokes, slipping, pulling, heaving themselves up the opposite bank. Pa was waiting there, a fire already started for the midday meal. While Phillip and Henry helped Rasiaga outspan the oxen, he called to Ma and Katie and Mary Ann.

'Get your buckets and follow me.' He walked upstream for about a hundred yards from where they had crossed the river. 'I must show you how our people take the water,' he said. 'In my homeplace there are no springs such as we had in Uitenhage or tanks as in Kimberley. There is only the river. But we are not animals that drink just anywhere. We take our water thus.'

He lay down with his feet at the water's edge, stretching his arms above his head to scratch the bank a body's length from the river. Then, squatting beside the mark he had made, he scooped up several handfuls of sand and waited until water seeped up into the hole. From this, he filled a cup with water and poured it into Katie's bucket.

'It is forbidden to drink straight from the river, you hear? If you do, my people will laugh at you and call you lazy when you get the water sickness.'

'I've never heard of this water sickness,' Katie said.

'Nevertheless, it is there in the river. But not here, not in this hole. This our mothers have taught us, and our mothers' mothers before them. And I tell you true, no one in my homeplace gets this water sickness – only the white hunters and strangers who drink from the river.'

'We'll waste a whole day gathering water in this manner,' Katie whispered when he was gone.

'Ssh,' Ma warned, nodding at Mary Ann. 'We will do as he showed us. It is the custom.'

She waited patiently, her face serene. With water to gather and food to cook, her uneasiness left her, and when their buckets were full, she hurried the two girls back to the fire. Here she began stirring the mealiemeal into the pot as soon as the water boiled, and then carefully sliced strips of dried venison from a buck Pa had shot a few days before.

After they finished eating, Rasiaga slept in the sun. Katie wiped the last grains of porridge out of the pot and took it down to the river. Pa was pointing at the muddy bank, and telling Henry: '—the spoor of a duiker. Fresh. We frightened it off. And there! Zebra prints. But look how deep. Something made them bolt while they were drinking. We should look for the marks of a lion.'

'Lion!' Katie cried out. 'Are there lions here?'

Pa nodded, his eyes moving intently over the ground.

Henry was filled with excitement. 'Lion! Wildebees! Eland! Kudu! Pa's going to teach me how to hunt.'

Katie made sure Pa was carrying his gun before she dipped the pot into the water, washed it hurriedly and ran back to the fire. Phillip was throwing sand on the coals and Ma was already seated in the wagon. Katie climbed up beside her. 'Did you know there were lions roaming about in this place?'

'Pa told me they kill the cattle,' Ma said. 'But we don't have to worry about them; Pa says they don't like people.'

Nevertheless Katie was not convinced. She was almost as frightened of lions as she was of magic spells and strange medicines and old men who did not like Christians. She tensed up in alarm when she heard a thump behind her, but it was only Henry, flinging himself over the side of the wagon.

'Pa sent me for his clothes. He's washing himself in the river.' Henry pushed past her with Pa's suitcase and leapt down to the ground. In a few minutes Pa returned, dressed in his white shirt and black coat and trousers.

'How do I look?' he asked Ma.

'You look very good, but where are your shoes?'

He wriggled his toes in the dust. 'They pinch my feet. I'll carry them until I'm almost there. You think I look good? Like a Christian? Like an educated man?'

Ma nodded. 'When the Old Man sees you, he will be very proud. I think he will say to everyone, "Look at my son who comes back such an important man."'

'You think so?'

It worried Katie, seeing Pa standing there as nervous as a young boy.

'You will make the Old Man proud,' Ma repeated. 'But you had better go immediately or else the wagon will reach the village first.'

'Yes,' Pa said. He stopped for a moment to speak to Rasiaga and then strode off into the veld, his tall, thin body erect, his chin high, never pausing to search out a path, because in spite of the long years of his absence and the many changes in this land, he had not forgotten his way home.

A wide river curled through the valley below. Beyond the dense bush which grew along its banks, there was an open field where a few men were throwing wood on a blazing fire. Rasiaga called back to Ma and pointed with the handle of his whip.

'I see my cousin has already reached the Old Man. There will be much feasting tonight.'

On the other side of the field, mealies were sprouting up in gardens planted on the side of a bare rocky slope, and above these gardens twenty or thirty round mud huts with pointed thatched roofs clustered among the outcrop of yellow stone, each hut joined to those about it by a low walled courtyard. There were no trees or flower gardens, but the red mud walls were painted with blue and white designs which gleamed brightly under the late afternoon sun.

Rasiaga lowered his whip and shouted in that high sing-song which carries over the hills, and immediately the men around the bonfire began to shout back. Women and children appeared among the huts and began running between the low walls, leaping down from one courtyard to the next, racing between the gardens to the open field where they waited, laughing, jostling, waving and calling out greetings. One woman, however, kept on running. She splashed through the river, pounded on in the dust, her red clay ringlets swinging about her face, her empty breasts dangling limp and naked to the top of her leather skirt.

'There aren't any Christians here. No one properly dressed,' Katie said flatly.

Ma said nothing, yet her face creased into a smile as that one woman neared. She, like Ma, was no longer young, but she leapt nimbly up on the wagon and balanced herself on her knees between Ma and Katie, her wire bracelets clinking as she clapped her hands.

'Anna, I rejoice to see you. I am Madawo. My hut is waiting.'

'Our mother is very kind,' Ma replied.

'Not "mother"; "sister." It was your husband's cows that were given for me.'

'Oh, no!' Katie exclaimed.

From behind her Henry, too, gasped with shock. 'Pa's a Christian, he can only have one wife. He cannot pay *lobola* for another.'

Together Ma and Madawo burst out laughing. 'You must excuse my children,' Ma sputtered at last. 'In some ways they are very ignorant.'

'Yes,' Madawo said. She looked at Henry and smiled. 'I am wife to the Old Man. Whenever a son was born to him, he set aside one cow; and all the calves born to that cow, and in turn the calves they bore, belonged to that son. By the time your Pa left this place, he was already rich in cattle, and since he's been away the herd has grown. Thus, when the Old Man took me for his wife, he used the cattle from your father's herd for *lobola*. And in return, when my daughters marry, the cattle they bring will belong to your father.'

'Oh,' Katie murmured. She did not fully understand either Pa's wealth or this woman's special relationship to Ma, but it was clear that with Pa's own mother dead, Madawo considered herself responsible for their comfort. As the wagon came to a stop near the bonfire, she helped Ma down from the wagon and whispered quick explanations as the other women stepped forward.

The Old Man's senior wife, Mompiwe, came first as was proper. She was taller than Madawo, and very thin, with deep lines running from her nose down to her chin.

'I see you,' she said, 'but I do not see your hoe. Don't you women from the Cape work in the fields?'

'We work,' Ma answered, 'and I have my hoe in the wagon. But why do I need it here? I see plenty of oxen. Don't your men know how to plough?'

'They know but they are not always willing,' Mompiwe said.

Moihabo, the baby wife who was no older than Katie, stepped forward, bobbed her head at Ma, giggled at the children, and climbed up on the spokes of a wagon wheel to peer in at the boxes.

Then other women surged around Ma. Katie stood awkwardly to one side, clutching little Mary Ann's hand, looking around for Pa. But he was at the other end of the field with Phillip and Henry. And John was already tossing his football among a group of young boys who were jumping up in the air to catch it. Katie felt alone, forgotten, until a group of girls approached, their short beaded skirts swinging around their hips. One of them reached forward to unbutton her blouse, another lifted up her skirt to look at her petticoats As Katie crossed her arms over her breasts and cringed back from their poking fingers, the oldest girl spoke out sharply to the others.

'Do you forget the courtesies?' and then, 'I'm Mayila. You must forgive my sisters, but you dress like Mrs Davidson up at the store and we've often wondered what was underneath her clothes.'

The girls fell back as Mayila spoke, and Katie knew at once that she was their leader. There was something about her – perhaps the way she threw up her chin – that reminded Katie of Charlotte. Like Charlotte, Mayila demanded answers.

'What do you have underneath?'

'A chemise. Petticoats. Knickers.'

'Will you show us?'

'Later, when I undress for the night.'

'You take off those clothes when you sleep?'

'Yes. I have another dress for sleeping.'

'*Hawu!*'

At that moment Madawo called to Katie and motioned for her to follow. The girls fell back except for Mayila, who walked at Katie's side.

'The Old Man waits,' she whispered.

Katie hung back. 'I'm afraid.'

'Of the Old Man?' Mayila giggled. 'Do you think he will eat you up? But he has no teeth in his mouth any more.' She grabbed Katie's arm and pulled her forward, up, up between the narrow walls to the highest hut.

Pa was there in the courtyard, squatting down with Phillip, Henry, John and Rasiaga. Some distance away, Ma knelt back on her heels with little Mary Ann in her lap and Madawo, Mompiwe and Moihabo kneeling beside her.

The Old Man was seated on a stump of wood between the men and the women, his back resting against the warm mud wall of his hut.

He was old, very old, and between the strips of furry hides which hung down from his waist, his legs angled out, bent at the knees like broken twigs. The skin of his chest hung loose and wrinkled over protruding ribs, and only a few clumps of white hair were left around his shrivelled ears. A grey film covered his eyes so that he pinched up his face as he laboured to see.

'Come closer, child, that I may touch your face,' he commanded. In spite of his age, his voice, like Pa's, was deep and strong.

Katie felt Mayila's hand in the small of her back, pushing her forward until she fell to her knees in front of the Old Man. His hand was shaking and paper-dry as it moved across her cheeks.

'It is beautiful, this face,' he said, 'like the moon which rises late in the night. You have come very late, my child, but although I am old and useless, my heart is glad because my son's daughter has come home.'

As the days passed, Katie felt that even though she was a Christian girl, she belonged among the heathen Batlokwa. It seemed to her that all the years of her life had been one long journey home to Soekmekaar.

She missed Charlotte of course, but when she thought of her, Mayila's face came between them, and it was Mayila's voice she heard calling to her soon after first light. While the old women took Ma into the bush to search for anthills to grind down and mix with clay for the walls of the house Pa was building, Katie roamed the hills with Mayila and the unmarried girls. They gathered mushrooms, wild spinach, berries and fruit, and twice a day they carried their sheepskin water-bags down to the river. While they waited for the drinking water to seep up into the holes they had dug, they told Katie stories about Huveana, a little man who lived in the reeds and tossed a magic spell on anyone who came too near. In return Katie told them of all the wonders she had seen in London. The girls laughed at her stories, knowing such things to be impossible, just as Katie laughed at theirs.

During the hottest part of the day they sat in the mottled shade of thorn trees stringing their beads in the old patterns, or weaving copper wire into bracelets for arms and ankles, or burning the scrapings from the insides of amarula pips to form a thick black salve to rub in their hair. Often the girls spoke of the men they were going to marry. Since their earliest years they had known who were to be their husbands, for among the Batlokwa it was the custom for a girl to marry her father's sister's son. Only if he died was her father free to choose her another man. A few of the girls envied Mayila, because her father's sister had no son, but these were the rebellious ones who wanted to marry someone not of their fathers' choosing.

Therefore Mayila, as leader of the girls, was very strict and saw to it that none of them, not even Katie, wandered out of her sight. This was not easy. Soon after her arrival, Katie saw that Mayila was having trouble with Damarra, a short, plump, fun-loving girl who was always trying to sneak away to meet a young man by the name of Hlope, who worked for the storekeeper, Mr Davidson.

But in spite of all Mayila's warnings, Damarra shamed them all. 'I saw her creeping down to the river very early,' Mayila announced one morning to the other girls, 'and when I followed I saw her lying in the water and pressing down on her stomach. But her baby would not come out. Even when I tried to help her the baby would not come, so now I must go and tell the old mothers.'

Some of the girls said nothing, just looked at Damarra with sly curiosity. Others scolded angrily because now there would be no wedding parties. Instead, the old mothers would go tonight to pull all the thatch off Hlope's hut and take away the fattest of his father's cows and perhaps a sheep as well. Thus Hlope, too, would be disgraced and he would have to come and take Damarra for his wife, and his mother would be angry and make her work very hard until her baby was born. Poor Damarra. Yet, although Katie pitied her, she could not help thinking that she was luckier than her friend Elizabeth in Kimberley who had been driven away with sticks by her father and mourned by her mother as though she were dead.

But the girls soon forgot about Damarra in their excitement over the crochet-hooks and thread Katie ordered from Mr Davidson. Soon after her arrival Katie crocheted a tam o' shanter for the Old Man to shield his bald head from the sun. He wore it all the time. When Ramokgopa admired it, she made another one for him. Immediately all the men wanted tam o' shanters. In time, anyone in Pietersburg could tell a man who came from Ramokgopa's Location because of the tam o' shanter on his head.

Of all the girls, Nsabula was the quickest with her crochet-hook. She had almost finished her second tam o' shanter when the man she was supposed to marry sent his friends to negotiate with her father about *lobola*. Already the women were brewing beer for the betrothal feast, and for the first time Katie felt left out of village life. Ma and Pa would never let her attend the festivities because of all the heathen dancing and drinking of beer. Caught up in her own discontent, she did not notice that Nsabula's fingers had grown clumsy.

Two days before the betrothal feast, Nsabula disappeared. In the late afternoon Ramokgopa pounded on the door of Pa's house and accused him of helping Nsabula escape.

'I know nothing about her,' Pa said. 'I've been hunting all day. You can see for yourself the buck I killed. If the girl disappeared, you should only blame her father for trying to force her. Perhaps she's already been eaten by the crocodiles.'

Ramokgopa stiffened. 'You saw her?'

'No,' Pa said, 'but long ago I saw my second sister – you remember, she threw herself into the crocodile pool because she did not want to marry the man who was promised. That's why I'm still saying we should not force these girls.'

Ramokgopa's eyes glared. 'Do you go against me?'

Pa stared back at him for a moment and then his shoulders drooped. 'No,' he said slowly, 'I do not go against my chief.'

'Then you will help us search?'

'Yes.'

Ma said nothing, only watched Pa leave, then turned back into the house. Katie followed her, feeling very frightened by all that talk of crocodiles, but Ma whispered to her not to worry.

'Do you know where Nsabula is?' Katie asked.

'Ssh.' Ma made sure that Henry and John were still outside and that little Mary Ann was sleeping. 'I saw her this morning. She was hiding in the bushes behind Mr Davidson's store. I think it was Mr Davidson who helped her because he sent his wagon into Pietersburg today.'

'Oh.'

'You mustn't tell, not even Mayila. Mr Davidson is a good man, but if Ramokgopa suspects him, then pretty soon we'll have another storekeeper.'

Katie nodded. She would not tell. Not even Mayila. Especially not Mayila, for she was the leader of the girls and it was her duty to keep them from rebelling. If she knew of anyone who was helping the girls escape, she would have to tell the old mothers, and they in turn would tell Ramokgopa. And perhaps he would come again to accuse Pa.

Ramokgopa and Pa had hunted, danced, drunk beer together when they were young, and fought side by side in the first war against the Boers. Now that they were old they remained friends in spite of Ramokgopa's distrust of Christian missionaries. Because Pa could read the newspaper and write letters and speak the language of the Boer farmers and policemen, Ramokgopa appointed him his first adviser and consulted him on all important matters. The Old Man was pleased. Now that Pa had come home, he no longer bothered to have the young men carry him across the hills to Ramokgopa's council tree but waited instead for Pa to report to him. Every day when Katie came back to the village with Mayila and the other girls, he would be sitting quietly in the sun, and she would stop to greet him.

At the sound of her voice he would always smile and motion for her to sit. Sometimes he would question her about her travels or else speak of the days long gone when the rains were plentiful and the grass grew thick and high on these dusty hills, never willing to let her go until the night wind stirred and one of his wives called him for his evening meal. One afternoon while she was sitting with him, Ramokgopa's third wife – the one who was Pa's own sister – came to visit, bringing with her a calabash of beer for the Old Man; yet all the time she spoke with him, she kept looking at Katie with a sadness in her eyes.

Katie was puzzled and asked the old man why she grieved.

'Because of Matthew,' he said.

'I've never heard of Matthew. What's he got to do with me?'

The Old Man looked down at her through the grey film over his eyes. 'He was the son of the third hut. And because of you, Ramokgopa sent him to the mission school. But last year – or perhaps it was the year before – he went down to the valley when the fever trees were in bloom and he died of the fever.'

'Oh,' Katie gasped, remembering what Mayila and the other girls had told her. The son of the third hut. The son of Pa's sister. The man who, according to custom, should have been her husband. Wondering idly what kind of a man he'd been, she spoke without thinking. 'But what if I didn't choose him?'

'Choose him? You? What foolishness is this?'

'I mean what if – if –'

'I don't know your if–if,' the Old Man said flatly. 'He was the son of the third hut.' He sighed and looked down towards the valley as though he could almost see the tall pale trunks of the fever trees which once again were breaking into bloom, and his sorrow came between them like the ghost of that unknown Matthew. For the first time, as Katie sat there, sucking nervously at a blade of grass, she felt uneasy in his presence. Would this blind old man have pressed her into a marriage even if – but he knew no ifs. The pattern of his life had been set from the day he was born, and in spite of the battles and the dangers of the hunt and the threat of sickness and the fear of magic, he had never questioned the old ways or fought against the customs of his people. Katie sat with him for a long time without speaking, but when the mountains began eating up the sun, she rose to her feet and started home.

Halfway down the hill she looked back. He was still sitting where she'd left him. Was he thinking about Matthew, she wondered, or was he worrying that she, being a year past twenty, was already old for marriage?

That night Katie asked Pa if he had known about the Matthew who should have been her husband. He nodded as if this was a matter of no importance.

'He's dead. I knew this before we came.'

'Then if he was still alive, you wouldn't have pressed me into marrying him?'

'No,' Pa said. 'If he was still living, I would have left you in Johannesburg with your aunt or sent you to America with Charlotte.'

'But what if the Old Man wants you to find me another husband?'

'Don't worry, Malubisi. I won't permit you to marry a heathen.'

'But what if he finds me a Christian husband?'

'There aren't any Christians here.'

Katie stared at him for a moment and then looked away. He had not answered her question. Perhaps for all his cleverness, he wasn't brave enough to go against the Old Man's wishes.

Was it because he had drunk the blood of a leopard while it was still alive that everyone – even Pa and Ramokgopa – waited in respectful silence for the Old Man to speak? In all of Ramokgopa's Location there was no one who did not hurry to carry out his wishes – no one except Ma.

Ma was determined to convert the Old Man before he died. As soon as Pa left the house – the first square house in Ramokgopa's Location – she unpacked her sewing machine and made the Old Man two long shirts to cover his heathen nakedness. He was very proud of those shirts and wore them all the time, but only for warmth and not for Christian modesty.

Every Friday he felt his way down the hillside, leaning heavily on one walking-stick and feeling his way with the other until he reached the bare swept ground outside the kitchen. There Phillip helped him take off his dirty shirt, wash himself in a basin of warm water and then slip the clean shirt over his head. Because of his coming, Friday became a special day for Ma. In the early morning Phillip was sent to gather wood for a fire under her clay oven, and when it was hot she and Katie made those little English cakes the Old Man liked to munch with his tea.

Phillip was seldom at home on other days but rode alone over the hills on a horse Pa had given him, or hung around the store talking to Mr Davidson about his pigeons. Because he had no skill in hunting and was not allowed to drink any beer, he was very restless in Soekmekaar. He wanted to go to Johannesburg. But Pa insisted that he stay to help with the building of the house, then wait until Henry and John were properly settled in school at the Lutheran mission. And on Fridays Ma wanted him to stay in the kitchen and listen to the Old Man. Even little Mary Ann was kept inside to play with her doll.

Only Pa was missing. Ma never tried to keep him from his hunting. She seemed relieved when he left, because he fidgeted nervously when Ma spoke her true thoughts to the Old Man, urging him to give up his superstitions and bow down before the Lord God Jehovah.

The Old Man nodded in agreement. 'I, too, believe in Modimo. He is above everything.'

'But our Lord God and your Modimo are not the same,' Ma argued. 'Our God is the one who loves us, each one of us, and if we're in trouble He Himself protects us. He doesn't set Himself so high that He cannot see us.'

'*Hawu,*' the Old Man replied, 'then your God must be kept very busy. I don't think I should bother Him. It's better for me to call on my ancestors.'

When Ma told him about the many beautiful mansions up in heaven and the angels always singing and how he would know these things if only he became a Christian, he would nod again.

'That sounds like a very fine place. I would like to see it, but I don't want to stay up there. It is better for me to remain in the Land of the Dead. Then if there is danger, I can come back to keep you safe.'

'How can you do that if you live in the Land of the Dead?' Katie asked.

'I will come back just as my own grandfather came back and cured me of a sickness many years ago.'

'I thought it was the blood of a leopard which cured you.'

'That was later. This first time I was burning up with a fever, and a great green mamba came down out of the thatch of my hut and curled up around my skin to make me cool. At night it went away, but in the morning it returned. So I knew this was no ordinary snake. Therefore I put out some milk and an egg for it to suck and told it how I wanted to get well. For many days that mamba came to cool my skin, until one night the fever left me. That snake never came again. It knew I was cured.'

'Oooh,' Katie shivered, 'I've never heard of such a thing. If I had been in your place, I'd have died of fright.'

The Old Man sighed. 'Ah, Malubisi, you make things very difficult for me. What am I going to do with you Christian grandchildren after I've joined my ancestors? How can I come to protect you if you are going to die of fright?'

Katie laughed softly. 'You can come back, but not in the form of a snake. Please not in a snake. Come in the form of a lamb or a – a dove.'

'Katie!' Ma said sharply. She would never permit anyone to joke about religion or the spirits or the things that happen after death.

But on the Friday after Nsabula disappeared, the Old Man stood in the doorway, unsmiling. He was looking directly at Ma and his voice was full of authority. 'Anna, where is she gone?'

'Why do you ask me? I did not help her escape,' Ma said.

'But you know where she is.'

'No one told me she was running away or where she was going. I can only guess.'

'You think she has gone to the Lutherans?'

'They are the closest missionaries.'

The Old Man nodded and held out his arm for her to lead him to the chair by the kitchen table. 'I did not think you would go against me. But if you teach these girls to rebel, I will have to send you away.'

'I know, Father. And I do not speak against the old ways,' Ma said. But her eyes were troubled. 'Yet I feel sorry for these girls. It is not right for a man to take many wives. This only leads to trouble. Too many women living all together do nothing but tear one another's happiness apart.'

'The old ways are best,' he said firmly. 'Because there aren't enough husbands to go around. Too many men are killed in battle. What can we do with all these women who are left over?'

'When all people are Christians, there won't be so many wars,' Ma replied. 'And you could stop the fighting. If only you'd accept our Lord God, then others would follow you.'

'I'm too old to change my ways. And anyway, do you forget Mompiwe, Madawo and Moihabo? My other wives have died but these three are still married to me. Do you want me to choose one and throw the others away?'

'No, you cannot throw them away,' Mama said slowly. 'But you can still pray to our Lord for forgiveness.'

Again the Old Man shook his head until Ma burst out, her voice rising, 'Do you want all your other sons and your sons' sons to live in heathen ignorance?'

The Old Man grinned. 'I want my other sons and also my sons' sons to find some extra wives who are clever like you. The ones they have do not sew these shirts, but they do not pester me with words either.'

'It's because I was raised a Christian that I'm clever with my sewing,' Ma said.

The Old Man shook his head. 'I've known other Christian women who are not so clever. There are the Dutch Reformed at Modjadji and the Lutherans on the way to Pietersburg, but among them all I've never seen a woman as clever as you. Is it because you are Presbyterian that you're so clever?'

There was nothing Ma could say. She could not speak against the other churches (although they permitted the drinking of beer, and she did not approve of this) without seeming to speak against Christians in general. And so she remained silent.

'But my son is also a Presbyterian and he is not always so clever,' the Old Man went on, pressing his advantage. 'You are his one wife and yet he does not always keep you content. Just this morning I heard you grumbling because he's built no house for your chickens. If I was a young man I could keep you contented – yes, you and all my other wives as well. Even now if I could see, I would go into the bush and cut the sticks to make a chicken house that even you could sleep in, it would be so fine. *Hawu,* daughter, why did you come so late? I'm old and useless and I can no longer do anything except sit here by your fire and gossip like an old woman.'

'Do not say you are useless. Everyone listens to you. Even when I pester you with words, I am still listening to you.'

The Old Man smiled and reached out for his walking-sticks. The shadows were growing long when he left the house, and Mompiwe was already starting down the hill to meet him. Ma and Katie watched him move slowly up the path, the tails of his flannel shirt flapping around his spindly legs. He leaned very heavily on his sticks, and every few steps he paused for breath.

'I wonder—,' Ma began and then swallowed her words.

Katie, too, was wondering. She knew that no man could live forever, and yet – and yet the blood of a leopard must have been very strong medicine.

Every Friday, Katie half expected to see Mompiwe or Madawo coming down that long hill to bring the Old Man's dirty shirt and take back the clean one to his hut, yet still he managed to come himself. He liked to argue with Ma. No one else ever defied him openly. Sometimes he grew impatient when she spoke out against the old ways, but like a cunning hunter he set his little traps by telling riddles and stories until Ma, in her confusion, would admit that one custom was good, only to find that by admitting this she was saying that another custom was good also. Then the Old Man would pounce on her words and make her laugh before they started to argue again.

Thus it was that Ma, Phillip and Katie were sitting in the kitchen with the Old Man one Friday afternoon when suddenly they heard a scream from the river. Katie recognised Mayila's voice, and without thinking she rushed through the dining-room and out the door.

Halfway between the house and the crocodile pool she could see Mayila struggling against her father and two of her brothers, Fika and Lithalo, and shrieking, 'No, no! I would rather die. Let me go.' Fika threw Mayila down on the ground and caught at her legs while Lithalo held her arms, and her father began tying her up with thorny vines. Mayila was still shrieking that if they would not let her go, they should kill her quickly because she would never be wife to old Rasiaga.

As she ran towards them, Katie found a big stick in her hands, though where or how she picked it up she did not know. But seeing it there, she raised it up and brought it down on Lithalo's shoulders. As he let go of Mayila's arms to turn and grab the stick, he brought up his foot and kicked Katie's stomach so that she fell on her back against the ground. She did not remember getting up or being thrown down again. She just remembered the taste of blood as she bit, scratched and clawed, the dry dust in her throat and the smell of body sweat. She did not know if it was she who was screaming or Ma, but suddenly Ma was there amongst them with the Old Man leaning on her arm.

'Are you such brave warriors that you have to fight with women?' the Old Man asked contemptuously. Mayila's father and her two brothers stepped back and glanced uneasily at one other and then at the Old Man, their courage draining away in the face of his terrible anger.

As Katie leaned over to pick the thorns out of Mayila's skin and help her to her feet, Phillip galloped up on his horse. Hardly stopping, he grabbed Mayila's arms and swung her up in front of him; then he continued on towards the river, splashing through the ford and up the hill towards Mr Davidson's store. While the Old Man listened to the hoof-beats, Katie lifted up her apron to wipe her face and found it covered with blood. She could hardly see out of one eye, and her shoulder was beginning to hurt where she'd hit the ground. Yet at the same time she wanted to laugh because Fika and Lithalo and their father were staring down at the ground in shame.

The Old Man waited until he could no longer hear the sound of the horse galloping, then turned to Mayila's father and brothers. 'So! It takes three men to fight one poor girl. In battle I would rather have Mayila beside me than you.'

'She's a wild one,' Mayila's father complained, 'and this one too.' He turned angrily on Katie. 'Why do you Christians always interfere? This was none of your business. Mayila was defying me, her own father. That's why she was running here. She thought you'd help her escape; and when my sons were catching her, she turned towards the river like a crazy girl and told them she'd rather marry the crocodiles than Rasiaga. It's all your fault—'

'Silence!' the Old Man said. He straightened his shoulders and stood there full of dignity in his long flannel shirt and crocheted tam o' shanter. 'You should have come to me when Mayila defied you, and I'd have told you then that Rasiaga is an old man and should take himself a widow-woman as a secondary wife, not a wild young girl like Mayila. I haven't time to listen to your excuses.'

Mayila's father stared into the Old Man's rheumy eyes and then bent down to pick up his sticks and motioned to his sons. The Old Man remained standing until Ma whispered for him to come back to her kitchen.

'Have they gone?' he asked.

'Yes, Father.'

He sighed then, and his ancient bones seemed to crumple up. Ma and Katie caught him before he fell. His body was light like that of a child as they carried him back into the house and laid him down very gently on a blanket in the warmth of the kitchen. Ma heated up the tea, hot strong tea with plenty of sugar in it, and spooned it into his mouth. And then while he slept, she washed the cuts on Katie's face with salt water and tied a wet cloth over her swollen eye. Now and then, as they waited for Pa to come home, she licked her fingers and held them over the Old Man's mouth to make sure he was still breathing.

Late in the afternoon Mompiwe, Madawo and Moihabo came to fetch their husband and waited while he slept. But when Pa came home, he was sitting up and laughing at their worry. But he had no strength to walk, and was quite content to be seated on a chair and carried up the long hill to his own hut.

He lived for two days. On Monday when Pa came back from Ramokgopa's council tree to report to him, the Old Man sighed. 'I've been waiting for you,' he said, and turned his face to the wall.

There was an emptiness in the land after the Old Man died, and an emptiness in Katie's heart. She couldn't sit on the front stoep without looking up the path and thinking of that old bent figure leaning on his walking-stick or the many spoonfuls of sugar in his tea. Sometimes the band of unmarried girls came calling for her to search out the mushrooms and spinach, but everywhere she went she seemed to hear the echo of his voice. The wind slurring through the tall reeds was the dried cackle of his laughter, and the pale green trunks of the fever trees became the stillness of his sorrow for that Matthew who should have been her husband.

One day when she and Ma were returning from Mr Davidson's store, a small black mamba reared up in their path, its forked tongue flashing in and out of its mouth. Ma raised her stick as though to kill it, but Katie grabbed at her arm.

'No,' she said, and kept hold of her arm until the snake lowered its head and slithered off into the grass.

'You're crazy in the head!' Ma exclaimed angrily. 'Why did you stop me killing it?'

'I knew it wouldn't hurt us,' Katie said slowly, but the disbelief in Ma's eyes kept her from speaking of the Old Man. Afterwards Katie was frightened by what she had done, because she knew his spirit could not come back in the form of a snake. Perhaps she was going a little crazy, she thought. And what would become of her if her heart kept telling her things which she had always known were impossible?

She knew then what she must do. As they were preparing the evening meal, she told Ma that it was time for her to leave Soekmekaar. 'My money is almost finished, and look how my clothes are torn. If I'm to dress like a proper Christian, I must go to Johannesburg to find some work.'

'I still have cloth. I can make you a new dress.'

'I must go.'

'So soon? I thought you'd stay until Charlotte comes home.'

Charlotte! It was a long time since Katie had thought of Charlotte, but now, remembering, she knew that Charlotte too would say it was time for her to go.

'No,' she said, 'I am here too long already. Sometimes in the night my belly aches for children, but there is no man here among these heathen to make me a fitting husband. I must go and find him among the Christians in Johannesburg.'

'We will talk with Pa,' Ma said.

'Malubisi is right,' Pa said when he came home from his hunting. 'It is time. Ramokgopa is my brother, but he is not like the Old Man. He listens to me, yes, but he listens to the others also, and many have not forgotten Mayila. They accuse us of teaching the young girls to rebel; there are even some who are now saying that my little Malubisi needs a husband to teach her obedience.'

Katie giggled, thinking of Fika and Lithalo who were very fine to look at, but had already failed to make her obey them.

'I'm not making jokes,' Pa said abruptly, and there was that look on his face which stopped her laughter. 'You are a grown woman and soon you will be too late for marriage. If Ramokgopa thinks of this, perhaps he himself will find you a husband.'

'You wouldn't let him, Pa?' Katie cried out.

'You could make things very difficult for me,' Pa said slowly, biting his lips. 'And so I say it is right for you to leave us now and go to live with your Auntie in Johannesburg. In two days Mr Davidson is sending his wagon into Johannesburg to buy supplies.'

Ma sat down in her rocking-chair and began to weep. Katie started forward to comfort her, but Pa caught her arm. 'Go and pack up all your belongings.'

'But—'

'I said go.'

Tears came into her own eyes as she looked over at Ma, but Pa's hand pushed her towards her room. As she opened her suitcase she could hear him talking to Ma. His voice was low and she could hear the worry in it but she could not catch the words. When she went to the door to hear him better, she saw him squatting in front of Ma, whispering earnestly, and she, wiping her eyes, was staring at him and saying something in reply. Pa chuckled softly and spoke again in his low voice. Ma tried to smile. They did not see Katie standing there. At last she turned back and reached for the small carved jewellery-box in which she kept her pearl necklace, her gold watch, her silver bracelet shaped like a snake, and all the other treasures which had been given her in England. These things were all she had. Ma and Pa were already shutting her out of their lives. Charlotte was far away. Mayila was now living with one of

Pa's brothers in Pretoria. Phillip was learning to be a shoemaker in Johannesburg. Henry and John were in school at the Lutheran mission. The Old Man was dead.

Outside, the shadows lengthened. She heard little Mary Ann shouting beyond the kitchen and Ma calling her in to wash herself before she went to bed. It would soon be dark and there was much for Katie to do. She wrapped her jewellery-box in the green street dress, folded the white gown and long white gloves she had worn only once since her return to Africa, packed her last pair of shoes, her Bible and the one paisley shawl which she had not given away. Tomorrow she would wash her only cotton dress that wasn't torn, air her blankets, and mend her English coat with the fur on the collar. It would be cold on that wagon at night.

Durban
1954

'Did you ever go back to Soekmekaar?' I ask as Katie settles down on her chair and picks up the microphone.

'Yes, I went back twice.' She hesitates for a moment and then, with a light laugh: 'But not until I had a husband to protect me.'

'Were you really afraid Ramokgopa would force you into marrying someone from his village?'

'Pa wouldn't have let him,' she said, but there was a tinge of uncertainty to her voice. 'That's why he sent me to my Auntie.'

'Weren't you sorry then that you hadn't gone to America with Charlotte?'

She shook her head. 'No, I'd already gone to England and lived too long among strangers. Now I wanted to stay among my own people. Some of Ma's friends from Kimberley were living in Johannesburg and Auntie knew many Christians. If I was ever going to meet an educated man who needed a wife, that was the place to go . . .'

8

Johannesburg

1894–1895

After the bone-weariness of the long wagon journey from Soekmekaar, Katie's months among the Batlokwa were like a dream remembered. In her eagerness to see Phillip, she pounded on the door of Auntie's house in Doornfontein and shouted out the news of her coming. There was a rush of bare feet inside. The door opened so suddenly that she lost her balance and fell against her cousin Fanny, who greeted her, helped her up and pulled her in, all at the same time.

'Is Phillip here?' Katie asked.

'I'm here,' he called out, leaping up from the couch in the dining-room. 'But why have you been so long? I thought you'd thrown yourself to the crocodiles.'

'Me?' Katie said. 'Why should I do that? Nobody's going to marry me off to some heathen stranger. I've come here to choose my own husband.'

Phillip's laughter sounded then, deep and rhythmic like a distant drumbeat, and in her joy at seeing him, Katie began to stamp her feet and move her body like the young girls in Soekmekaar. Suddenly a shocked voice cut into the room: 'Katie! What have they taught you in that heathen place?'

Auntie hurried in from the kitchen. She was a small woman, round and black like Ma but very strict. No dancing was ever allowed in her house.

'I'm sorry, Auntie.'

'When did you last eat?'

'Early this morning.'

'Then come. The coffee is hot.'

The coffee was always hot in Auntie's house, and the smell of fresh bread drifted from her kitchen. Every day she baked bread and cakes for Height's Hotel in Ferreirastown, Johannesburg. Now she cut two thick slices, dipped them in bacon dripping and set them on the table in front of Katie.

'Eat.' She waited until Katie was finished and then asked, 'Your parents, are they well?'

'Yes.'

'And you?'

'I've come to find some work.'

'There's a Mrs Height, the wife of the proprietor of Height's Hotel, who needs a nurse-girl. A woman in our church told me. Her brother is cook in that house and she thought perhaps Fanny – but Fanny likes it where she is. If you want a job, you'd better go there tomorrow.'

It was still dark when Katie woke up the next morning, but the smell of boiling coffee drew her out of her blankets. Quietly she picked up her suitcase and tiptoed into the kitchen, where she hooked up her English corset and slipped her green street dress over her head.

Auntie looked up from her basket and gasped. 'You can't wear that.'

'Why not? It's the only clean dress I have.'

'It's much too grand.'

Katie pulled off the green dress, brought out her black serge skirt which was already shiny with wear, and held up the one blouse she had left. Still Auntie shook her head, pointing at the lace insertions down the bodice.

'That's too fancy for a nurse-girl. If you have to earn your money as a servant, you must dress like a servant. Wait.' She hurried into Fanny's room and came back with a blue striped flannel dress that looked like a nightgown. 'You can borrow this. And leave off your shoes. Servants don't wear shoes.'

The sun was just rising when Katie reached the big double-storeyed house in smart Saratoga Avenue. She sat down on the back steps, shivering in the cold morning air and wondering what the time was.

She had taken out her watch to wear but Auntie had looked at her in amazement. 'You can't wear that. If a policeman sees you wearing a gold watch, he'll arrest you and put you in jail.'

'But it's mine. It was given to me in England.'

'Do you have a letter to prove it? No? Then hide it away and tell no one. I don't want any thieves or policemen coming into my house to make trouble.'

Auntie's talk of thieves and policemen had made her nervous. When the door to the servants' quarters opened, Katie thought for a brief moment that the man approaching her was a baboon dressed up in a servant's uniform. His white tunic stretched tightly across his chest. His legs, protruding from his white shorts, were very thin, and he moved unevenly. When he saw Katie, his face twisted as though in anger.

'Who are you? What you want?' he said in English.

'I'm Katie Manye. If you are the cook, then your sister told my Auntie that your Missis needs a nurse-girl. I'm looking for work.'

His suspicious manner disappeared and now he spoke rapidly in Xhosa. 'My sister sent you? Then I'll speak for you. She's very funny,' gesturing towards the door behind Katie. 'Many girls have come, but this one is too fat and that one's dirty and another looks sickly. Perhaps she'll think you're too small.'

Katie answered him in his own language. 'But I'm strong. Give me something to lift and I'll show you.'

'If my sister sent you, then I know you're strong; but now you're cold. Wait until I start the fire.'

Soon he came out of the kitchen with a tin cup of steaming tea. 'Drink this quickly.'

Katie warmed her hands around the cup until he repeated again, 'Quickly.'

'Why so quickly?'

'So I can wash the cup before she comes down.'

'If she doesn't like me to drink her tea, then take it back. I'm not a thief.'

Charlie laughed at her. 'Don't be silly, girl. Have you never worked in Johannesburg before? This isn't like other places. Here the white people have forgotten their manners.' He sounded like Auntie.

'Why do you say that?'

'Because I know it. I see it. Here the white people think only of gold. They fight over it and steal it from each other and lock it up in their banks where it's useless. *Hawu!* The gold makes them into thieves, and so they think that we're thieves also.'

'But aren't you a thief to steal this tea for me?'

Charlie's face twisted into a scowl. 'You have a tongue like a wasp, and if you don't take care it will poison you.'

'I didn't mean—'

'I can see I must teach you many things, so drink your tea quickly and listen carefully to what I say. The Missis will not like you if you act too proud. So when she comes down, you stand like this.' He dropped his big shoulders to make himself small and cast his eyes on the ground like a naughty child. 'And when she speaks to you, say "Yes, Missis" and "No, Missis" and "Please, Missis" and "I'm sorry, Missis," and you'll get along all right.'

His play-acting made Katie laugh so much that she choked on her tea, and while she sputtered for breath, they heard the sound of a door closing upstairs. Charlie grabbed her mug and disappeared into the kitchen.

There were more sounds of movement, and a bell tinkled beyond a window to the side of the kitchen. Katie could hear Charlie's uneven footsteps back and forth, the mumble of English voices and the crackle of bacon frying. Behind her, beyond the servants' quarters, a young boy led a saddled horse around the side of the house. Then a woman's clear voice sounded. 'Yes, Charlie, what is it?'

'Please Missis, pardon me, Missis,' Charlie said, and Katie was astonished. She had thought he was play-acting when he told her how to speak, but now she knew that inside the house he was standing with his shoulders drooped and his eyes cast downwards. 'My sister is outside.' As he spoke, he raised his voice as if to make sure she heard the things he was telling his Missis. 'She looks for job. Always before she worked on farm near Pietersburg. Looked after children since very young. Washed, ironed, sewed clothes.'

'Why did she leave there?'

Charlie did not pause but spoke rapidly as though he knew the reason. 'Because farm sold. People gone.'

'Tell her to wait. When I have time, I'll talk to her.'

It was almost noon when Mrs Height called Katie into the kitchen. She was a tall American woman, almost as tall as Pa, and very thin, with darting eyes and nervous hands. 'So you're Charlie's sister. You don't look like him.'

'She baby sister,' Charlie said quickly.

'Be quiet!'

'Yes, Missis.'

'And you. Have you worked before?'

'Yes, Missis.'

'Where?'

Katie repeated what Charlie had already said, stammering with discomfort at the lies.

'What did you do on that farm?'

'I looked after the children. I made the food for the baby and put him to bed. I also washed, ironed and mended the clothes.'

'You can sew?'

'My other Missis taught me.'

'How is it you speak such good English?'

'I went to school, Missis. To Standard Six.'

Mrs Height frowned, thought a minute and then said firmly, 'I'll try you out for a week. Before breakfast you will help Charlie clean. In the mornings you'll do the laundry. In the afternoons you will fetch my little girl from school and look after her for the rest of the day. If you work well, I'll keep you.'

'Please, Missis, how much pay?'

'Five shillings a month, your food and two uniforms, a clean one for each day.' She nodded a dismissal and turned to go.

'Please, Missis, what time do I have off?'

Mrs Height whirled around, darting those eyes and creasing her forehead. 'You haven't even started work and already you are asking for time off.' Behind her, Charlie was rolling his eyes and shaking his head.

Katie drooped her shoulders as he had shown her and looked down at the floor. 'I'm a Christian girl, Missis. On Sundays I go to my church.'

'Oh. We'll see about that.'

As soon as she was gone, Charlie began to scold. 'You must learn to keep a rope on your tongue. If you ask questions, you're going to find yourself in big trouble.'

In spite of Charlie's warning, it was the lies he told in his effort to help her that gave Katie the greatest trouble. Often she forgot that she was supposed to be an unspoiled country girl who knew nothing of the world. Once when Mrs Height called her into her sewing-room to pin up the hem of a dress, Katie said without thinking, 'Please, Missis. I think there's too much fullness at the shoulders. In England the leg-of-mutton sleeves have gone out of fashion.'

'Really, Katie! What do you know about fashion?'

'When Mrs Keithley—' She stopped suddenly. How could she explain that just a year ago Mrs Keithley had her dressmaker take out the sleeves of all her dresses and cut them over? 'Where I worked before,' she stammered, 'my other Missis showed me pictures.'

'Oh,' Mrs Height said, but there was a funny look on her face as if she did not quite believe her.

Another time when the little girl, Doreen, showed her a picture of Buckingham Palace and announced that that was where Queen Victoria lived, Katie again forgot herself.

'Yes, that's where she lives when she's in London, but when she wants a holiday she goes down to Osborne on the Isle of Wight.'

'Does she have a palace there too?'

'A kind of palace. Not nearly so grand as Buckingham but much prettier.'

Mrs Height put down her embroidery. 'Katie! Whoever told you that?'

'I don't know, Missis.'

'Then stop filling Doreen's head with such nonsense.'

Charlie made Katie's life difficult in other ways as well. In spite of the English words he knew, he was very slow to understand Mrs Height's instructions. He often made mistakes, and then Mrs Height would scold them both for being lazy or stupid. Afterwards he would grumble not only about Mrs Height but about all the white people in Africa.

'It's their fault I am almost a cripple,' he said. 'During Cetshwayo's war they shot my legs full of bullets and left me to die.'

'But if you were fighting—'

'I wasn't fighting. I was still a young boy then. But their soldiers made a sport of shooting us. I tell you, Katie, the white people love their dogs and horses better than us. You can't trust any of them.'

'But the missionaries—'

'Ah, the missionaries! They're the worst of all. They came to teach us to put away our spears, but when we did this, they brought in the storekeepers to cheat us and then the policemen to put us in jail. I tell you, it would be better if the missionaries had left us alone.'

'Left us in heathen ignorance?'

'Yes, they liked us better when we were ignorant. In those days they sat with us on our mats and ate with us out of our bowls. But now that we have chairs and dishes like them, they call us dirty and will not eat our food.'

Poor Charlie with his funny weak legs and his 'Please, Missis' and 'I'm sorry, Missis'. But he was too proud to pretend humility forever. One day his anger boiled up inside him.

It was on a Wednesday afternoon. Mrs Height had invited some very important ladies for tea. All morning she ran around the house, fixing the flowers, calling to Katie or Charlie to polish this table over again or move that chair to a different place. She herself came into the kitchen to make a cake, scattering pots and spoons and spilling flour, scolding because the oven was too cold and then worrying because it was too hot, and, when the cake was done at last, telling Charlie to hurry with the Master's dinner because it was almost one o'clock.

'How can I cook when she leaves us this mess to clean?' he muttered under his breath.

The Master came home early that day, and they could hear him asking impatiently why dinner was late.

'I don't know,' Mrs Height told him wearily. 'The servants have driven me mad this morning, even Katie. I've had to make them do everything over twice, and Charlie was slower than usual. Sometimes I think he deliberately tries to irritate me—'

'What's that she says?' Charlie asked Katie fiercely.

'Ssh! She's just trying to pacify him.'

'She spoke my name. What did she say?'

How could Katie tell him what Mrs Height had said when they had both been working so hard since six o'clock that they'd had no time to eat? It wasn't fair, the way Mrs Height excused herself by blaming them, but even though Katie thought this, she didn't want Charlie upset any more and pretended not to hear his question.

After he had served the meat and potatoes and vegetables in the dining-room, Katie spooned up their porridge. She felt better once they had eaten. While Charlie was cutting the crusts off the bread and making pretty little sandwiches, Katie went back to her room to change into a clean uniform. When she returned to the kitchen, Charlie had finished piling up the sandwiches on a plate, tucking sprigs of parsley here and there and sprinkling chopped lettuce over them to keep them fresh. But when Mrs Height came out for a last inspection, she was not satisfied.

'Charlie! That's my everyday plate. Why do you think I put out the silver tray?'

'You didn't tell, Missis,' he replied sullenly. That was the first time Katie had ever heard him try to explain.

'Haven't you any sense at all? Why don't you use your head once in a while?'

'I'm sorry, Missis,' he said. A muscle began to twitch in his cheek and he forgot to cast his eyes on the floor.

'Never mind, Katie can fix the trays while you change your clothes. It's almost time for people to come and I want you to look your very best.'

The first carriage was rolling up the driveway when he returned to the kitchen, looking very smart indeed, his hair still glistening with the moisture from his washing, his tunic crisp and clean, and his long, black Sunday trousers hiding his funny legs. But when Mrs Height saw him, her face grew very red.

'How dare you,' she almost shouted. 'Do you think you're the Master in this house to wear long trousers? Why do you think I buy you uniforms? Go back this minute and put on your shorts. When I ring the bell for tea, I'll expect you to be dressed properly.'

Charlie's proud smile crumpled into blankness. As he turned to leave the kitchen, he glanced back at her just once, and there was such hatred in his eyes that Katie's knees began to shake.

'You shouldn't have said that, Missis,' Katie said.

'Now don't you get cheeky. You know I can't have that silly fool strutting around like a white man.'

'But you told him to look his best.'

'Of course I did.' Her hands touched nervously at her hair as the front knocker sounded. 'You go to the door and show the ladies into the lounge.'

Another carriage sounded in the driveway, and then another and another. For a few moments Katie was so busy opening and shutting the door she did not have time to think. When it seemed that all the guests had come, she started down the hall towards the kitchen, but the knocker on the front door sounded again.

This lady, the last to arrive, had brought her little boy, who was about two years old. As she entered with him, Mrs Height told Katie to take the child into the garden. But the child cried and clung to his mother until Katie smiled at him and began to wiggle her fingers to make him laugh. While she was doing this, Mrs Height rang her tea bell.

There was a great clatter in the kitchen, which startled the ladies and frightened the child. As Katie was trying to calm him, Charlie entered the lounge. She heard a gasp of horror from someone, a nervous giggle over in one corner, and then a shocked silence. Little caterpillars of fear crawled up Katie's back as she turned around to look.

Charlie was standing with the big silver tea-tray in front of Mrs Height. He was wearing his dirty old uniform, one side of his face was smeared with mud, and even halfway across the room she could smell the horse dung on his feet.

For a moment it seemed that everyone stopped breathing, then Mrs Height said very quietly and distinctly, 'Get out of here, you filthy beast.'

Charlie just stood there looking stupidly down at the floor until her voice rose to a scream. 'Get out of here! Don't let me see your face again.'

'Yes, Missis.' He dropped the tray on the table in front of her and turned to go, paying no attention to the teapot, which fell over, or the hot tea splashing on her new dress.

The little boy's mother picked him up in her arms. Katie crept across the floor towards the Missis to mop the spilt tea with one of the clean serviettes which she had ironed just that morning, then rose to her feet and picked up the tray.

'I'll bring more.'

'Yes. Fresh. In a clean pot.'

But already the ladies were making their excuses and crowding into the hall and out the front door.

There was no sign of Charlie in the kitchen when Katie went to heat more water. When she returned to the lounge, Mrs Height was all alone, slouched over the table with her head in her arms, crying as if her heart would break.

She did not notice Katie pouring milk and tea into a cup and holding it out to her. 'Drink this, Missis.' After a moment Katie touched her shoulder and repeated, 'Please drink this, Missis.'

Mrs Height groped for her handkerchief to wipe her eyes and then looked up. 'Oh, Katie, why did Charlie do that?' Her lips began to quiver. 'Now everyone is laughing at me.' But she gulped down the hot tea as though it were medicine, waited while Katie poured another cup, and drank that more slowly. Then she sat up straighter in her chair and set the cup firmly on its saucer.

'Bring Charlie in here.'

Her fingers were tapping impatiently on the table as Katie ran to the servants' quarters. The door to Charlie's room was open and he was tying up the last of his belongings in his blanket. He was dressed again in his long black Sunday trousers. Both his clean and dirty uniforms were piled on the floor.

'What's the matter with you, Charlie? Have you gone mad?'

'No.' He began to laugh.

'Then why did you do such a crazy thing?'

'To teach that white woman a lesson. She wanted me to look my best, so I wore my long trousers to show respect for her and her important friends. But she didn't want me to be altogether dressed. She scolded – you heard her – because she wants to keep us naked and dirty. So I showed her friends how she wants to keep us. Did you see their faces?' He began to laugh again.

'You showed her nothing. Now I think you've lost your job.'

'I haven't lost it. I've thrown it away.' He wriggled his fat shoulders into his coat, picked up his blanket-roll and balanced his hat on the back of his head.

'Stay well, Katie.'

'But the Missis wants to talk to you.'

'Why? She told me not to show my face again. I'm finished here. And you, Katie, are you going to stay and work for someone who likes to shame us?'

'I need to earn.'

'Not me. Not here. I'll find my money somewhere else.'

'But where, Charlie? Where will you go?'

'To my sister's house.'

Katie stood for a moment watching him limp down the driveway and wondered what would become of him in this mixed-up town. Just before he reached the road, he looked back and waved. Although he no longer had any job, he seemed younger and stronger than before, so that in spite of his foolishness she could not pity him. When he was out of sight, she trudged back slowly to the big house.

The Missis was still tapping her fingers on the table. 'It's taken you long enough. Where've you been? Where's Charlie?'

'He's gone, Missis.'

'Good riddance!'

'Please, Missis. He needs his money.'

'Money? What on earth are you talking about?'

'His wages, Missis. It's almost the end of the month.'

'After what he did, he doesn't deserve anything except a good thrashing.' Her lips thinned into a cruel line.

Katie felt a bubble of anger rising up in her stomach. Charlie was right. The Missis didn't care what happened to him. She only wanted to cheat him out of his pay.

'Don't stand there gawking like an idiot,' Mrs Height snapped. 'Get that tray out of here and clean up the kitchen.'

She went on giving orders, but Katie kept hearing Charlie's voice: 'In this town the white people have forgotten their manners.'

Mrs Height did not look for another cook to take Charlie's place. Instead she raised Katie's pay to fifteen shillings a week, taught her new ways to prepare the food, and hired another nurse-girl.

Each morning at dawn Katie pulled on the previous day's clothes and ran into the big house to make the fire and prepare tea to take to the upstairs bedrooms. Then, while the nurse-girl scrubbed and waxed the floors, she dragged the carpets out to the back fence and beat them with her broomstick until a cobweb of dust rose up to catch at the glints of red and gold which streaked across the sky. She was happiest in those early mornings. In the summer-time the wind-still garden was like a last long drink before the journey into the day's heat; in the winter-time the sharp clean smell of trees and grass promised new growth.

The *thump, thump* of her broom against the carpets roused the insects, chickens, horses and dogs, and the sun's rays reached down and warmed her skin until the sweat loosened her muscles and the yellow dust swirled round her feet.

After the Missis finished her breakfast and was making out her shopping list, there were windows to shine, the bedrooms to tidy, the kitchen to clean, and the special jobs for each day – washing, ironing, mending, baking, polishing the silver. At last when all the work was done, Katie cut two loaves of bread, measured out the jam, made fresh tea and called the stableman, the gardener and the nurse-girl to the back stoep for their first meal of the day. Afterwards it was time to cook the midday dinner and change into a clean uniform for the Master, who came home promptly at half past twelve.

In the afternoon the Missis gave Katie her shopping list. On the way to the stores she met other maids and cooks who worked nearby, and as they walked together they gossiped about their families: Mrs Johnson was taking her daughter home – meaning England – for a holiday, she said, but her maid had seen how that girl's corset no longer pinched in her waist and her tread was heavy. The Pattersons were always quarrelling, and often Mrs Patterson slept alone behind a locked door. Mrs Grimshaw stole money out of her husband's purse when he was drunk, and Mr Wilson was storing rifles and bullets in his stable as if he expected a big war. Katie listened and laughed with the other servants about the hidden lives of these white people who thought they knew each other at their fancy teas and big receptions and yet were altogether ignorant.

Yet there was also sadness among those white people. One morning when the Missis called her to help with some sewing, Katie forgot herself and wondered aloud what Mr Frye would do with his young children after his wife was dead.

'Don't be silly, Katie. Mrs Frye just has indigestion. She eats too fast.'

But Mrs Frye's maid had told Katie that Mr Frye had sat in his big chair and cried after the doctor had come and gone. Now why would a man do that unless the doctor had told him that his wife's sickness was very bad? Yet, in spite of Katie's warning, Mrs Height was surprised three weeks later when she heard of Mrs Frye's death.

'How did you know when no one else knew?' she asked Katie.

'The doctor knew. And her husband.'

'And I suppose they told you?' the Missis said with a touch of sarcasm.

Later, when the Master came home, she heard him suddenly burst out laughing. 'Listen to me, Sam. It's not only that she predicted Dorothy Frye's death. There are other things too. Sometimes when I'm talking to her, she will say the oddest things. About England. Things she couldn't possibly know. Things I don't know myself. But then when I check up on her, she's always right.'

'She probably just repeats what she has heard.'

'Heard from whom? She never sees anyone except other natives, and how can they know all the details she describes? The other day she told me that in the Crystal Palace they have machines that turn out copies of songs while you wait. I'd never even heard of them, but Doreen's music teacher said it was true.'

'Well, I'm sure there's some perfectly logical explanation. But if she'd tell me what Consolidated Mines is going to do—'

'Sam, don't laugh. Katie's no ordinary servant. And one does hear such extraordinary stories about native witchcraft. Yet whenever I ask her any questions about it, she grows very sullen and uncommunicative. I know—'

Her voice dropped again and Katie could not hear the rest of what she said. She did not want to hear any more. Everywhere she went it seemed that she was set apart – in England because her skin was black, in Kimberley because she had lived too long among the English, in Ramokgopa's village because she was a Christian, and now here in her work because Mrs Height thought she had magic powers.

But Katie soon forgot everything when Mr and Mrs Height went away for a few days and gave her some time off. Since she had come to work for Mrs Height, she had never had a holiday, but now she would have three whole days to visit Auntie and her friends.

Perhaps, yes, perhaps three days would be time enough to find herself a husband.

The sun was setting by the time she entered the African location, and she started to run. It was late to be walking alone in those parts. The air was heavy and sweet with the smell of mealie beer in the backyard shebeens. A woman stirring an iron pot over an open fire eyed her curiously, and a group of idlers shouted after her as she passed. A drunk stumbled through a broken gate and grabbed at her arm. She wrenched herself free and started to run. Just then she heard a scream in the distance, followed by shouts and thuds. The drunk slouched off into the bushes. The group of idlers disappeared. Here and there doors slammed. The sound of fighting came nearer, the crack of knobkerrie against knobkerrie, the thrashing of bodies, hoarse shouts, snapping branches. Katie lifted up her taffeta skirt with no thought of modesty and began to run even faster until hot gusts of breath knifed into her chest. Soon there would be the whistles of police coming to gather up the bodies and question anyone they saw.

She hurried on, around a bend in the road, past the church, past the minister's house, past an open field, and at last stumbled up onto Auntie's veranda. She paused for a moment to catch her breath and dust her shoes. Inside the house people were singing. Often on Saturday nights Auntie's friends gathered together, for Auntie knew many musicians and, like all Fingoes, she loved to sing.

Auntie looked up in surprise when Katie came through the door. 'How is it you come tonight? Have you lost your job?'

'No, I have a little holiday.' Her knees were still trembling as she dropped down on the floor next to her cousin Fanny. 'There's been a big fight down the road.'

'Anyone killed?' Phillip asked from across the room.

'How do I know? I was too frightened to look. I just ran.'

'You're safe now,' Auntie said. 'And it's lucky you came, because we are greeting John Bokwe.'

'He's here?' Katie said softly, looking round at the men and women crowded into the dining-room. She had never met Bokwe before, but she had heard about him all her life, for Mama and Auntie had known him in the Cape when he was young. Now he was a famous musician. Auntie nodded toward a tall black man sitting in an armchair and called out, 'Here is Katie, my sister Anna's daughter.'

'One of the two who went to England to sing before the Queen?' he asked.

'Yes,' Katie said shyly. 'We sang your "Vuka Deborah" and she liked it very much.'

John Bokwe had brought another composer, Enoch Sontonga, to visit Auntie. It was one of his songs that Katie had heard while she stood on the veranda. Now Auntie suggested that he teach them another.

'I have one in my head but it's not quite right,' he said. He hummed a few notes and began, 'Nkosi sikelel' iAfrika' – God bless Africa. He glanced at John Bokwe, who nodded and began humming also, and as he repeated the phrase Auntie's friends joined in. Without her thinking of it, Katie's voice rose up out of her throat, an octave higher than the others, until Enoch Sontonga nodded, satisfied, and hummed a few more bars, paused, shook his head. 'It's not yet right,' he said.

John Bokwe nodded. 'Not yet, but it is a good song. When the notes come right in your head, you will know it is finished.'

Auntie went out into the kitchen for a pot of steaming coffee and a tray of tin cups. Someone asked Sontonga if he was going to stay in Johannesburg, but Katie did not hear his answer. Fanny was whispering in her ear, 'Can you keep a secret?'

'You know I can.'

'Don't tell anyone. Not yet.'

'I won't.'

Fanny leaned closer. 'I think pretty soon I'll get married.'

'Who? When?'

'A man in our church who told Phillip he wants to marry me.' She giggled. 'Phillip told him he's got to work very hard because I'm worth many cows.'

Fanny's happiness filled Katie with envy. All the girls she knew would soon be married. Even Charlotte had written in her latest letter about an African student at Wilberforce University, a Mr Maxeke, hinting that perhaps she would come back from America with a husband. It seemed to Katie that only she was left out. Although she had met many good Christian men in Auntie's church, they were either married or courting some other girl. It was not so easy to find a husband when she was shut up all week in Mrs Height's house.

Fanny chattered on until a loud voice blotted out her words. 'My boss calls him a stupid, pig-headed old fool. I tell you, pretty soon the English people here in Johannesburg are going to make war with Oom Paul Kruger.'

'Yes,' a waiter at Height's Hotel spoke up, 'I hear those Uitlanders talking while they drink their whisky and smoke their cigars.'

'Then we should pray for peace,' a little man sitting beside Phillip said slowly, 'because if the white men fight each other, then we will be fighting also. Some of us will help the Boers and some will help the English, and there will be suffering everywhere.'

Katie stared at him in amazement because he was speaking her own thoughts exactly. He was not a handsome man but there was something about his face – the crooked nose and the crinkles of laughter around his mouth – that made her happy just to look at him.

He glanced up at her as he finished speaking, caught her eye and held it, and they gazed at each other across the room for a long time, not moving or smiling. Then, without taking his eyes away from her, he leaned over and spoke to Phillip, who nodded. They both stood up and made their way carefully around Auntie's table to stand in front of her. 'Katie, this is my friend, Mr Makanya,' Phillip said.

'I see you,' she replied, moving closer to Fanny so there was room for him to sit beside her.

'Are you well? You no longer look as frightened as when you first came. Until I saw you I didn't know a woman could look so frightened and still be so beautiful.'

Katie smiled, remaining silent as he sat down. In time there would be much to talk about with this man, but for that first moment she was content to sit quietly, knowing that he was there beside her. She did not need to ask him questions, because from the way he looked at her, she knew he did not have a wife.

'I like to hear you sing,' Mr Makanya went on. 'When I went to school, I wanted to sing in the choir, but my voice was not good enough.'

'But it is. I like the sound of your voice and the way you speak.'

'Then I wish you'd been my teacher.'

Her pulse quickened. He was an educated man. 'Where did you go to school?'

'At Adams mission.'

'Where's that?'

'At Amanzimtoti. Near Durban. Close by my homeplace.'

'But that's in Natal!' Katie felt as if a cold wind was blowing between them. Natal was the land of the Zulus.

'Yes. Miss Manye, what's the matter? You're shivering.'

His voice sounded far away. A grey mist blurred her eyes. Katie leaned one arm on the floor to brace herself as she clambered awkwardly to her feet and pushed past the shapeless forms of people she could not see. The voice of her old ancestor echoed from her childhood: 'He's a Zulu; run, Katie, or he will eat you up.'

It was many years since she had last thought of that old woman with the yellowed bone showing through her hair. Was it just the heaviness of her years or was it possible that she did have some mysterious power to know what others did not know? Katie shivered again as she stumbled into the kitchen and pushed her knuckles into her mouth to stifle her sobs. Why did he have to be Zulu, this man who had touched her heart's tenderness before she knew him? Why did he have to appear so gentle, so kind, when he came from a nation of such cruel and terrible warriors?

Through the thin wall she could hear the voices in the dining-room, the splatters of laughter, and the sound of the front door opening and closing as people came and went. She did not hear Mr Makanya speak again until almost everyone had gone. Then, so close that he could have touched her if the wall was not between them, he said to Phillip, 'Your sister, we were talking together until suddenly she did not look at all well.'

'She looked all right to me,' Phillip said. 'Maybe she's tired. It's a long way from Saratoga Avenue, where she works.'

She heard the shuffle of Mr Makanya's footsteps, his muttered goodnight to Auntie. He was gone now, out of her life, and tomorrow she would speak firmly to Phillip about the friends he brought to meet her. He must learn to keep drunkards like Gershom out of her sight and see his Zulu friends at some other place, because she was not so clever about men. Without Pa to advise her, she could not trust her foolish heart.

But when she woke up in the morning, Phillip had already gone to his shoe-repair stall opposite the Johannesburg railway station. Fanny had left for her work, and Auntie had not yet returned from delivering her cakes and bread to Height's Hotel. Katie did not want to waste her holiday by staying all alone in an empty house; she also needed to buy cloth for a new dress. Then she could stop to ask Mrs Mashaba if she could use her sewing machine.

By the end of the afternoon Mrs Mashaba had finished all the seams of her new dress and basted up the hem. All that was left was the handwork. Back at Auntie's house, Katie heard Phillip's voice before she saw him, but he stopped talking when she came into the kitchen. Auntie's round fat face was creased in smiles, and Fanny's eyes gleamed with surprise and curiosity.

'Phillip has some important news,' Fanny said eagerly.

'A letter from home?'

Phillip shook his head, leaning against the wall and grinning at her curiosity. 'Mr Makanya has asked permission to court you. He brought his friends to speak with me because our father is not here.'

'What did you say?'

'I told him I would speak with you tonight.'

'Then tomorrow you can tell him I do not care to see him.'

'Don't be so quick to throw him away,' Auntie said. 'He's a good man.'

'How can you say that?' Katie replied heatedly. 'You know Ma would never agree. Don't you remember the warnings of our old ancestor?'

'The Zulus are different now,' Auntie said calmly. 'Since the time of Cetshwayo they have lived in peace. And there are many Christians among them.'

'Nevertheless, I don't want to know—' She did not want to mention Mr Makanya's name, for there was a saying, Do not speak of the lion or it will jump on you.

'Then you're a foolish girl. Already it's past time for you to marry.'

'I'm old enough to know I don't want to marry any Zulu.'

'Makanya has a good job at the saddlers Greatrex,' Phillip said. 'He doesn't waste his money. His wife will be very lucky.'

'Then let him go and find his lucky wife. That's no business of mine.'

Phillip frowned. Auntie sighed. Fanny looked disappointed. Although Katie did not want to think about that Zulu, she kept wondering what he had said.

'What did Mr Makanya say exactly?' she asked Phillip.

He laughed.

'Don't you dare laugh at me. Anyway, I don't want to know, I don't want to see him.'

But she had already spoken his name!

Mr Makanya came to the Presbyterian church on Sunday afternoon. From her seat in the choir between Auntie and Mrs Mashaba, Katie saw him pause in the doorway until he saw her. He smiled and then nudged a tall thin man beside him and nodded in her direction.

Against her will she felt a gladness in her heart at seeing him. Perhaps the Word of God had really softened his Zulu blood. But even as she thought these things, he beckoned to another man outside the door, a tall, fat man who towered above him and his other friend and swaggered down the aisle to one of the front benches. She did not like the look of the big man – too bold and proud. He sat up very straight with his huge shoulders thrown back, as though he carried a spear inside his shirt. He made all the other people in the church look weak and helpless.

She twisted her hands nervously in her lap before the choir rose for the hymns. Her knees shook so, she could hardly stand. But suddenly, as the pastor began his closing prayer, she thought of a way to escape. Waiting until she was sure that the three Zulus had bowed their heads and closed their eyes, she pushed past Auntie's fat legs, slipped stealthily out the back door of the church, picked up her skirt and ran through the open field towards a distant road. She ran faster than ever before, and did not return to Auntie's house but followed a roundabout way to Saratoga Avenue.

Yet even there in her own room she could not escape from Mr Makanya. He whispered to her out of the moonlight, and in her dreams he came to her shyly without his two fierce friends. When she woke up on Monday morning, the happiness of her dream caressed her in the warmth of her blankets until the sharp knowledge of the day brought back her loneliness. She leapt out of bed and hurried into the big house; but it was not until the Missis returned in the afternoon that she felt safe. Then, with all the clothes to wash and fresh bread to make, she was too tired that night to dream of anyone.

Uitenhage *c.* 1880. The town's red corrugated-iron roofs and green trees could be seen from Katie's family home, five miles away in the rolling countryside. (Photo: Port Elizabeth City Library)

The African Native Choir, which toured England in 1891–1893, posing in their best Victorian attire. *Top row:* Josiah Semouse, —, Johanna Jonkers, Wellington Majiza, —, —, Katie Manye, —. *Middle row:* John Xiniwe, Mrs. Paul Xiniwe, Paul Xiniwe, —, Albert Jonas. *Bottom row:* Charlotte Manye, Anna Gentle.

The African Native Choir in London, 1891, posing in tribal dress. *Top row:* Wellington Majiza, Paul Xiniwe, —, Josiah Semouse, —, —, —. *Middle row:* —, Johanna Jonkers, Katie Manye, Mrs. Paul Xiniwe, —, —, Charlotte Manye. *Bottom row:* Mr. Letty (choir manager), John Xiniwe, Albert Jonas, Mr. J. H. Balmer.

Adams Mission Station, 1916, in the hills above Amanzimtoti. Arriving here in 1902, Katie "gazed out over the rolling hills. The sugar-cane was bright green under a blue sky, and the earth was a deep red. Dark green bushes marked the river winding through the valley." (Photo: Brueckner papers, Killie Campbell Africana Library)

The Amanzimtoti Institute at Adams Mission. This school was attended by the
Makanya children. (Photo: Brueckner papers, Killie Campbell Africana Library)

The call to service at Adams Mission. Worshippers walked from afar, and often changed into "Christian" dress before reaching the church. (Photo: Brueckner papers, Killie Campbell Africana Library)

Dr. James McCord with his motorcycle, which Katie detested. "The Doctor always drove very fast, laughing into the wind . . . , never noticing that Katie winced every time he jounced over a pothole."

"Sometimes the Doctor would be called to some homestead in the hills to treat a patient who was too sick to come to a dispensary." (Photo: Brueckner papers, Killie Campbell Africana Library)

The Mission Nursing Home, which Dr. McCord opened in March 1909 on the hill overlooking Durban. (Photo: Brueckner papers, Killie Campbell Africana Library)

Pastor William Makanya, Katie's brother-in-law, conducting a service with some of the patients on the hospital balcony in 1911. (Photo: Natal Archives depot)

The American Board Mission chapel in Beatrice Street, Durban, photographed in 1902. Dr. McCord's dispensary was located in a building to the right of the chapel. (Photo: Inanda papers, Killie Campbell Africana Library)

Dr. McCord with his assistant Garnett Mtembu (on his right), who helped mix medicines and changed dressings on male patients, and (on his left) Thlambesine Ngcobo, an African traditional doctor whose treatments and medicines Dr. McCord became interested in. (Photo: Natal Archives depot)

Dr. McCord in 1940, shortly after his retirement.

The author and Katie Makanya, Durban, 1954.

9

Johannesburg

1895–1897

On Tuesday morning, Katie's three-day holiday seemed like another life. As the familiar pattern of her day unfolded, she felt secure and easy in her mind. Until the post came.

Mrs Height handed her the envelope with her name written in a neat, careful script. Katie did not have to be told who was writing to her. His characters were small, like Mr Makanya himself. She could not stop his letters but she did not have to read them. Quickly she threw the envelope into the fire.

Another letter came on Friday, and another on Saturday. She burned them both unread.

On Sunday she was afraid that Mr Makanya would come again to the Presbyterian church and afterwards to Auntie's house, so she went to visit Mrs Mashaba. She wandered around the garden sucking the juice from the blossoms of a honeysuckle vine before Mr and Mrs Mashaba returned from the service. Yet even they gave her no peace.

'I'm told Mr Makanya is courting you,' Mrs Mashaba smiled.

'No, he's not courting me. I don't want him. I don't want any Zulu.'

'He is a good Christian,' Mr Mashaba broke in, 'and he works hard in his church.'

'I don't care. I can't trust any Zulus.'

'You can trust Makanya,' Mr Mashaba said. 'He has spoken to Phillip and also to me because I am your father's friend. Would he do this if he was deceiving us?'

Would he? Katie did not want to find out. She did not want to have anything to do with him. Yet on the way back to Saratoga Avenue, each spindly bush by the road reminded her of his thin body. The night wind was like his breath on the back of her neck.

Letters came on Monday, on Tuesday, on Wednesday.

On Thursday Mrs Height asked her if she was sick.

'No, Missis,' she said.

'Then what's the matter with you. This morning there was no salt in the porridge, and just look at those tables all covered with dust.'

'Yes, Missis. I'm sorry, Missis.'

When another letter came in the post, Mrs Height wanted to know who was writing to her.

'Just a silly man who is wasting his money on stamps,' Katie said.

'What does he want?'

'I don't know. I throw his letters in the fire.'

'Aren't you curious?'

'No, Missis.' She slipped the envelope into her apron pocket intending to throw it away when the Missis wasn't looking.

But when she undressed in her room that night, she heard the crinkle of paper in her pocket, pulled out the letter and touched its corner to her candle. A little flame spurted up, burning her finger so that she dropped the letter quickly to the floor, and the flame went out.

She stood there, sucking the pain out of her finger and thinking how strange it was that the paper was not burned up. Perhaps it was a sign that God wanted her to read it. She leaned over, picked it up, and sat down on her bed. He had written in English:

> Dear Miss Manye,
>
> Your brother tells me you do not like me because I am Zulu. He says the Zulus chased your ancestors out of their homeland in the time of Tshaka. My ancestors too suffered at the hands of the warrior chiefs. In the time of Dingaan my father's father was Duzi, chief of the Makanyas in the Qwabe clan. Dingaan did not like the Qwabes so he sent out his regiments and told them: 'Whenever you see a man come home and put his fire right, then kill him because all the Qwabes like their fire.' There was much killing. Duzi himself was killed, but his baby wife, Mbalasa, escaped with some of the others, and they fled across the Tugela to find safety with the English. So you see, my ancestors, although themselves Zulu, were also driven from their homeland.

It came to Katie then that her reason for hating the Zulus was now like a rope binding her to this man. She went on reading about his job at Greatrex and about his work for the Reverend Mr Goodenough. 'If you think I am telling you lies, you should go and ask him,' he said. And he signed his name, Ndeya Makanya.

'Ndeya.' Katie did not know Zulu, but it was much like Xhosa, and she heard the meaning of that name: 'the Little One'. A gentle and unassuming name like the man himself.

On Friday she asked for time off.

'Why?' Mrs Height asked.

'I have to see my missionary,' Katie said. Then, when Mrs Height hesitated, she added, 'And tell him about the man who is writing me letters.'

Mr Goodenough was very deaf. When he came to the back door of his house, he was carrying a large horn, which he put to his ear.

'I've come to ask about Ndeya Makanya,' she shouted into the horn.

'Why do you want to know?' Mr Goodenough asked.

'He wants to be married to me. But I'm told the Zulus are fighters and drunkards. I only want a husband who is a good Christian and educated.'

Mr Goodenough dropped his horn. 'I've known Ndeya since he was very young. I can tell you this: he is one of the best members of my church. He did very well in our school at Adams Mission Station.' Mr Goodenough's blue eyes twinkled. 'But you, are you a good girl? Ndeya's family is far away, so I must make sure you will be a good wife.'

'Yes, I'll make him a very good wife,' Katie shouted back.

But before she answered his letter, she had to write to Ma.

She saw Mr Makanya for the third time on Sunday afternoon when he came to Auntie's house after church. His coming was like the sun rising after a cold and rainy night.

'You've read my letters,' he said softly when Auntie and Fanny found work in the kitchen to keep them busy and Phillip thought up reasons to go outside. 'That day at your church, you looked at me as if I had a spear to throw, and then you ran away.'

'It wasn't you who frightened me. It was your friends: the big fat one who looks so fierce, and the tall thin one.'

'Mbambo!' he laughed, 'He's not so fierce. He doesn't like to fight, only to joke. Wherever he goes, he makes people laugh. You wait and see. And Mngadi, he's not a joker. His thoughts are very deep. If Mbambo or I get into trouble, we go to Mngadi. We went to school together, we three, and we're like brothers.'

But she did not want to hear about his friends, only about himself, about his family and his homeplace in Natal. One day he would take her there, but she would not tell him this, not yet, not until she heard from Ma.

It was Pa who answered her letter in his large sprawling hand. It was the first letter he had ever written to her. Although he had learned to read in night school, he found it difficult to pen his words and remember his spelling. She wept to think of the long hours he must have spent in writing that letter, and she also wept to think that Ma had not been able to bring herself to write.

> Your mother grieves, because as you know she does not trust the Zulus. But I cannot tell you not to marry this man. When you were young, you obeyed me in the matter of Gershom. Now you are old, I can only pray that God will guide you and watch over you.

It was an honest letter with no pretence of pleasure in it, but no anger either, and no threat that he or Ma would shut her out of their lives. Carefully Katie folded up the sheet of paper and slipped it under the cover of her Bible. And then, although her face was still wet with tears, she took out her pencil, licked the end to make her letters black, and began to write: 'Dear Mr Makanya, I am willing to get married to you. But first I must give a month's notice.'

Katie saw Ndeya just once more before their wedding. He brought his friends, Mr and Mrs Nyati, to drink tea with her in the servants' quarters behind Mrs Height's house, and he told her that he had to go down to visit his family in Natal for three weeks. 'We'll be married as soon as I come back,' he said. 'Mngadi will make all the arrangements.'

Katie hid her disappointment in front of Mr and Mrs Nyati. 'Yes,' she said, but later she complained to Fanny.

'That Mngadi. If he wasn't married already, I'd think he was my husband. Never asking what I want, only telling me the plans he's made with Mr Goodenough. He's even gone himself to hire Mr Makanya's clothes.'

'At least he didn't hire any clothes for you,' Fanny said, glancing over at Katie's wedding dress hanging on the back of her bedroom door.

Auntie had wanted Katie to make over the white gown she had worn for the concerts in England. But Katie wanted her wedding to be just like the wedding of that English girl in the City Temple in London where she had earned a pound with her singing. Instead of listening to Auntie's advice, she made a special wedding dress out of white watered silk, which she bought for eight pounds down at the Indian stores. The skirt was full, the bodice tight, and little white roses were embroidered around the neck. She whipped narrow lace to the edge of a large square of mosquito netting for a veil and even found a wreath of artificial orange blossoms to wear on her head. She also spent five pounds for cream-coloured satin for Fanny to wear as her bridesmaid, and almost two pounds for the flour, sugar, eggs and dried fruit from which Auntie made her a wedding cake. And although Auntie told her to pick lilies down at the river for her bouquet, she ran instead to Market Street to buy white roses and maidenhair fern for herself and pink roses for Fanny. When she paid the vendor his seventeen shillings and sixpence and told him those flowers were for her wedding, he gave her a bonsella of three white carnations for Ndeya, Phillip and Mbambo to wear in their buttonholes. Auntie was very cross when she returned with the flowers.

'One day you'll need all that money you've thrown away,' she warned. 'When your husband is sick or loses his job or gets thrown in jail, then you'll wish you had it.'

'Mr Makanya is perfectly healthy and he won't get thrown in jail.'

'Poor girl, you know nothing,' Auntie sighed.

At two o'clock on Wednesday, 24 July 1895, Auntie buttoned up the bodice of Katie's wedding dress and pushed her towards the looking-glass in the kitchen. Phillip stood in front of it, turning this way and that to make sure his frock coat hung right over the grey striped trousers, and tilting his grey top hat backwards and forwards on his head.

'You've stood there half the morning. Do you think you're the one who's getting married today?' Auntie said impatiently.

While Phillip arranged the white carnation in his buttonhole, Katie ran back into the bedroom. She knelt down, pulled her carved jewellery-box out from under the bed and fumbled inside for the string of pearls which Lord Knutsford had given her. They gleamed against her black skin like drops of moonlight on a darkened pond, and even Auntie nodded pleasantly and said they looked very nice.

The older people left first. Then, escorted by Fanny and her friends, Katie walked slowly to Ndeya's church, nervously fingering her pearls and wondering what Lord Knutsford and Mrs Keithley would say if they could see her now.

The church did not look so big from the outside, but the way to the pulpit where Mr Goodenough waited seemed very long. At first, coming in from the bright sunlight, she could not distinguish the faces of all the people crowded in front of the benches or leaning against the walls. As her eyes grew accustomed to the dim light, she saw the massive shoulders of Mbambo towering above everyone else, but she did not see Ndeya. For a moment, panic curled at the edge of her mind and she clutched at Phillip's arm. Then she looked again at Mbambo. With a brief flash of surprise she wondered how she could have feared him that Sunday afternoon two months ago, for now he seemed as safe and sure as a mountain which breaks the force of wind and storm. If Mbambo was here in the church, then she knew Ndeya would be here also. Indeed he was, standing straight and proud, yet looking very small beside his friend.

As Ndeya reached out his work-roughened hand for hers, the joy of his presence wiped out the heartache of marrying against Ma's wishes. Of the whole service she remembered only the feel of the gold wedding-ring being pushed over the knuckles of her finger and the way Ndeya's arm trembled when they turned and walked together down the aisle into the sunlight.

The minister followed them, and then the European guests – a lady whose name she did not know but who ran the night school where Ndeya sometimes taught, a Mr Curzon who worked with Ndeya at Greatrex, and some Americans who were visiting the Goodenoughs.

While Mr Curzon congratulated Ndeya and wished Katie well, the Americans were whispering hurriedly together, and after Mr Goodenough had introduced them, the last gentleman to be introduced paused in front of Katie.

'We had no time to choose a wedding present,' he said, 'so you must choose your own.'

He reached out his arm towards her, and Katie, cupping her hands in the manner of her people, waited for the thrust of coins. Instead she felt a crinkle of paper money.

'You are very kind,' she murmured, not yet daring to look down until he followed the other Americans towards the table where Auntie and the women from the Presbyterian church were already laying out refreshments. Then Katie looked at the money in her hand.

'How much?' Ndeya whispered.

'Five pounds,' she gasped.

'*Hawu!*' he said, hardly believing their good fortune.

They looked at each other in amazement, and then spoke out their thoughts at the same time.

'We can save it for our chil—,' Katie began.

'We'll buy a cow—,' Ndeya said.

They began to laugh together in their happiness, dismissing this first little disagreement between them as unimportant.

There was no more time for private words together, for Auntie was calling out that it was time to cut the wedding cake before Mr Goodenough left with his friends, and Mrs Mashaba was beckoning to them to hold up their wedding presents, and Fanny was carrying glasses of lemonade around. Amidst all that confusion Mbambo's laughter kept rolling out as he moved among the people; wherever he went he left the men chuckling and the women laughing. Katie waited eagerly for him to come close so that she too could hear his jokes, but he did not come while she was cutting the cake, nor even when she opened up the big red blanket which he had given them for their bed. He did not come until all the food was eaten, the presents displayed and her knees aching from standing so long.

Suddenly, when Ndeya had stepped away from her to say goodbye to Mr Curzon, she felt the presence of Mbambo behind her. She turned quickly. Her head came only to his chest, so she had to bend backwards to see his face. He had put away his laughter and was looking straight down at her.

'You're tired,' he said. 'It is time for Ndeya to take you home.'

'Yes,' Katie replied, wondering why it was he and not Ndeya who knew this.

'Don't worry about your presents. Mngadi and I have a little cart, and we'll bring them to your house.'

'Yes.'

'And Katie, I'm sorry I frightened you that other time, that Sunday in your church. Ndeya told me you think I'm too fierce.'

'Not now, just that first time. You seemed so big, so strong.'

'I'm not as clever in my head as Ndeya and Mngadi but I am strong. And my strength belongs to my friend and—,' he hesitated, 'and the wife of my friend.'

'Yes,' Katie said softly, and for a long time they just looked at each other without any need for words. Ndeya returned to Katie's side, and Mbambo's laughter boomed out again. 'So Makanya's an old married man now. He won't be able to run to this place and that with us younger chaps. He'll always have to go home to his wife.'

'We'll see about that,' Ndeya retorted, and the banter went on between them until Katie signalled to Fanny to open up the small sack of rice.

'Come,' she whispered to Ndeya. Throwing the train of her wedding dress over one arm and clutching at her skirt with the other, she began to run, her head bent to escape the shower of rice while the old people clapped and the younger ones followed a little way to the house that Ndeya had built on land belonging to the church. They were laughing and breathless as they ran through the door and closed it firmly behind them.

Katie kicked off her white satin shoes and sank down on one of the dining-room chairs which Phillip had made. It felt good to rest her feet. She glanced up at Ndeya, who was leaning with his back against the door, staring at her, while he listened to the shouts of their friends outside.

'They'll go soon,' he said.

'Yes.'

They were alone together in that house, alone together for the first time, and suddenly Katie didn't know what to say to this stranger who was her husband. Yet she did not feel uncomfortable without any words between them.

'Mbambo said he and Mngadi would bring our presents. What a big clown Mbambo is, calling you an old married man. Are you really older than him?'

Ndeya smiled. 'We're the same age. He just likes to joke because of the grey in my hair.'

'Why isn't he married?'

'He has a wife. She stays in their homeplace.'

'Why doesn't she come to him?'

Ndeya shrugged, not interested in Mbambo's wife.

'How many children?'

'No children.'

Poor Mbambo, Katie thought. Such a big strong man to have a barren wife. But they would be lucky, she and Ndeya. They would have many children. She knew this in her blood, for already, beneath the white watered silk of her wedding gown, her belly waited, trembling, for a child to grow. She glanced up eagerly at Ndeya across the silence which had fallen again between them. Half-smiling, she reached up to remove the wreath of artificial orange blossoms and the veil, and then slowly unclasped her pearls from around her neck. Ndeya watched her all the time, saying nothing, and suddenly Katie wanted to laugh because in spite of his grey hairs he looked very young and uncertain.

'I don't hear anyone outside,' she said. 'You no longer need to guard the door.'

'No. Anyway I have a key.' He pulled it out of his pocket to show her, and then reached behind him to turn it in the lock. As he moved forwards, more confident now, Katie's heart began to throb in her chest. She did not notice her pearls dropping to the floor until he stooped to pick them up. She didn't think of the wedding presents which Mbambo and Mngadi would bring. She thought only of this man who was now her husband and of the children she would bear him. Yet even these thoughts scattered like the petals of a rose caught up in the wind when he closed his arms around her and forgot his shyness.

Two days after their wedding, Ndeya brought Albert Makanya home.

'This is my brother,' he told Katie, 'the son of my father's half-brother. He'll sleep here until he finds a job.'

'Yes,' Katie said and turned quickly into the kitchen to hide her dismay. A visitor so soon, when she and Ndeya were just beginning to know each other!

For three months Albert Makanya slept on their dining-room floor and ate their food. Nevertheless, he was an honest man, and as soon as he began to earn, he would bring Katie a sixpence or a shilling. In time he had paid her well. He was not the only one who lived with them. Sometimes there were three or four of Ndeya's friends or relatives from Amanzimtoti sleeping on that floor. At the end of each day the men would sit around joking with Ndeya while Katie worked quietly in the kitchen. Sometimes, watching her husband, she felt as if she was alone in a concert hall watching some singer whose every song and gesture were known to her but who still remained a stranger.

One night when Ndeya closed their bedroom door and prepared to sleep, Katie whispered to him plaintively, 'All day I've wanted to talk privately with you, but your friends take up all your time.'

'You can talk to me now,' he mumbled.

'I'm with child.'

'With child already?' Ndeya sat up in their bed, and even in the darkness Katie could sense his excitement. He caught her hand and held it tight, unable to speak for a moment, then suddenly he leapt up and flung open the door.

'Albert! Ntshebekazi! Ngwenyana! All of you! Katie's with child.'

Those foolish men roused themselves from their blankets. They punched Ndeya in the shoulder and laughed with him like a crowd of schoolboys. Katie lay alone in the bedroom, almost weeping one moment because her husband had gone to rejoice with his friends, and laughing the next because he was so proud that he wanted to shout out the news to all the world.

But for all his excitement, Ndeya had little time to plan for their child. It was not only the friends staying in their house who took up his time, but all the others who came to him when they were in trouble, especially when they needed money. Ndeya believed every tale of woe and never hesitated to reach into his pocket and give away whatever money he had.

Although Auntie talked about policemen who arrested people for no reason, Katie had not known the truth she spoke before she came to live with Ndeya. One of the deacons in the church disappeared for two months. Then he returned. He had been in jail, but for what reason he did not understand. There were so many laws that no one could know them all. Many of Ndeya's friends had been in jail. They laughed and joked about it with no feeling of shame. Even Ndeya himself did not think that going to jail was a disgrace.

Once in the middle of the night a man tapped on their window. Ndeya did not ask any questions. He just jumped out of bed, ran to the kitchen and opened the door. Katie lit their candle and followed him, but as soon as he saw the light, he told her to blow it out.

'Why?'

'Put out the light, I said.'

She snuffed out the candle, but not before she glimpsed a thin, breathless figure who sidled into the house.

'This is Umfinyela, he comes from my homeplace,' Ndeya told her. 'He's running from the police. Tonight they won't think to find him here, and tomorrow he can go to a certain white man and buy a false pass. Then he can travel safely by another name.'

A shiver of fear rippled up Katie's neck. 'What's he done?'

'It's better not to know.'

'Then we can't hide him,' she said. 'If he's done nothing, he can explain this to the magistrate. If he's sinned, he can be punished.'

For the first time Ndeya raised his voice in anger against her. 'Do you shame me in front of my friend? I told you he came from my homeplace. Tonight we'll hide him and perhaps tomorrow also.'

Katie was glad of the darkness, because she didn't want the stranger to see her tears as she stumbled back into bed. A few moments later Ndeya climbed in beside her and pressed his body close, but she lay stiff and unyielding. For a moment she hated him for risking the welfare of her unborn child to help his no-good friend. All night long she listened to the rustle of the wind outside and waited for the rush of footsteps and the thunder of policemen at their door.

After Ndeya left for work, Umfinyela roused himself and came into the kitchen. Katie cut four pieces of bread and poured out a cup of coffee.

'You'd better eat before you go.' She watched him stuff the bread into his mouth. 'If you come from my husband's homeplace, how is it I've not seen you before?' she asked. 'You haven't been to our church.'

'No,' he said, 'it's too far from my workplace.'

'Oh,' Katie said, but she could hear in his voice that he was only making excuses. Her impatience boiled up within her but she did not want to scold, because Ndeya had called him a friend. Yet Ndeya called everyone friend – rogues and drunkards and sometimes even those he did not know – as long as they came from Natal. Umfinyela looked out the window and then leaned back in his chair.

'The police don't know where I am. That's good. Now as soon as I find the money to buy that pass, I can take my troubles off your back.'

'Find the money? How are you going to find it if you're hiding here?'

'Ndeya will bring it.'

'If the police don't find you first.'

'They won't look for me here.'

'Not now, but this afternoon? Tonight? How much money do you need?'

'Two pounds.'

'Then wait.' Katie ran into the bedroom, opened her jewellery-box and counted out a one-pound note, five half-crowns, six shillings, four tickeys, and twelve pennies. It was the last of the five pounds which those Americans had given her when she was married.

'Here,' she said to Umfinyela when she returned to the kitchen. 'Go quickly and buy your pass. And take the rest of this loaf to feed you as you travel. But remember, when my husband visits his homeplace again, you'll still be owing me this money.'

'I'll remember,' he promised. Nevertheless, as she pushed him out the door and watched him disappearing down the road, she knew that her words and her money were lost. He wasn't to be trusted, that one, but at least he was gone.

Umfinyela was not the only one who twisted Ndeya's thoughts. He was always buying from strangers on the road and bringing her presents she did not need. 'Some day the police will come to arrest you for stealing things some no-good rascal has tricked you into buying.' But even though Katie scolded she could not teach him to leave such things alone. She knew that some day she would find herself in trouble if Ndeya went to jail and there was no money saved up for her and her child.

At last she confessed her worries to Mrs Nyati, who took in washing, and asked if there were white ladies who wanted to send out their laundry. Before long she was fetching baskets of dirty clothes and washing them down at the spruit. Her earnings she hid away in her jewellery-box.

Only once did Ndeya question her about the money she was saving. 'It's not for spending or giving away,' she told him. 'It's for the schooling of our child.' Or, she thought silently, to pay your fine to the magistrate when some policeman comes to arrest you.

Ndeya was indeed fortunate that he did not get arrested when one evening he and Mr Nyati drove home in a cart drawn by three beautiful black mules. At their gate Ndeya jumped down, unhitched one of the mules and pulled it into the yard.

'This animal cost only ten pounds, and he'll carry both you and your laundry. Nyati bought the other two and the cart as well.'

'These animals are worth more than ten pounds,' Katie said. 'Where did you get them?'

'From Joe Bhengu. It's true he sold them cheap – but he's in a hurry to go home.'

'Joe Bhengu? I've never heard of him.'

'He's my friend.'

When he spoke the word 'friend', Katie's heart sank into her stomach like a big lump of porridge. Suddenly all those presents he had brought her, all those no-good friends who had cheated him and taken his money, were too much for her to bear.

'You're stupid to call him "friend." You'll not see that Joe Bhengu again. He's already vanished into Natal where the police can't catch him. They'll catch you instead.'

Nyati, watching from his cart, burst out laughing. 'Hawu, Makanya! I can see you're already in the fire. I'm going because I don't want your wife to burn me up. But don't listen to her, she's nothing.'

'You think I'm nothing!' Katie whipped around to face him. 'All right, but soon you're going to need this nothing to get you out of trouble. You wait and see.'

Ndeya pushed her into the house and told her roughly to shut her mouth. By the time he returned, the Zulus who were staying with them began to joke and laugh at him because they said he was married to a woman who thought she knew everything. Although the big pot of mealiemeal was already cooked for their dinner, Katie left it there on the stove and went into the bedroom by herself. She was too angry to serve them, or even to eat. She was too angry to speak further with her husband.

In the morning she said nothing about the mule. As soon as all the men were gone, she untied the animal and chased it out of their yard. She didn't feel easy until she saw it amble across the road and down the hillside towards the spruit. As she turned back to the house she heard a shout, and there came Nyati and his wife, full of importance in their new cart, calling out and waving proudly to everyone they saw. For one brief moment Katie could not help envying them. A mule would be a big help in carrying her laundry. But then she saw again the strength and beauty of those mules, and knew that they were worth more than ten pounds each, much more than either Ndeya or Nyati could afford to pay.

That afternoon the police came to Nyati's house, bringing with them a young boy who called the mules by name and pointed to certain markings on their ears to show they belonged to his master. Nyati explained how he had bought them, not knowing they were stolen, but the policemen didn't believe him.

'There were three. Where's the other one?' the young boy asked. Nyati shrugged helplessly and pointed down to the spruit. Then, seeking Katie out with his eyes, he slyly shook his head to show that he would say nothing about Ndeya.

This time Ndeya had been lucky. Nyati was a loyal friend. But Ndeya couldn't always count on luck, and there were many others, besides Bhengu, waiting to lure him into some new trouble. He was so trusting that even a child could trick him. A child! Katie began to laugh. She called over to Nyati's second son who was about ten years old.

'You know Greatrex where my husband works?' He nodded again. 'Run there quickly and find him. Tell him that the police have arrested your father and are searching for him also.'

The boy's face puckered with fear until Katie laughed again. 'This is only a joke. You know he bought a mule just like your father. Now I'm going to frighten him so that he won't throw his money away the next time some stranger tries to sell him what is not his to sell.'

'Oh,' the boy said, his eyes bright with knowledge. He was a clever boy, that one, and he ran as fast as he could to Ndeya and returned to Katie before dark.

'Mr Makanya said to turn the mule loose,' he told her.

'Did you tell him the policeman had already seen it tied up in our yard?'

'Yes, I told him also that one was waiting in the kitchen and another was looking for him on the road.'

'You've done well. Here are some sweeties and a piece of meat to take to your mother. She has plenty of worries and must eat well tonight.'

There was no sign of Ndeya among the workers streaming back through the twilight to their homes. There was no sign of any of Ndeya's relatives or friends. Katie sat on her front step waiting. Candles flickered in some of the houses nearby and a few stragglers hurried past her gate. The road emptied, and there was no sound anywhere except the bullfrogs croaking down at the spruit and the wind rustling through the leaves. Ndeya must be really frightened, she thought, pulling her shawl more tightly around her shoulders. She wondered where he was, if he was hungry and cold, and thought for a moment of walking to Mngadi's house to see if he was there. But if he came at all tonight, he would want his food. At last she went back into her kitchen, made a pot of tea, added an extra spoonful of sugar, and sipped the hot sweet liquid while she waited.

She must have dozed, for suddenly her head jerked and she was wide awake. Through the window she saw a shadow moving without any noise towards the back door.

'Who is it?' she called out, opening the door a little way.

'Ntshebekazi.'

'Sh. What do you want?'

'Ndeya sent me. Are the police still here?'

'Yes.' She tried to close the door but he reached out to keep it from closing. Quickly she moved her body in front of him so he could not see inside, and then called out loudly as though speaking to someone in the dining-room. 'No, there's no one out there. It's just the wind, but I don't think my naughty husband is coming home tonight. You'd better go look for him somewhere else.'

Ntshebekazi's foot slipped away from the door and Katie shut it quickly. She could not help laughing, and perhaps he heard and knew she was only pretending, because it wasn't long before Ndeya crept up to the back window, peered in, and then flung open the door.

'You!' he said, glancing around at the empty room. 'You *sangoma* – you witch. You bring me bad luck.'

'No,' Katie said, reaching out for the shoes he held in his hand, 'I bring you good luck. Didn't I chase away that mule before the police came? If my head had not told me that Bhengu was a thief, you'd be in jail with Nyati tonight.'

Ntshebekazi crowded in, as did the lodgers who had been afraid to come back when they thought her kitchen was full of policemen. Now they were all laughing at the joke she had played on Ndeya.

Poor Nyati had to pay a very big fine. His wife had to take all their money and sell their furniture besides, and still she had to borrow nine pounds and fifteen shillings from Katie before he could go free. But Nyati was an honest man. In time he paid back every penny, and he never called Katie a nothing again.

Ndeya too had learned his lesson. He did not buy again from strangers, but lost his money in other ways, less dangerous to himself and his family. He was a good man and very skilled at harness-making, but he was a dreamer and dreams cost money.

Katie's son was born on a Saturday morning when she was alone in the house. The pains started suddenly. Soon they came so fast that she grew frightened and stumbled over to the window to call for help. By the time Mrs Nyati reached her, Katie was crouched on the floor with her baby in her hands.

Mrs Nyati snipped and tied the cord, wiped the baby with a towel, wrapped him in a flannel sheet, and laid him in Katie's arms.

'What's wrong with him? He looks almost European,' Katie cried out in anguish.

'Nothing's wrong. All babies are light-skinned for a day or two. Just look at his ears. You can always tell by the ears.'

Katie looked at her baby's ears and saw that their edges were very dark. 'Then he's all right?'

'Very much all right.'

She smiled down at her son, remembering when her brother Henry was born. She was very young then, and she and Charlotte had been sent to play outside with Phillip. Then the old midwife called them in for food and told them to be very quiet. 'Your mother's very tired,' she said. 'All day she's been running in the bush to find a monkey and cut off its tail to make a baby brother for you.' Neither she nor Charlotte had wanted to see the monkey, and for a long time she did not like her brother Henry.

What foolish stories we tell our children, she thought, and then whispered softly, 'But I'll never tell you foolish stories, my son. I'll always teach you true.' She was hungry and tired, and as soon as Mrs Nyati had brought her a dish of porridge, she closed her eyes. She would sleep until Ndeya came.

It was Mbambo's laughter which woke her. Mrs Nyati was trying to shush him, but his happiness was like a strong wind lifting Katie out of her bed. Mbambo bent down to look at the baby and then straightened up to his great height, his laughter booming out and shaking the house. 'A proper Makanya. I must go at once and tell Makanya that we have a son.'

Katie smiled. Because he had no children of his own, he called Ndeya's son 'our' son, and his great strong hands slowed into gentleness when he touched him.

Ndeya chose the name of Samuel Knutsford Makanya. After his first son was born, he no longer called his wife by her own name but, according to custom, she became for him 'Mother of Samuel'.

Yet, proud as he was of Samuel, he spent little time with him. If he was not working in his harness store, he was busy in the church or talking to the people who gathered around him. He was like a honeysuckle flower around which the bees gathered, and wherever he went the buzz-buzz-buzz of conversation followed.

Katie had more time to talk with Mbambo than with her own husband. He was a wild one, that Mbambo, full of crazy talk, although he meant no harm. Often he brought bulbs or cuttings from his master's garden or a bag of toffees, and once when Mrs Mashaba was visiting he came with a pound of stewing meat. 'This is for Ndeya. I want to watch you cook it properly.' Another time he came when Anna Marutle was visiting from Kimberley. 'Are you Sotho too?' he asked. Without waiting for her to answer, he went on, 'I think Sotho women make good wives. I myself am thinking of taking a Sotho wife.' He glanced over at Katie and closed one eye quickly to warn her not to speak of the wife he already had in Zululand.

'I'm Fingo,' Anna giggled, 'and anyway, you're too old for me. How is it you're not married?'

'Me? Married? I'm too young. I am young enough to be son to Makanya.'

'Hawu! Mr Makanya's not that old.' Anna pointed at Katie, who once again was growing big with child. 'Katie's his first wife and she's still young enough to bear children.'

Mbambo laughed. 'And what of all those grey hairs on Makanya's head? And as for Katie, look at her wrinkles. She's an old woman.'

'But old women don't have babies.'

'You say that? And you a Christian! Don't you read your Bible? Haven't you heard of Sarah, who bore a child when she was threescore years and ten?'

'But that was a miracle.'

'Yes,' Mbambo said, 'and we still have miracles today. Katie's our miracle.'

After he left, Anna was still giggling. 'Are all Zulus as crazy as that one?' she asked.

'No,' Katie said, 'Mbambo is himself. There's no one else like him, not any-where.' No one, she repeated to herself, for who else would call her a miracle, who else could fill her lonely heart with laughter. For her, his great round laughing face was as beautiful as the cactus blooming on the dry veld.

Now that Katie was the mother of a Zulu, she no longer hesitated to speak out her mind at the meetings of the Women's Association in their church. It was on her way to one of those meetings that she met Mr Goodenough. He stopped to ask about Ndeya, and when he lifted up his big horn to hear her reply, she spoke to him easily in Zulu.

'Didn't you tell me you're Sotho?' he interrupted.

'Yes,' she said, half-turning so he could see little Samuel on her back, 'but my son's a real Zulu.'

He looked down at her intently. 'From your speech I would think that you are Zulu also.'

'I grew up among the Xhosa, and that language is not very different from my husband's.'

'You speak Xhosa also? Besides Sotho?'

'Also Dutch and English.'

'Then I have a job for you,' Mr Goodenough said. 'A friend of mine, Dr Dickson, has been hired by the Chamber of Mines to teach the people about the evils of drink. But he's an Englishman from the Cape. He knows none of the native languages. He will need an interpreter.'

Katie's interest stirred. There were too many drinkers among the migrant workers in Johannesburg. Many had left wives and children behind in what-ever part of the country they came from. In their free time they tried to forget their loneliness by seeking out the backyard shebeens to buy homemade beer or other more potent drinks. On Saturday nights no one was safe on the roads. Even on Sunday afternoons there were fights, sometimes right in front of the church, and on Mondays there were many accidents in the mines. Those who drank did not listen to the preachers, but perhaps they would lis-ten to this white doctor.

The first time she stepped up beside Dr Dickson and the mine supervisor on the little platform in front of the Salisbury mine, someone from the crowd of black men below taunted her: 'Where is your husband, woman? Is he already weary of your abuse that he sends you here to bother us with words?'

'Are you afraid of my words?' she shouted back in Xhosa. 'Then you are right to be afraid. Because my words are not the words of a woman. I am the mouth of the white *inyanga* who comes to warn you of the evil spirits waiting for you in all the drinks you buy from the old witches in this town. Pretty soon those spirits will burn you up inside until you die.' She paused a moment and then went on, 'And who is this white *inyanga*? you ask. He is a man of strong powers. He puts words in my mouth. Xhosa words if you want them, or Sotho, or Zulu. Tell me your language and I will speak to you in your own tongue.'

Dr Dickson had stopped talking to the mine supervisor and was looking at Katie in some alarm. 'What are you telling them?'

'Just to be quiet and listen.'

On the other side, the mine supervisor began to chuckle. 'Don't you believe it, Doctor. She's frightening the hell out of them by describing your magic powers.'

The men below were quiet now and ready to listen.

Dr Dickson worked very hard. Two or three times a week he took Katie with him until they had visited the Stanhope, Sheba, Robinson, Crown Reef and other mines. But the drinking went on. There was more and more fighting on the streets, more accidents in the mine shafts.

'Dr Dickson's a good man,' Katie told Mbambo, 'but the workers listen and grumble and soon forget.'

'Because he's a white man,' Mbambo said, 'and we are tired of white men telling us to do this and do that.'

In her despair, Katie wrote to Charlotte. 'It's no use working with the church pastors,' she said in her letter. 'It's only the American Board and the Presbyterians who forbid their members to drink. Other churches are not so strict. Even some of the Christian women are brewers.'

Charlotte wrote back, describing the Temperance Movement in America – the meetings, songs, picture books – and even told her of a white woman who ran around with an axe chopping down the doors of saloons.

At the next meeting of the Women's Association, Katie spoke her thoughts. 'It's useless to preach to the drinkers,' she said. 'They will call us nothings because we are women. But I ask you this: Who bring forth the children of our people? Women! Who plant the gardens and prepare the food? Women! And who brew these drinks in their shebeens? Women! I tell you, we are the strength and the weakness of our people. And those of us who are strong in Christ must wipe out the evils of our weaker sisters. We must join with women everywhere to start a Temperance Movement as they have done in America.'

In the months that followed, Katie was very busy visiting women in other churches, schoolteachers and pastors, and even the women in their shebeens, urging them all to join with her in her new Temperance Union. There were meetings to plan, parades to lead, and songs to teach to the children after school. At last her life was complete. Even without a high school education, she was doing important work. If Pa could see her now, he would be proud. Charlotte, too, would think she was doing an important work. At the same time, little Samuel was healthy and quick to learn, Ndeya's harness shop which he had set up was prospering, Mbambo was her friend, and again she was growing big with child. She was very happy.

Then the Zulus began to quarrel with Mr Goodenough, and all her contentment was shattered.

Katie blamed herself. Several years earlier, Katie had met Pa's cousin, the Reverend Mangena Mokone in Pretoria. As a young man Mokone, like Pa, had travelled south to find guns for the Old Man. He had got as far as Natal, and there he had been taken in by Wesleyan missionaries. Like Pa, he became a Christian, and in time was ordained pastor and sent to Pretoria.

But Mokone had a mind of his own. He told Katie the Wesleyans were like all other Europeans. Because he had a black skin they treated him as a child and would not listen to his suggestions. And so he wanted to break away and start his own church. To do this he needed money, and he asked Katie if she knew of any people in England who would help him.

'Why do you look to England? I think it would be better to tie yourself to the Negroes in America. You should write to my sister Charlotte.' Words thus spoken lightly at one time would come back to haunt Katie at another.

One of the people in America who had helped Charlotte get a scholarship to Wilberforce University was Bishop Turner of the AME – the African Methodist Episcopal Church. Mokone wrote to him at Charlotte's suggestion, and in 1897 Bishop Turner came out to Johannesburg to join Mokone's church to the AME.

Because the Bishop was a friend of Charlotte's, Katie and Ndeya gave a big party for him in their house, and they and their friends all went to his meetings. But after he left, only a few of the Zulus in Johannesburg joined the AME. When Mokone tried to draw them in, Katie objected. 'You have your own church now,' she said. 'But my husband and I are American Board. And we are very satisfied with Mr Goodenough. He's not like those other missionaries you told me about.'

At first the Zulus all agreed. When they originally came to Johannesburg, they had met in one other's houses to pray together on Sunday afternoons. In time they collected among themselves enough money to build a church. It was then that the American Board missionaries in Natal sent up Mr Goodenough to buy the land, supervise the building and choose a pastor.

Thus, when Mokone came to visit and claimed that the white missionaries owned the title-deeds to the church, Katie was not afraid to contradict him.

'What do the title-deeds matter? If we want something, we have only to tell Mr Goodenough.'

Mokone shook his head. 'If you want one thing and he wants another, then he won't listen. The church belongs to him and he will have his way.'

Many of the Zulus were upset by Mokone's talk of title-deeds and went to consult with Mr Goodenough. And so the arguing began.

Eventually, Mr Goodenough removed his big horn from his ear so that he could not hear them and told them to *thula,* to shut their mouths, as though they were children. He was a stubborn man who would not discuss the matter further. But Mbambo, Makanya and some of the others were just as stubborn. On Sunday they refused to enter the church and went to the Pastor's house instead and formed their own Zulu congregation. Katie wept when Mbambo and Ndeya told her what they had done.

'How can you leave Mr Goodenough?' Katie asked Mbambo indignantly. 'He has known you since you were young. He was one of your teachers at Adams College. How can you throw him away?'

'Because he told us to *thula* and treated us with disrespect,' Mbambo replied.

'Only because his ears are all blocked up and he did not fully understand.'

Mbambo pretended to take down a big horn from his ear and shouted *thula* at her. Then he turned to Ndeya. 'Don't listen to her. She's crazy in the head. She helped Mokone break away from the Wesleyans because he's from her own people. But she won't help us break away. Not even you, Ndeya, so leave her alone. She's not one of us.'

'You're stupid,' Katie said angrily. 'You forget too soon. You forget how the Reverend found Nyati another job and how he called us to his house for Dr Dickson to cut our arms and rub in medicine to save us from smallpox. But *I* don't forget these things.'

Ndeya looked at Katie uncertainly until Mbambo laughed again. 'Among the Sotho it is the women who tell their husbands what to do. Are you Sotho, Makanya?'

Ndeya muttered angrily that he had already decided to join the Zulu congregation. But he could not make Katie leave the church where they had been married and where their son, Samuel, had been christened. It was not right for her and her husband to worship separately, Katie thought, and that was all Mbambo's fault. But the real reason she was angry with him was that he had told her husband, 'She's not one of us.'

The next Wednesday afternoon, as Katie was singing a lullaby to Samuel, she felt the presence of Mbambo. He was standing under a tree in front of their yard, a streak of sunlight shining down through the leaf shadows on his face.

'What are you doing here? You know Ndeya's in his harness shop,' she shouted at him.

Mbambo shook his head slowly like a man startled out of a dream. 'It's Wednesday. I've come to see our son.'

Katie lifted Samuel up. 'Now you see him.'

'But he cries. He wasn't crying when you were singing. Ah Katie, I did not know a song could make the hair on my neck stand straight.'

Fury rose up through Katie's chest and harshened her voice. 'I do not sing for you, Mbambo. You set me apart. To my own husband you said I'm not one of you.'

'I never meant—'

'You said it. To my own husband you said it. Since then I do not want to speak with you, Mbambo.'

She shut the door quickly against him and sat down in the rocking-chair to quiet Samuel. For many minutes Mbambo remained standing outside. At last he turned and walked down the road, his shoulders drooping and his feet hesitant like those of a blind man. Her own eyes blurred with tears at his going, and her throat tightened up, so she could no longer comfort Samuel with her singing.

10

Soekmekaar & Johannesburg

1897–1899

Mbambo no longer came to play with Samuel on Wednesday afternoons. And he did not come home with Ndeya to see 'our' daughter when little Charlotte was born. Katie kept telling herself that she did not care and threw all her energy into her work, interpreting for Dr Dickson and organising meetings and parades for the Temperance Movement.

Samuel was big and strong for a two-year-old. He loved everyone. Baby Charlotte was different. If Katie left her for just a minute, she began to cry. But she was still so small that Katie could carry her on her back wherever she went. And she was as healthy as Samuel. But one Friday morning, when she was almost a year old, she whimpered all day and refused to eat. That night her little body grew hotter and hotter and her legs began to jerk. Katie and Ndeya bathed her in lukewarm water. For a time she was quiet. Ndeya went to bed and did not hear Katie's call when Charlotte again went into convulsions. This time she died.

Katie, not yet believing, held her in her arms and sat down in the rocking-chair by the window, until Ndeya came in the morning and took the child from her. Katie did not hear what he told her or what was said by those who came during the day and stood beside her chair and went away again. Only once did she speak. Auntie was dressing Charlotte's little body before laying her down in her coffin.

'She must wear her red coat,' Katie said.

'No, Katie. You should save that one. Her old coat is good enough.'

'The red coat is warmer. Without it my baby will be so cold under the ground.'

Katie waited while Auntie laid little Charlotte in her coffin. She looked so pretty in the red coat with her eyes closed as if asleep that Katie still could not believe she was dead. Even after the funeral Katie kept listening for her to wake up in the night. Once, when Samuel whimpered, she jumped up and ran to Charlotte's empty crib before remembering. Katie could not weep. She just sat in her chair by the window, too numbed to move her body or think or speak. Auntie often sat with her through the long afternoons although Katie hardly knew she was there. Mr Goodenough prayed with her but Katie did not listen. Fanny came with Phillip and Mrs Mashaba. Mngadi and his wife brought sweet potatoes and stew. Dr Dickson came with medicine. Even Mbambo came. Katie was unaware of their presence.

How many days or weeks she sat uncaring in that chair, she did not know. But at last it was Mbambo that roused her from her apathy. He squatted on his heels in front of her and spoke out harshly.

'You're a wicked, selfish woman,' he said.

'Yes,' she answered dully, 'God has punished me. He has taken my baby.'

'And now you don't care if the other one dies also?'

'Samuel?' Katie started up in alarm. 'What's happened to Samuel?'

Mbambo pushed her back into the chair. 'He's on his sleeping mat. I myself lay down beside him while he cried himself to sleep.'

'But Samuel never cries.'

'Tonight he cried,' Mbambo told her, more gentle now that she was listening. 'When I said to him "Let us pray," he said, "I don't want to pray to Jesus. He's a naughty man. He ran away with my sister into the clouds so I cannot see her and now I have no one to play with. So I won't pray to him lest he take me also." He's afraid, Katie.'

'I'm frightened too, Mbambo. My God has forsaken me.'

'Have you forgotten what the Bible says: "What the Lord giveth the Lord taketh away"?'

'So cruel!'

'Why do you call Him cruel when you still have Samuel?' Mbambo's voice quivered. Looking down, Katie saw the pain in his eyes. Poor Mbambo had no child to call his own.

'Yes, we still have Samuel,' she said.

'And Ndeya. Don't forget Ndeya. See how thin he is because you do not feed him.'

Katie looked over Mbambo's head to where Ndeya was standing, his one hand resting on the table, his shoulders bent as if he were very tired and his face as lined as an old, old man's. Her tears came then, and her sobs wrenched at her chest as she poured out her grief. Ndeya ran over and pushed Mbambo aside so that he himself could hold her still. And in the comfort of his arms, her love stirred again for him and Samuel. And also for Mbambo.

Several weeks later, Phillip brought her a letter from Ma, the first word she had had from Soekmekaar since her marriage. 'My heart grieves for your sorrow,' Ma wrote. 'I can only pray that the good Lord will look after you and your firstborn.' She did not mention Ndeya.

Slowly she folded up the letter and pushed it back into the envelope. 'Ma still cannot forgive my husband for his Zulu blood,' she said sadly.

'Because she does not know him,' Phillip said. 'I think if you took him for a visit— '

'No,' Katie said sharply. 'He is not invited.'

Phillip brought out another letter. 'Read this.'

In her letter to Phillip, Ma complained that Henry would not stay in his Lutheran school. He kept coming home to hunt and dance. He drank beer. He smoked dagga. Ma did not know what to do.

Phillip waited until Katie finished reading, then said, 'While you work for temperance here in the city, your own brother gets drunk in the country. You should go home and make him change his ways.'

Katie shook her head sadly. 'I cannot leave my husband.'

'I think when Ma sees Samuel she'll forgive you.'

'Phillip is right,' Ndeya interrupted quietly.

'I won't go without you.'

Ndeya laughed. 'Then I'll close up my store for two weeks and take a holiday.'

The next day Katie wrote to Pa. Ndeya, too impatient now to wait for Ramokgopa's wagon, hired a cart and two mules. They travelled more quickly in the mule cart than by ox-wagon. Soon after they passed the Lutheran mission, Pa and Henry came riding out on their horses to meet them. Katie could not believe it was five years since she had seen Pa. He still sat very tall and straight on his horse, and there was less grey in his hair than in Ndeya's. He did not look much older than Henry, who eyed Katie warily and galloped away after a brief greeting.

The mountains were eating up the sun by the time they reached the dancing ground between the huts and the river. Katie could smell the roasting meat from an ox Pa had slaughtered. Already people were gathering around the glowing ashes. Among them Katie noticed several women who wore proper dresses, and at the far end of the dancing ground she saw a square house with a steeple.

'You've built a church,' she said to Pa.

'Yes, we have a number of Christians now. And once a month the Presbyterian missionary comes from Pietersburg.'

'And Ramokgopa? Has he become a Christian?'

'No, not Ramokgopa. He says the old ways are good for him. But he doesn't work against us any more.'

Katie looked for Ma but she was not among the women running forward to greet them. She was leaning on a stick and waiting quietly some distance away, holding on to the hand of Mary Ann. Katie gasped with pain at seeing the change in her. Her hair was streaked with white, and she had lost all her teeth, so that her cheeks were sunken in, and the lines around her mouth made her look stern and old. Katie jumped down from the cart and ran to throw her arms around her, laughing and crying at the same time.

'Oh, Katie,' Ma murmured, holding her close. But when Ndeya approached, her body stiffened and her voice grew as hard and cold as the frozen rain.

'My husband rejoices that you bring our daughter home. His house is ready for you.' But no word of her own pleasure.

Ndeya answered her quickly before Katie's anger pulled her away. 'We too rejoice to bring your grandson home to you.' He stepped forward, thrusting Samuel towards her. After a moment's hesitation Ma took Samuel in her arms. When he whimpered in all the confusion, Ma began to smile and comfort him with soft words. Within a few hours she was calling out to all her friends, 'Come pay your respects to my Zulu grandson, or else he will eat you up.' Even when the night came she would not let him go but took him into her bed to sleep beside her.

After all the feasting was over, Ndeya rolled out their sleeping mats and unfolded their blankets while Katie stood at the window looking up at the stars. The sky seemed very close. The soft breeze of the summer night touched lightly at her cheeks and rustled the grasses on the veld. Somewhere a small night-hawk was calling out cheerily. Down by the river the bullfrogs were croaking, and everywhere the darkness echoed with the soft tinkling trill of the cicadas.

'It's so peaceful here in the country,' Katie murmured. 'Soon Ma will know you and be glad. At last my heart rests easy.'

Ndeya blew out the candle and patted the sleeping mat beside him. 'Then come and rest your body.'

At first Ma spoke to Ndeya only as courtesy demanded and in her careful English, because he came from Natal. But within a few days she forgot her suspicions and addressed him as *umkwenyana,* which means son-in-law, and Katie knew then that she had forgiven him his Zulu blood.

During the next two weeks Ndeya mended all the goatskin water bags belonging to the tribe. He repaired a saddle for Mr Davidson. Even in Soekmekaar there was much work for a harness-maker, and Ramokgopa offered him land for a house if he would stay.

Ndeya shook his head. 'I cannot forget my store in Johannesburg.' But later he admitted to Ma that when the Batlokwa tried to talk to him, he could not understand. Even with Pa he was not altogether comfortable. He could not understand Dutch or Sotho, and Pa's English was slow and halting. Only with Ma could Ndeya talk without the need for Katie's presence. Ma spoke to him in Xhosa, the language of her girlhood, which is much like Zulu, and when she used a word which was strange to him, they laughed together, repeating this or that in English until the meaning was clear. Often she questioned him about the customs of his people at Amanzimtoti, and later reported to Katie what she had learned.

'If he takes you back to his homeplace, you must know what is expected,' she said. 'It is not always easy to follow in ways that are strange to you.'

Poor Ma! Katie sensed her loneliness. Life was not easy for her in Soekmekaar. Mary Ann was a sickly child, making much extra work. 'Ever since the smallpox when Mr Davidson cut our arms and rubbed in muti to save us, Mary Ann has been sick,' Ma said. 'Every so often her head aches and her throat is sore. Sometimes she has sores and rashes on her body.'

Ma worried also about Charlotte in America, Phillip in Johannesburg, and John, who had won a scholarship to a boarding school in the Cape. But most of all she worried about Henry.

'The teachers at the Lutheran school told me he's a troublemaker,' Ma said. 'He's older than John but fell behind him in school. He doesn't want to study his books. The last time he ran away, the Lutherans would not take him back. But what can he do here among all these heathen?'

'Perhaps you should send him down to Blinkwater to live with Grandfather,' Katie said. 'He won't need so much book-learning to be a fruit farmer.'

'It's so far. I'm afraid he'll get lost on the way,' Ma said wearily.

'Not if I take him back to Johannesburg and put him on the train.'

Pa was relieved at Katie's suggestion, and Henry was excited at the thought of visiting her in the city and then travelling down to the Cape. Thus it was that he left with Katie and Ndeya when they returned to Johannesburg.

After their visit to Soekmekaar, Ma wrote to Katie every week. Henry was doing very well in Blinkwater. But soon after Katie's third child, Ethel, was born, Ma began to worry about John.

John did not like his new teachers. He said they were stupid. They in turn considered him disrespectful, and were threatening to take away his scholarship and send him home. 'He wants to be like Charlotte and go to America,' Ma wrote, 'but we have no money to send him.'

'Then he must come to work in Johannesburg,' Katie wrote back. 'He can live with me and give me what he earns so I can save it up until he has enough.'

As soon as John arrived, Katie took him at once to see Mr Curzon, the white man who had worked with Ndeya at Greatrex and had come to their wedding. He too had left Greatrex and was now caretaker of some flats. Because he was Ndeya's friend, he gave John a job as janitor. From six o'clock in the morning until half past seven at night, John was under the eye of Mr Curzon; but in the evenings Katie never knew where he was.

He went everywhere, to meetings, to different churches, to study groups, to night school, and when he could not think of anywhere else to go, he would bring his new friends home. He had many friends from different tribes, as well as Europeans, Indians and even one Chinese man, and all of them would sit in Katie's dining-room and speak long words and read to one another out of the newspapers and talk economics and revolution. John was never without his newspapers. He bought them on the streets and he sent away to Cape Town and other places for papers, which came to him in the post.

John was seventeen years old but he had never learned to droop his shoulders or look down at the ground when a white man spoke to him. When Katie warned that unless he pretended humility, some white people would think him cheeky and make trouble for him, he talked earnestly about injustice and oppression.

Once he went with her to the post office to help her carry back a box of chickens Ma had sent her. When Katie showed the clerk the invoice, he said the chickens were no longer there.

'But they must be,' Katie said. 'See? It says on the invoice.'

'Not any more. We never keep anything more than a week. That's the rule.'

'There were ten hens and three roosters. You don't throw away live chickens. You must have sold them. If they are not here, you should give me the money for them.'

'I know nothing about your chickens. Now get out.'

John stepped up angrily, speaking Dutch to be sure the clerk understood.

'Those chickens were worth three pounds and fifteen shillings. It says so on the invoice. We are not getting out until you give us that money.'

The clerk shook his head and said that was too much.

'It's not too much,' John said. 'Unless you are stupid you sold them for more than that. If you refuse to give us the money, I'll go to the magistrate and he'll make you pay.'

The clerk's face grew very red. Katie was afraid he would lean across the counter and hit John in the face, but instead he went behind the wall of postboxes to talk to someone she could not see, and after a few moments he came back and threw the money down on the counter.

'Now get out. And don't have anyone send you any more fowls by post.'

John scooped up the money, gave it to Katie and turned back to the clerk. 'Dankie,' he said. Then, with an air of defiance, he added in English, 'Tomorrow, if I wish, I'll order more fowls by post but I'll have them sent cash on delivery so that you won't be able to steal them.' Katie had to pull at John's arm to get him away before he infuriated the clerk even more.

She warned him constantly to keep his angry thoughts to himself. Although he would not listen, he always brought her his money when he was paid, and she would give him a little to spend and saved up the rest so that he could go to America. She was anxious for him to go. There was more talk of war between the Boers and the English; if John waited too long she was afraid he would be caught up in it and never get to America at all. In her impatience she took ten pounds from the money she had saved from her laundry and added it to the twenty pounds put aside from his earnings, telling Mr Curzon that he would leave his job at the end of the month. At the month end she walked with him to Park Station and bought him a ticket to Cape Town.

A week later John sent word that his passage on the ship would cost eleven pounds and he would need the rest of his money to travel to Wilberforce University, where Charlotte was waiting. Katie immediately went with her children to the post office to telegraph it.

As she drew the money out of her purse and stepped up to the counter, she recognised the clerk who had grown so angry with John over the chickens. Although he did not recognise her, she felt nervous. In her confusion she started to explain in English that she wanted to send some money to Cape Town, until the frown on the Boer's face made her remember and she repeated herself quickly in Dutch.

The clerk's frown disappeared. 'Don't worry. It will reach there safely. Just wait. In half an hour or so a message will come and it will be like a receipt.'

'*Dankie, baas,*' Katie said humbly. While she stood there, thinking of her young brother going so far away and wondering if she would ever see him again, tears came to her eyes. The clerk looked at her sharply, glanced at the baby on her back, hesitated a moment, then lifted up the counter and motioned her to a chair.

'*Dankie, baas,*' she repeated, although inside herself she was laughing in spite of her tears. The Dutch were a strange people. If you acted out of foolishness or sorrow or ignorance, they could be very kind. But if you held your head straight they grew angry.

It was a great relief to Katie to know that John was on his way to America, safe if war broke out between the English and the Boers. Every day, it seemed, she heard some new rumour: Englishmen were storing arms and provisions in the shafts of the Ferreira mine. The Boers were sending a truck loaded with dynamite to blow up the Consolidated Goldfields building. Mr Rhodes was sending a big army to march on Johannesburg.

By September 1899 many people began leaving Johannesburg. Dr Dickson went down to the Cape, Mr Goodenough was packing up his things to return to Amanzimtoti, Phillip closed his shoemaking stall and went back to Soekmekaar. Auntie took Fanny and her family down to Blinkwater, Mr Nyati sent his wife and children to Amanzimtoti, and even Ndeya's friend, Mngadi, decided that Johannesburg was no longer safe.

'We should also pack up our things and go back to your homeplace,' Katie told Ndeya.

'No, I think the English learned a lesson from the Jameson Raid. They won't send their soldiers to fight the Boers again.'

However, a few days later he came home early and told Katie a Boer commandant had come into his store and taken down a saddle that belonged to someone else. When Ndeya objected, the Boer raised his whip and threatened him.

'Now are you satisfied to leave?' Katie asked.

Ndeya nodded reluctantly. 'Yes, Mbambo also says it's time to go. He says we must take our things to Park Station early in the morning, and he will meet us there.'

That afternoon Katie brought out her tin trunk and packed up all their dishes, tablecloths, the clock that chimed, the picture of the sea that Fanny had given them when they were married, the knives, forks, sheets, blankets – everything except her jewellery-box in which she kept the money she had saved and the string of pearls Lord Knutsford had given her. It was dark by the time Ndeya finished digging a deep hole in their backyard. He called Katie to hold the lantern while he buried the trunk and stamped down the earth with his feet before covering the place with stones and twigs.

At dawn she woke the children and dressed them in all their clothes – Samuel chortled with delight because baby Ethel looked so fat. Katie wore her serge skirt, both her blouses, and over them all three of her dresses as well as the two shawls and her coat with the fur collar that Mrs Keithley had given her in London. Ndeya put on his Sunday suit but he threw his two jerseys, his overcoat and an extra pair of trousers on a chair.

'It's still early. I should collect some money which an Englishman owes me.'

'But it's already six o'clock, and you said Mbambo—'

'It won't take me long. I'll be back in an hour and then we'll go.' Ndeya hurried out the door before Katie could argue further.

After he was gone Katie picked up her jewellery-box and all the food she could cram into a basket to carry with her. Now there was nothing more to do except wait. Katie looked around the dining-room. In a corner was the pile of clothes she had been ironing for Mrs Mitchell when Ndeya came home the day before. Perhaps Mrs Mitchell would tell Mr Goodenough that she was a thief if the laundry was not delivered. Mrs Mitchell lived only a little way beyond the American Board church. Katie could deliver the clothes and get back before Ndeya returned.

She tied baby Ethel to her back, lifted the laundry to her head, took Samuel by the hand and started up the road. Halfway to Mrs Mitchell's house she saw Mbambo running towards her, his fat cheeks dripping with sweat and his chest heaving while he gasped for breath.

'Where's Makanya?' he shouted.

'Gone to collect some money owed him.'

Mbambo slammed one fist into the palm of his other hand. Then he, who never spoke evil of his friends, blurted out, 'That stupid fool! I told him to bring you to the station early. Since the first light I've waited. There's only one more train and it's going as soon as it's full. Come on.' He grabbed Samuel and swung him up on his shoulders.

'But I'm taking this laundry—'

'Forget your laundry. All the white people are running away. One train left yesterday and I saw a white man sitting on the top of a carriage holding his dogs.' He caught her arm. 'Hurry!'

'But Ndeya, he won't know where we are.'

'Don't worry, I'll come back for him.'

'But I've got nothing, no money, no food. It's all at home.'

'I have money enough.' Holding Samuel firmly with one hand, he started running back the way he had come.

Already he was some yards away with Samuel on his shoulders. Katie tossed the laundry off her head, leaving the shirts and dresses which belonged to Mrs Mitchell scattered on the road, and thought only of this man who would not leave his friends behind. Mbambo knew what he knew, and she must do as he said.

She ran faster to catch up with him. Ethel was jolted awake and began to cry but Katie paid no attention. Mbambo did not speak. His khaki shirt was black with sweat and the muscles of his neck bulged like knots of rope, but he did not stop running. Even when he coughed – great racking coughs which shuddered through his body and rocked Samuel on his shoulders – he did not slow his pace through the deserted streets. The sound of his cough jabbed sharp pains into Katie's own chest as she gulped for air, but his heavy footsteps were like drum beats urging her on.

As they turned into Commissioner Street, they could see the smoke from the train and a mob of people, both black and white, pushing their way into Park Station. Mbambo dragged Katie through the crowd of jostling, shouting people, past the first- and second-class carriages, until he reached a long line of open cattle cars in which Zulus were squeezed together. He stopped beside the first one and called out to a woman he knew. 'Makanya's wife. Can you make room?'

'Yes,' she said, and he leapt up, caught his feet in the iron bars which held the boards together, and climbed up to drop Samuel into the woman's arms. Once the child was safe, he reached down to Katie and pulled her up beside him. She threw one leg over the edge of the cattle car, balancing there with Ethel still tied to her back until Mbambo could heave himself up those last few iron rungs.

But instead he loosened his hands and jumped down to the platform.

'Mbambo, what are you doing?' she cried out.

'I must go to find Ndeya.'

The train whistled. More people rushed along the platform, frantically trying to climb up the sides of the cars. In all this confusion Katie still clung to the topmost bar. She had to yell down at Mbambo to be sure he heard.

'There's no time to find him. And you with so much coughing. You mustn't be left behind.'

'Ndeya's my friend. I cannot leave him.'

'Let him learn to take care of himself. Please Mbambo, come with me now.'

Mbambo hesitated and, for just one moment, fire blazed in his eyes so that it seemed as if the whole world was in flames. Then he shook his head and she was left alone in a cold wind, with him so far below that she could not even reach down to touch his hand.

'Mbambo, what am I going to do without you?' she shouted, not caring who heard. 'Always when I'm in trouble and my husband is running this way and that, you've come to keep me and my children safe. I'm afraid without you, Mbambo.'

'You've nothing to fear,' he said. 'When you get to Durban you must go to William, Ndeya's eldest brother, the one who's pastor of the American Board church in Beatrice Street. He'll keep you safe until we come.'

'Until you come? But what if you get caught up between the bullets in this white man's war.'

The train whistle sounded again and the cars bumped together, jerking forward. Samuel shrieked in fright. Ethel screamed. Katie almost fell off the edge of the cattle car into Mbambo's arms. Perhaps, if it had not been for her children, she would have let herself fall. But Samuel's shrieking was like a chain pulling her down. Mbambo reached into his pocket and pulled out two one-pound notes, pushing them at her; then he ran along the platform as the train slowly began to move.

'Don't worry about me. I'll dodge between those bullets—'

'But what if you get killed, Mbambo?'

'Even if I'm dead I will keep on running and running until I find you,' he shouted above the clanging of the iron wheels and the rush of the wind.

The train was moving faster now but still he ran beside it, gulping for breath and smiling encouragement.

Katie tasted salt in the tears pouring down her cheeks as the train gathered speed. She lifted up her chin and her voice rang out, loud and clear, 'Ujehova abe nawe, akuphathe ngomusa size, sibonane futhi' – God be with you till we meet again. She kept on singing as long as she could see Mbambo running along the platform, and even after the train rushed across the open veld she kept on singing.

▽△▽▽△

Part Two

Durban

1954

Katie seems tired this morning. She leans more heavily on my arm as she climbs the steps to my front door. I wonder if she is strong enough to continue our daily sessions. Yesterday, when she had recalled Mbambo's final journey to Umgeni, her eyes had filled with tears and she had lapsed into Zulu as though she had forgotten my presence.

'Auntie,' I say gently when she is settled in her chair, 'you know that I grew up in town and never learned to speak Zulu properly.'

'I know,' she says, and her eyes flash with remembered exasperation. 'I tried to teach you but you were always too impatient.'

'Then do you realise that sometimes, instead of speaking English, you lapse into Zulu or Sotho, depending on whom or what you're talking about?'

'If I do that, you should interrupt and ask me what I'm saying.'

I shake my head. 'When I was a child, you taught me it was rude to interrupt.'

She laughs. 'I won't scold you any more.'

But it's not the fear of scolding that will stop me. It's the fear of interrupting her train of thought. As she picks up the microphone, I know that on occasion I will have to replay the tape to the Zulu and Sotho nurses in my father's hospital and rely on them to translate the words I do not know.

11

Durban

1899–1902

When Katie arrived in Durban, all she could tell Pastor William Makanya was that Ndeya and Mbambo had remained behind in Johannesburg.

Pastor William nodded. 'I'm told there are ten thousand Zulus left behind.'

However, a week later word came that a train filled with Zulus was coming from Vryheid. But neither Ndeya nor Mbambo was among the passengers.

'Perhaps Mr Marwick knows where they are,' someone told Katie, pointing to a white man in crumpled trousers and a torn shirt.

'Please, Mr Marwick, have you seen my husband, Ndeya Makanya?' Katie asked. 'Or his friend, Mbambo?'

The white man rubbed the bristles on his cheek and furrowed his brow. 'Perhaps, but in all this crowd I can't remember one man from another.'

'You'd remember Mbambo. A very big man, as tall as you and wide in the shoulders; always joking.'

'Someone like that was carrying a man on his back when we marched into Vryheid, but I don't know his name. He may be on the next train.'

While Katie and Pastor William waited they heard people talking about Mr Marwick. They called him uMuhle, which means Kind One, because after the last train left Johannesburg he sent his messengers to pass the word that he would be at a certain place at a certain time and any Zulu who wanted to go back to Natal should meet him there. Thousands came, carrying their belongings. 'Throw away everything you've brought,' uMuhle told them, 'except the clothes on your backs and the money in your pockets. There are no trains, carts, horses or mules to be had anywhere. We will have to walk together.' And he walked with them that night and the next day and the next, and he slept in the fields with them and shared his food until it was finished, and gave his coat to an old man without any shirt. He walked twice as far as anyone else because he marched up and down the long line of people, encouraging those who lagged behind and cheering up those who were hungry. And when at last they reached Vryheid he collected food from the farms, found a doctor to examine the sick, and arranged for trains to carry them all to Durban.

'We will praise him to our children and our children's children and his name will be remembered,' the people said.

Katie and Pastor William waited at the station until the second train arrived. The first man out was the husband of a woman Katie knew. As soon as she asked if he had seen Ndeya or Mbambo, he began to laugh.

'Mbambo! That crazy clown. When we complained that we were hungry and cold and wet with the rain, he shouted out in his loud voice, "Let us rejoice because the Lord God has run out of manna and he sends us drink instead."'

'Don't tell me his jokes,' Katie said impatiently. 'Tell me where to find him.'

'I haven't seen him since yesterday.'

Katie ran along the platform, peering into the cars until, almost at the end of the train, she saw Ntshebekazi and another man bumping each other as they climbed backwards down the steps of a carriage. They gripped the ends of a stretcher, and behind them, gripping the other ends, she saw Ndeya and Mgwazeni. 'Ndeya!' she called out, and ran forward. Only then did she see the long form of Mbambo lying on the stretcher.

'What's happened?' she gasped, looking down at his face. Mbambo tried to laugh but only a rasping breath and a few splatters of blood came out of his lips.

'Oh, Mbambo,' she wept, wiping the blood from his chin with the edge of her dress.

'You worry too much,' he managed to whisper.

His friends carried him out of the station, across the road, and laid him down on a patch of grass.

'We must get a doctor,' Katie told Ndeya.

Mbambo raised his head so that he could look straight at her. 'It's no use, Katie. Mgwazeni must go find a wagon. It's time for me to go back to my homeplace.' He fell back against the stretcher as though exhausted.

Katie took off her coat with the fur collar and tucked it around his shoulders. While he slept, she sat beside Ndeya and waited through the long afternoon.

'When did he get so sick?' Katie asked.

'Two days ago. Before that, he was coughing but he said it was nothing. Even when it rained and we had to sleep all night in the mud, he did not complain. He just kept joking and helping to carry the old and the weak. He was still coughing after we crossed the border into Natal. Just outside Vryheid he fell down and had no strength to get up. That was when I saw the blood on his lips for the first time.'

Ndeya fell silent, and they sat there together, yet separately, both of them wrapped up in their own sorrow for this man who lay quietly in the warm sun, the laugh wrinkles about his eyes smoothed out by sleep, his mouth half open, his breath coming too quickly, too shallow for a man his size. At last Mgwazeni arrived with a wagon and two oxen. Mbambo coughed again, stirred, and tried to lift himself on his elbow.

'Umgeni is far and the night is cold,' Katie pleaded. 'You can travel tomorrow.'

'It's better for me to go now. My wife will be waiting,' he said.

'Ah, Mbambo,' she murmured in despair, knowing that when he wanted to do one thing, no one could persuade him to do another.

He reached out his hand for hers and held it for just a moment. Then he grinned. 'You'll remember what I told you.'

'I'll remember, Mbambo.' Her voice dropped to a whisper. 'And I will be waiting for you always.'

'Then stay well.' Mgwazeni cracked his long whip, the oxen turned, and the wagon moved slowly down the long road leading out of Durban towards Umgeni.

As soon as Ndeya was rested after his long journey, he set out to look for work. He did not return that night. In the morning he was still missing. For two weeks Katie looked for him everywhere – at the Addington Hospital, the courthouse, the jails – but no one had seen Ndeya. Two weeks later a letter came in the post.

Ndeya had gone to the army barracks and asked one of General Buller's soldiers if he had saddles that needed repair. Instead, the soldier pointed to some mules and told him to inspan an ammunition cart. When Ndeya said he did not know how, he was told to learn quickly because he was in the army now. He would have to drive the ammunition cart until the English won their war. For two years there was no more word from Ndeya. There were no letters from Ma either, because Soekmekaar was in enemy territory, nor was there any news from Charlotte, who had sailed for Africa from New York just a few days before the war started.

In Durban, Katie had no money, no friends, no family of her own; only Pastor William Makanya. With his help she found a job as washer-woman for an Englishman in Essenwood Road. He paid her ten shillings a month, gave her a ration of food each week, and a room above his stables where she could live with Samuel and Ethel. Her next baby was born in that room. She named him Sagila, after those heavy sticks called knobkerries which make very good weapons when two men fight each other.

Sagila was a strong, healthy boy, but Ethel was sickly. One morning just after she was two years old, she cried out in her sleep and her skin felt hot. Katie, frightened by the memory of little Charlotte's death, ran with her to the nearest doctor. She was waiting outside his surgery at eight o'clock.

When the doctor's nurse arrived, she motioned Katie to the back steps to wait her turn. Although Katie had come before anyone else, the doctor saw his white patients first, then a Coloured man. About noon, a light rain began to fall. Katie huddled on the steps trying to shield Ethel's blanket with her body, but by two o'clock they were both soaking wet. Still she had to wait while the nurse beckoned two Indian women.

'But it's my turn,' Katie cried out in desperation.

'Don't be cheeky,' the nurse said, 'or you won't see the doctor at all.'

At half past three the doctor listened to Ethel's chest, charged Katie two shillings and sixpence, and told her to take the child to the Addington Hospital.

Two days later Ethel died of pneumonia.

There was no longer any Mbambo to remind Katie of her other children, and no Ndeya to comfort her in her grief. There was only herself. Somehow, during the months that followed, she found the strength to keep on tending Sagila, answering Samuel's questions and washing the Englishman's clothes. In time the sharp pangs of her sorrow burned away in a flame of anger at the white doctor who had kept her waiting all day in the rain.

When Ndeya returned unharmed at the end of the war, Katie told him bluntly she would stay no more in Durban. 'And not in Johannesburg either. I don't want to live among white people any longer.'

'Durban's no good for me either,' Ndeya said. 'The sea air makes me wheeze. We'll go to Adams mission. I can start a little store in the hills above Amanzimtoti.'

'Yes,' Katie said, 'it's better for the children in the country.' And better for me also, she thought. She could plant mealies, pumpkins, beans, pineapples and pawpaws in her garden, and search out mushrooms and wild spinach the way she used to do in Soekmekaar. At night, when Samuel and Sagila were sleeping, she could sit in her house with Ndeya and listen to the bullfrogs and cicadas and the rustle of trees outside and know that she and her children were safe.

12

Amanzimtoti

1902–1904

They left the Umbogintwini railway station behind them and trudged nine miles along the dusty road which led up into the hills, their few possessions in a basket on top of Katie's head, and Sagila tied in a blanket to her back. Ndeya walked a few steps ahead, holding Samuel's fingers with one hand and grasping his stick with the other. They rested often because of Samuel. As they sat by the roadside, Katie gazed out over the rolling hills. The sugar-cane was bright green under a blue sky, and the earth was a deep red. Dark green bushes marked the river winding through the valley.

'This land is beautiful. How could you ever have left?'

'I needed to earn, and there are few jobs here for an educated man. Only work in the cane-fields.'

'But now you'll build your store and we'll never leave.'

Ndeya's relatives were waiting for them at his brother's house. 'This boy's a real Makanya,' his brother shouted, holding Samuel up for all to see. The women reached for Sagila, passing him from the arms of one to the arms of another, only returning him to Katie when she unbuttoned her blouse to put him to the breast.

In the days that followed, Ndeya and his brothers built a house of mud and wattle at the edge of his brother's freehold land. Katie and the women gathered bundles of grass for the roof and broke down anthills to mix with cow dung to build the floors. When at last her house was ready, Katie looked around at the sleeping mats on the floor, the wooden boxes to sit on, the rough table which Ndeya had made out of some old boards that the Indian storekeeper across the road had sold him for a few pennies, and felt altogether content. As soon as Ndeya went up to Johannesburg to claim their things, she would be properly settled.

But when Ndeya returned to their old home behind the American Board church in Doornfontein, he found it in ruins. All their furniture had been stolen, and only a gaping hole remained in the backyard where he and Katie had buried the tin trunk. But it was useless to yearn for her lost possessions. At least she would have no worries here about thieves and policemen.

Samuel started school at Adams mission station on the other side of the river. Katie loved that river. After all those years in Johannesburg where she'd had to buy their drinking water from the water-cart, she never tired of filling her pots at the Amanzimtoti River, so named because the water was clear and sweet. She loved the sound of the summer rains and kept an extra rain-barrel outside her kitchen door to catch the drips from the roof. At night she would slip into the darkness with her soap and towel and crouch down in the barrel until her whole body was covered. Sometimes, after she had worked hard in the fields all day, she liked to stay for a long time in the water. Ndeya would come out and sit on the stoep and talk. Once he asked her if the water wasn't too cold, and she said no, it was still warm from the afternoon sun.

'Still warm?' he said. 'But that's not possible.'

'But to me it's warm.'

'That's because you're *utokoloshe*,' he teased, pretending she was one of those mischievous water sprites who live in rivers.

'So, you think I'm *utokoloshe!*' She splashed water at him so that he jumped backwards.

'Yes, because you are always bothering me with your foolishness. But I'll teach you a lesson.' He grabbed her dress and towel and stood at some distance, ignoring her pleas for her clothes.

'You'll have to come and get them.'

'But I'm naked. I have nothing to cover myself.'

'You're *utokoloshe!* You don't need clothes.'

'But I do. The moon's too bright. What if someone sees?'

'It's late. There's no one.'

'But I'm not a heathen girl to walk around naked.'

'No, you're *utokoloshe*.' He would not even throw her the towel, so she had to climb out of the barrel and run for the door. But he caught her, and although her skin was wet, he would not let her go.

'If I was really *utokoloshe*, I would use my magic to run away,' she whispered.

'No, you'd use your magic to make me big and strong. You could change me into a giant and I could do anything.'

'Not here, Ndeya. Take me inside where no one can see.'

'There's only me, and you're so beautiful in the moonlight.' He laughed again, recklessly, like a young man without any grey hairs; and the warm smell of his body, the soft night air and the twigs prickling into the skin of her back as he pulled her down to the ground made her, too, feel young and wild and free.

Katie's body grew strong at Amanzimtoti. All day long she hoed and weeded her garden, and fertilised it with cow dung and chicken droppings so that the pumpkins grew big and the sweet potatoes ripened. That first year she produced twenty-five bags of mealies from her fields and so many other vegetables that she had to borrow a cart to carry them all to sell at the market in Isipingo. And still she had time left over to gossip with her new friends while they washed their clothes at the river, and go with them to the Mothers' Meetings, Women's Association and choir practices at the mission church.

The other women often talked about the missionaries at Adams. Katie knew Mrs Wilcox, who came to meetings of the Women's Association, but she had only seen Mrs McCord at the mission church on Sundays. She was the youngest of the missionary ladies – 'the same age as me,' Katie said to herself, 'and with glasses just like mine!' Although Mrs McCord tried to look older by pulling her light brown hair severely up into a bun on top of her head, she laughed too quickly to appear altogether dignified. Katie was curious because she heard her neighbour Umgqibelo address her as Nkosazana, or Daughter of a Chief.

'Why do you call her that when she is wife to her husband? You should call her Nkosikazi,' Katie said when she met Umgqibelo at Jeena's store.

'Because she *is* Daughter of a Chief,' he told her.

'How can an American lady be daughter to a chief?'

'But she is. She was born at Umsunduzi. Her father was also a missionary: the Reverend Mr Mellen. When the old chief died, his two sons fought with each other to take his place. Some of us wanted one and some wanted the other. But while we were arguing among ourselves, the hut tax came due and we had no chief to collect the money for the government. So our headmen asked Mr Mellen to collect the tax.'

Umgqibelo began to laugh. 'A clever man, the Reverend. He told us that if he collected the tax, then he would be our chief and we would have to obey him.'

'And the people agreed?'

'Yes, and he called a meeting every Sunday at the church. That's why we have many Christians at Umsunduzi.'

'Is he still chief?'

'No, he went back to America when Nkosazana was very small.'

Katie was eager for a chance to talk to Mrs McCord when she brought boxes of clothing to Esther's house for distribution, but on that day Sagila fell sick. Katie was afraid to take him out into the cold air, so she sent Samuel in the hope that he would be given some trousers or a shirt to wear to school.

She did not know whether it was Samuel or Esther who told Mrs McCord that Sagila was sick, but Mrs McCord walked all the way across the fields. When Katie did not answer her knock, Mrs McCord opened the door and came inside.

'I hear your child is sick,' she said.

'Yes,' Katie said, looking around quickly to make sure her house was clean.

Mrs McCord came directly over to the box on which Katie was sitting and felt Sagila's face.

'Yes, he has a fever. You must take him to see Dr Edwards in Isipingo. I'll send Umgqibelo over with the donkey-cart to take you; when you get there, tell the doctor I sent you.'

Katie shook her head.

'Don't you understand?' Mrs McCord said impatiently. 'The baby needs medicine. Only a doctor will know what kind.'

'No,' Katie replied, staring straight at her even though her grey eyes grew dark like thunder clouds.

'Katie, you must.'

'No. If I take him to a white doctor, he will die.'

'Now, Katie, you know better than that. I tell you—'

'No.' Katie closed her ears. She wanted this white woman to go away, this Mrs McCord who stood there in her house as if she knew everything. But Mrs McCord went to the door and stood yelling across the fields until Esther came running with some of the other women after her.

'Esther,' Mrs McCord said, jerking her head in Katie's direction, 'tell her she's got to do as I say. I don't think she understands.'

'I understand very well,' Katie said.

Mrs McCord wheeled around. 'Then why won't you go to Dr Edwards? He is a clever doctor. I called him when my own child was sick.'

'Your child is white. And these doctors – they're all the same. First they love the European patients, then the Coloureds, and after them the Indians because their hair is straight. They don't bother about us until they've taken their money from everyone else. By that time we're dead.'

'That's not true.' Mrs McCord gasped as though Katie had struck her in the face. 'And your child may die without treatment.'

The two young women faced each other, the one with chin uplifted and black eyes fired with anger, the other with stubborn jaw and pursed lips.

At last Katie spoke. 'I put my trust in the Lord. If He hears my prayers He will cure him.'

Mrs McCord's face softened. 'Perhaps the Lord has sent me to you. Now tell me quickly: How is the baby sick? And for how long?'

'Three days. It's the fever. First his body is hot, then he sweats and shivers with cold; and he doesn't sleep. Nor does he suck when I put him to my breast.'

'Give him water with sugar in it. Just a few drops from a spoon as often as you can.' She grabbed a mug off the table, dipped it into the tin of drinking water and put it on the floor. 'Where's your sugar?'

Katie nodded at the food box which Ndeya had hung from the inside roof. Mrs McCord opened it up, took down the bag of sugar, and dumped some into the mug.

'Keep giving him this, drop by drop, until I return.'

Within an hour she came again, her face flushed and wet from the heat, so that her spectacles kept sliding down her nose. In her right hand was a bottle. Without speaking, she poured some medicine from it into a teaspoon which she carried in her other hand. Then she leaned over Katie and pinched Sagila's nose so that he opened his mouth for breath. As soon as he did this, she dribbled the medicine down his throat. He choked and sputtered and began to whimper.

'Give him more water and medicine. Every three hours you must give him this medicine all through the night.' She looked around at the mats, table, boxes. 'Do you have a clock?'

'It was lost in the war,' Katie said.

'Then I'll send Umgqibelo over with one,' Mrs McCord said, thrusting her arm in front of Katie's face and pointing to the watch on her wrist. 'Do you know how to tell the time?'

'Yes.'

'Good. Then at eight o'clock you must give him another spoonful of this medicine. Just one spoonful, you understand? No more. And then again at eleven o'clock; and again at two o'clock and five o'clock.'

'Yes.'

Katie dipped the spoon into the mug and dropped water in Sagila's mouth as she had been told. When she looked up again, Mrs McCord had gone. But the sense of her presence remained all through the night, and the ticking of the clock Umgqibelo brought was like the sound of her voice saying 'eight o'clock – eleven o'clock – two o'clock – five o'clock.'

Just before first light, Sagila slept.

Each morning Umgqibelo came with more medicine, and in time Sagila was like himself again. When she was sure that he was perfectly well, Katie caught her fattest hen and chose her best pumpkin and left them for Mrs McCord.

A few days later while Katie was hoeing her garden, Mrs McCord came across the fields. 'I've come to thank you for the hen and the pumpkin,' she said.

'It's nothing,' Katie replied.

'But that's not the only reason I've come.' She sat down on one of the wooden boxes beside the table. 'Katie, I need to talk to you.'

'Please, I must wash myself first. My hands are dirty from hoeing.'

Katie ran outside and leaned over the rain-barrel to splash water over her hands, then laid twigs and sticks across the embers in the fireplace outside the back door, and sent Samuel to Esther Ngcobo's house to borrow a proper teapot and a china cup and saucer. By the time he returned, the water was boiling. She made the tea and carried it into the dining-room, where Mrs McCord was still sitting. 'When I came the other day, I knew nothing about you,' Mrs McCord said as Katie poured the tea. 'Just that your child was sick. Now I hear you've been to England. Mr Goodenough tells me also that you can speak many languages.'

'Only five,' Katie said.

Mrs McCord smiled. 'My husband speaks only one. He studied Zulu for six months, but his ears are too small to hear the differences between some words. And since he's been in England, he's forgotten what he learned. He'll need an interpreter.'

'Then you should talk to Esther Ngcobo or—' Hurriedly, Katie tried to think of the various women she knew who had been to school and understand English.

'No,' Mrs McCord said, 'he needs not only someone who knows English perfectly, but also someone who can help him with his Zulu. Someone like you.'

'My Zulu is too slow,' Katie began, not wanting to work for any white doctor. But Mrs McCord started to laugh, because all this time they had been talking together in Zulu. When Katie realised this, she began to stammer. 'I mean – I'm Sotho.'

'You can't fool me, Katie. You know Zulu as well as I do.'

'Then why don't you be his interpreter?'

'I can help him with the medicines and in other ways as well. He will need us both.'

'But I have no time. My children are small.'

'Mine also, but Laura Nyuswa takes good care of them when I am busy. She can take care of Sagila, and when Samuel comes back from school he can play with my Jesse and Mary and Bobby.'

When Katie kept shaking her head, Mrs McCord asked abruptly, 'Don't you trust me?'

'I trust you.'

'Then you must trust my husband also. He's coming to be a doctor for the Zulus – for the Zulus first, you understand. Before the Indians or the Coloureds. And he does not treat any white people at all, except the other missionaries.'

'I'll have to think about it,' Katie said, turning her head away for fear those piercing grey eyes would see into her private thoughts. She did not want to work for any white doctor, even if he was a missionary, even if he said he was for the Zulus first. If he was really clever at doctoring, the white people would come to him with their money, and they always had to be seen to before anyone else. Moreover, she still did not feel comfortable with the American Board missionaries because of the way they ignored Ndeya.

But when Mrs McCord wanted something, she pressed very hard to get it. She was too clever to argue with Katie and risk a blunt refusal, so she spoke to the other missionaries. All urged Katie to work for Dr McCord.

Even Ndeya surprised her. 'Yes, *uDokotela* needs you,' he said, smiling in that gentle way he had, and nodding his head. 'Do you forget his wife saved our child, Mother of Samuel?'

Thus, in the end, it was her husband who sent her to talk to the white American doctor.

One Wednesday morning in 1902 Katie walked along the road toward the mission, feeling at peace with herself. God had given her a very good excuse for refusing to work for the white doctor: she was again with child.

A few patients were already sitting about on the grass behind the dispensary when she got there. Some were listening to the drone of Umgqibelo's voice as he read out of the Bible, some were dozing. One woman was trying to hush the crying of a baby in her arms. Beyond the back veranda, the door to one of the rooms was slightly ajar, and Katie could hear the voices of three men inside. She recognised that of the Reverend Mr Kilbon, who talked as though he had a burr in his throat, and the nasal twang of the Reverend Mr Bunker, but the third voice was strange to her. That must be the doctor, she thought idly.

Suddenly a boom of laughter thundered out which shook the house and made the door frame rattle. Katie gasped. The figures around her blurred into a mist; her heart thudded with a sound like running footsteps. No one anywhere laughed like Mbambo!

Then, as suddenly as it came, the laughter was finished. The house stopped shaking and those American voices sounded again; the door to the room swung wide open. Mr Kilbon and Mr Bunker stepped out of the shadow into the sunlight, and she saw them both quite distinctly. But the third man remained behind, a ghostly presence in the dim light. His massive shoulders filled the doorway, his head almost touching the top of the frame. Katie waited calmly. She did not fear Mbambo.

Then the ghost stepped into the sunlight. So convinced was she that Mbambo's spirit had come to find her that she did not comprehend what she saw – a man with skin the colour of ocean sand and eyes of pale blue fire. She stared at him until the woman with the crying baby nudged her, '*UDokotela* calls you.'

'*UDokotela?*' Katie mumbled, still confused.

The ghost was calling out to her. 'Umgqibelo tells me you're my new interpreter.' But he was no ghost. He was the new doctor. She knew this by the long white coat worn over his shirt and trousers.

'Yes, sir. No, sir,' she muttered.

'What's that? Speak up.'

'Yes, sir. I'm Katie.' She threw back her head to look at this white man, this husband of Mrs McCord. There was a faint biting odour about his person that tickled her nose, but she lifted up her chin and looked at him straight.

'And no, sir, you'll have to find another interpreter.'

'But I thought it was all arranged. I'll pay you sixpence an hour and you can leave your chil—'

'No, it was not arranged.'

'Oh!' Sounding perplexed, he turned to Umgqibelo and, motioning to the patients on the grass, asked, 'What are we going to do? My wife can't come today.'

Umgqibelo looked reproachfully at Katie. She heard again the crying of the baby. She saw the wasted body of an old woman and a grimace of pain on the face of a young boy. It was not fair for them to be kept waiting all day while the doctor ran around searching for another interpreter.

'Just for this morning I'll help you,' she said. 'But tomorrow you will have to hire someone else.'

'Then come along.' He started striding up a path. Katie had to run to keep up with him.

'Where are we going?' she asked the back of his head.

'To the hospital.'

'Already you have a hospital? But you've just come.'

'Four days ago,' he corrected her, 'and Umgqibelo had patients lined up waiting. Already we've had three confinements, one amputation and the removal of a tumour.'

'Amputation? Tumour? What are these?'

'You'll see.'

In the first room Katie saw a long table, a chest of drawers, and on top of it a primus stove and a big shiny pot. The odour was stronger here but the Doctor did not seem to notice; he only opened another door.

'This is our women's ward,' he said, gesturing at four women lying on sleeping mats, three of them with babies beside them. Katie recognised Zenzile Ndlovu, a member of the mission church. A good woman but very unlucky! She had already borne many children but all of them dead. Now she held up a newborn baby, and although she was ten years older than Katie, her face was young with happiness.

'At last my husband rejoices,' she said to the Doctor.

'And well he should. You've a fine girl,' he replied in his halting Zulu.

'Did you hear about my mother?' Zenzile laughed.

'This morning she was waking everyone up with her praises. I hear she was a big nuisance.'

'No, that was the mother of my husband. My own mother saw you take out your knife. She was so frightened that she ran away and told everyone that I was being killed and cut up. At home all my people were mourning until my husband came and told how you had taken my baby out of my stomach. He said you were very clever and knew how to kill us and then bring us back to life.'

The Doctor turned to Katie and spoke slowly, with the heaviness of a schoolteacher. 'Tell her that although my muti is strong, it did not kill her. It only put her to sleep so she did not feel the pain of the knife.'

As they moved to the next bed and the next, two other women held up their babies for the Doctor to see. Then, at the fourth bed, Katie looked down on Ntotisa, a young girl who was hardly more than a child. She came from Zama's kraal. A few months earlier she had been bitten in the leg by a puff-adder. Her father had rushed to her side when he heard her scream, had knelt beside her in the grass and immediately cut out the poison with a piece of broken glass. Then he had carried her all the way to Umbumbulu to a famous *inyanga*, or doctor, who had rubbed one medicine into the wound and given her another to drink so that she would vomit up any poison left in her body. Thus it was that she did not die. Nevertheless, her leg was never right again, and after a time the flesh began to rot and fall off; the smell was so bad that no one wanted to be near her. Now she was here in the Doctor's cottage and there was no smell of rotting flesh, only that faint odour of the Doctor.

'Is the pain still bad?' he asked.

She nodded wearily.

'Ask her', he told Katie, 'if the pain is in the leg I cut off.'

She nodded again.

'Then tell her that each day the pain will be less.'

He held up his right hand, and Katie noticed for the first time that between his thumb and last two fingers there were only ugly white scars covering the knuckles. 'Tell her that when I was a child, younger than her, my two fingers were cut off. At first those lost fingers gave me much pain but in time the pain was lost also.'

Katie repeated his words; then he added, 'Tell her that when she is well again, I will give her a new leg.'

'You mean a crutch?' Katie needed to know his meaning exactly.

'No, a wooden leg with a foot that bends so she can learn to use it properly. Then she can run again.'

The girl's eyes brightened. 'Run? It's long since I could run.'

'Soon you will again,' Katie said firmly. 'The Doctor says so, and he is not a man who lies. So you must be grateful. And when you run you must show the people your new leg and call them to church so that they can praise the Lord for this miracle.'

'Katie, you talk too much,' the Doctor interrupted. 'I'm in a hurry. Leave the preaching to Umgqibelo.'

He moved quickly into another room, which he called his men's ward, where a man was sleeping peacefully with his wife sitting beside him. As the Doctor pulled down the blanket and looked at the bandages on his stomach, his wife jumped up and ran outside, laughing and shouting.

'What's she telling them?' the Doctor asked Katie.

'She says that her husband looks like he's wearing a corset because those bandages make his stomach small.'

'It's a lot smaller than when he came in. I took out a big inverted tumour this morning.'

'What's an inverted tumour?'

'A lump growing in the body.'

'And you cut it out this morning?'

'Yes, I like to operate very early, before breakfast. Now call that woman back. I want her to sit here and hold him if he moves.'

Back in the first room they had entered, the Doctor paused beside the chest and pulled out one of the drawers. Inside were rows of shining instruments laid out on a clean towel. Pointing at them, he told Katie he wanted her to learn their names. 'This', he said, 'is a gag for the mouth. This is a steam sprayer for antiseptic. These are forceps – artery forceps, high-traction forceps—'

'Please, Doctor, I need a pencil and paper.'

He pulled a gold pen from his pocket and a little notebook from which he tore a page and laid it on top of the chest, then watched as Katie drew a picture and wrote down *R-Tree forceps*.

'No, no. A-r-t-e-r-y. Do you know what an artery is?'

'No, Doctor.'

'It's a – well, never mind for now. Just remember the name.' He began to spell out other words until she shook her head in confusion.

'Please! There are too many to learn at one time.'

'Very well, but learn these now and tomorrow you can learn the others.'

In those moments in that little cottage hospital with the women holding up their babies so proudly and Ntotisa hearing that she would run again, Katie had forgotten that she was working for this doctor for only one day. And in her forgetting, she asked why it was necessary for her to know the names of the strange instruments.

'Because if we have an emergency and my wife's away, you'll have to help me – hand them to me when I operate.'

'Me! But I'm not a nurse. I know nothing about such things. I'm only an interpreter.'

He stared down at her, saying very slowly and heavily, 'You'll be what you have to be and you'll learn what you have to learn.'

'I'm not brave enough. I'll forget everything if I have to see you chopping off legs or cutting out tumours.'

'Then don't watch. Just look down at my instruments. And perhaps we won't have any emergencies. When my wife is helping me, you'll just be the dirty nurse.'

'Me! A dirty nurse. No.'

'What did you say?' His voice was as sharp as his instruments. Katie stepped back, frightened by his sudden anger, but she was angry too, because no white man, not even a missionary, had the right to insult her.

'I'm not dirty.'

'You're not—?' Suddenly he threw back his head and his laughter boomed out in the cottage, shaking the walls and the floor until she backed away. Then as suddenly as it came, his laughter was finished.

'You don't understand, Katie. I don't mean *you're* dirty. That's just what doctors call a nurse who doesn't wash her hands.'

'But I do wash my hands.'

'But not in the way I mean. When I operate or examine a patient, I wash my arms and hands with carbolic soap. My wife does this also. You'll see. But whoever wipes up the floor, who does the dirty work, doesn't have to wash so carefully. Therefore she's called the "dirty nurse," no matter how clean she keeps herself.'

'I don't care. I won't be called "dirty nurse." You'll have to call me something else.'

'What?' He seemed amused.

'Just Katie.'

'I'll try to remember. But when I'm busy I may forget.'

'Yes, it's easy to forget,' she replied. 'Perhaps when we're busy I, too, may forget the names of these.' She pointed to the instruments in the drawer.

She caught her breath. She had spoken too quickly without thinking. But instead of calling her cheeky, he said nothing, just twisted his lips a little to one side and pushed up one eyebrow higher than the other as he moved past her through the door. Again she had to run or else she would have been left behind.

At the dispensary the patients were still waiting on the grass. While he examined a patient, the Doctor waited for Katie to repeat his questions in Zulu and translate the answers into English. But she soon noticed that sometimes he already knew what they had said before she told him.

'I think you're fooling me,' she said at last. 'You don't need an interpreter.'

'Yes, I do. I understand some things and can often guess the rest. But I have to be absolutely sure. Too many words sound the same.'

'How do you mean?'

He smiled at her self-consciously. 'Yesterday I gave a woman some medicine and told her to give a spoonful to her iguana three times a day. She was very angry and went to my wife to complain, because she had no iguana, and if she found one she did not understand why giving it medicine would cure her child. Mrs McCord had to explain that I really meant her baby, her *umntwana*.'

'Oh, Doctor!' Katie giggled.

'You think it's funny? But to me, *umntwana* and iguana sound much the same. So you see, I do need an interpreter.'

Just before eleven o'clock Umgqibelo brought in a strong, fat heathen woman whose face Katie would always remember. Her nose was thin and straight, and above her large, beautiful eyes her hair was neatly woven with clay into a high rounded headdress. She stopped just inside the door, greeted the Doctor and announced that all she needed was the Doctor's red muti.

'He will have to examine you first,' Katie told her. 'He doesn't give out his medicines until he knows the sickness.'

'I can pay.' She opened a beaded leather pouch which hung down from her neck to the top of her cowhide skirt. 'And I already know my sickness. I have this lump here,' she touched her breast. 'It's like a lump my sister had in her neck, only smaller. The Doctor gave my sister his red muti just two days ago. Now I want some.'

Reluctantly she allowed the Doctor to examine the lump. Afterwards he looked at her solemnly, told her to sit in front of his desk, and then sat down himself in a swivel chair.

'Tell her', he said to Katie, 'that a lump in the breast is different from a lump in the neck. My red muti is very good for scrofula. But it won't cure her lump. I will have to cut that out because it may be a very bad sickness.'

'No,' said the woman. 'I want the red muti.'

'If I cut you now, tomorrow morning you will probably get better. But if you only take the red muti, then that lump will grow, and in time more lumps will come under your arms and then others, until even the cutting will not get rid of them.'

'I want the red muti,' she repeated, and although Katie argued with her for a long time, she would not listen. At last the Doctor sighed.

'It's no use, Katie. Just tell her that if she gets lumps under her arms, she mustn't come and waste my time. I won't be able to cure her then.'

After she was gone, Katie thought he looked very sad and tired.

'Shall I get you a cup of tea before I call in the others?' she asked.

He nodded. 'But give me three minutes first.'

'Three min—?' Already he had put his elbows on his knees, his head in his hands, and was sound asleep. She tiptoed outside, closed the door, made a cup of tea for herself, and sat down on the edge of the veranda to rest.

This Dr McCord was very different from that other white doctor in Durban. His hands were gentle when he examined the patients, and although he had worked very hard all morning, he hadn't complained or scolded anyone, not even the heathen woman who wanted the red muti. Moreover, Katie's own work that morning had not been difficult. She felt almost like a thief for taking sixpence for each hour spent gossiping with the people. She sat there for perhaps ten minutes dreaming of all the things she wanted to buy for her house, until the Doctor called her name.

'I'll have my tea now.' When she brought in his tray, he pointed to the chair against the wall and told her to sit down. 'There are certain things you've got to understand. First, when I say three minutes, I mean three minutes. Not five or ten. You let me sleep too long.'

'But you were tired—'

He glanced at her sharply. 'That's for me to judge.'

'Yes, Doctor.'

'Another thing. Tomorrow when the patients come, Umgqibelo will give each one a number. I want you to call them in the order of their coming.'

'Yes, Doctor.'

'That's all.'

By twelve o'clock only one patient was left, a woman with a big abscess above her knee. As Katie helped her up on the table, the Doctor took a little knife out of his carboliser. She knew he was going to cut, and so she turned her eyes away, but the woman jumped as he lanced the abscess and Katie had to turn back to hold her still. In turning, she saw the blood and pus pouring and smelled the foul stench of the infection.

Suddenly she wanted to vomit. The walls of the little room closed down on her. She heard the Doctor's voice as though from a great distance, telling her to put her head in her lap, but she could not see any chair, only the floor coming up to hit her. Then she was brushing away the cold water splashing on her face. But as she rose up, she saw a bloody smear on the Doctor's white coat and the walls began to close down on her again. This time, however, he did not let her fall but caught at her shoulder and pushed her onto a chair, then pressed down on the back of her neck so that her head was touching her knees.

When her head cleared, the stench of the abscess remained in spite of the open window and the faint smell of carbolic soap on his hands. The taste of vomit was still in her mouth as she stumbled out onto the veranda and sank down on the edge of a step.

She was glad she had told the Doctor to find another interpreter. She did not like to see that abscess and smell that pus. She had never seen such things when, as a girl, she had watched Ma bandaging a cut or a swollen ankle. How ignorant she was in those days, thinking a nurse spent all her time comforting the sick, giving out medicine and bandaging wounds. But after one morning in the dispensary she knew the work was not that easy.

In a few moments the Doctor followed and asked if she was feeling better.

'A little,' she said. 'But as I told you, tomorrow you must find someone else to help you. I'll never be able to stand—'

'Yes, you will.' He hesitated for a moment and then sat down beside her. 'The first time is always the worst. When I was in medical school in America, I had to watch a lot of operations before I ever held a knife. The first one was very hard for me. I kept wanting to faint, and every few minutes I had to put my head on my knees until I felt well enough to look again. But after three months I could watch anything, and my professor was calling for me to assist him.'

'But you're different. You're white.'

'I'm not any different. At first I thought I would never get used to it. But I wanted to be a missionary and I'm no good as a preacher. Then I read about David Livingstone—'

'You mean that English explorer in Westminster Abbey? The one whose servants cut out his heart and buried it in Africa?'

'Yes, he was a missionary too, a medical missionary. Like him, I thought I would be better at doctoring than preaching. So I had to get used to the blood and the smells.'

Katie looked down at her hands twisting in her lap, at the cement floor of the veranda and at a crack in it running from where she sat to where his right hand rested, that hand with the fingers missing. He sat very still, watching her. In the silence she felt confused, uncertain, until the crack in the cement took on the shape of a rope, and no longer thinking, she jumped up lest it bind her to him forever. 'I must go home.'

He took his big watch from his pocket. 'It's half past twelve. You've worked four hours.' He handed her a shilling, a sixpence and two tickeys. 'On your way home you'll pass the hospital. I want you to stop and tell the patients I'll come again before nightfall.'

'Yes, Doctor.'

'And I'll expect you here tomorrow morning at six o'clock.'

He did not see her shake her head, for already he was on his feet and moving back through his little room. She heard the bang of the front door, his quick footsteps on the outside staircase leading down to the road.

She had no intention of returning next morning. Yet, when she stopped at the hospital to gossip with Zenzile Ndlovu, the sight of her baby wiped away the memory of the other woman's abscess. Before she left, Ntotisa called her and wanted to hear again about her new leg. Oh, that Doctor was clever to send her back to see the joy of those women with their babies and the hope of that girl who would run again.

The sun was hot. On her way home, she stopped at Jeena's store. With the money she had in her pocket she could buy meat for Ndeya's dinner tonight.

The woman whose baby had an ear infection was standing by the roadside. As Katie approached, she said something to a woman nearby who spoke to another, and all three of them bobbed their heads in respectful greeting. Katie felt very strange, for she was not old enough for such deference. Even inside the store the other customers stepped back, clearing a path for her, and Jeena himself motioned her ahead of everyone else.

Katie liked Jeena, the Indian storekeeper. He was always friendly, and as he weighed out her shilling's worth of meat, he said he'd heard she was nurse to the missionary doctor.

'Not nurse, only interpreter.'

'Now you're earning, I have many things you'll want – blankets and dishes

– and I can show you some very good cloth.'

'Not today.' But the jangle of coins in her pocket made her think of all the things she wanted to buy to pretty up her house, and she was trying to rid herself of such thoughts when Ndeya came home. He'd seen Ndlovu, who was very big with importance because of his living daughter taken out of Zenzile's stomach.

'What's the matter, Mother of Samuel?' Ndeya asked.

'Nothing,' she said, measuring out rice and water and then running outside to her cooking-hut. How could she speak to her husband about this white man whose laughter boomed out suddenly to shake the contentment of her life at Adams, this man who moved so fast or sat so still, this man who was strong as a mountain even though he, too, had once almost fainted at the sight of blood?

When he later blew out their candle and settled down on his sleeping mat, Ndeya said, 'You'll go again tomorrow.' His words were not so much a question as a statement of his wishes.

Katie reached out for the comfort of his hand. 'Yes,' she said, glad of the darkness. Ndeya was so kind, so trusting, so proud to think she had found a way to serve his people that even had she told him, he would not understand the feeling in her heart. When she thought of the Doctor, she was afraid of the fire within him. Yet when she thought of Zenzile Ndlovu and Ntotisa and all the people at Jeena's store greeting her with such respect, she knew she would be what she had to be and learn what she had to learn.

There was much Katie needed to learn in her work with the Doctor. Every afternoon, after she had washed and ironed his long white coat and the blue uniform and white apron Mrs McCord had made for her to wear in the dispensary, she took home the papers on which she had drawn his instruments and written long medical words. Trying to memorise them was more difficult than any schoolwork. She studied them until her head ached. Yet she was in a hurry, for the Doctor was very impatient, and if she handed him an instrument other than the one he asked for, he would throw it against the wall and reach out his long arm to grab what he wanted, sometimes upsetting the tray so that all the other instruments fell to the floor. Then she would have a big job boiling them again in the carboliser before he could use them on another patient. She had been working in the dispensary only a week the first time this happened. His quick temper shocked her into clumsiness so that she forgot what she already knew.

'It's no use,' she told Ndeya that afternoon when he returned from his store at Empusheni. 'I'll never learn those instruments. The Doctor's too quick. He doesn't give me time to think.'

'Then you must know them without thinking.'

Ndeya called for Samuel to bring him some sticks of bamboo, then took out his knife and notched the sticks here and carved them there until in a little while he had fashioned toy instruments like those in the pictures she had drawn. When this was done he stood on tiptoes to make himself tall and announced that he was *uDokotela* McCordi. In English he asked, 'Will you please hand me the lance.'

Katie giggled in spite of her weariness. 'He's not so polite. If he has to cut, he just thrusts out his hand and calls, "The lance!"'

'All right.' Before she could catch her breath, Ndeya suddenly thrust out his hand and called sharply for the lance. She slapped it on his outstretched palm and he put it back on the table, then thrust out his hand again, calling for the haemostat. She had to think a moment, so he asked for it again and again, and then unexpectedly called for something else and she made a mistake. With a big show of anger he pretended to throw it against the wall. Soon they were both laughing out loud at his play-acting; the children, hearing their laughter, came running to join in their game. Every night in this way Ndeya helped her study the instruments until she knew them all perfectly.

Yet it was not so easy to hand them to the Doctor. When Katie saw the wounds he treated in his examining room, she often had to run for the chair and put her head on her knees. However, one day there were so many patients that the Doctor was not finished until half past three. After the last patient was gone, Katie took in his tray of tea.

'Bring a cup for yourself,' he said and reached down into the bottom drawer of his desk and brought out a tin of Baumann's Biscuits. 'We must celebrate this day together.'

'Is it your birthday?' Katie asked, knowing how much white people liked to have parties on their birthdays.

'No.' He waited a moment. 'Katie, think! Today you forgot something.'

'Forgot?'

'Yes, you forgot to faint.'

It was true. Not once had she run for the chair. She felt very proud to realise she was no longer afraid of the blood and the pus and the smell.

Mrs McCord always assisted her husband in the first room of the little cottage hospital, which he used as an operating theatre. She was very quick and often knew which instruments he needed before he asked for them. One of the other missionaries – Mr LeRoy or Mr Dorward or Mr Bunker – would give the anaesthetic. Mr LeRoy was the best, and the Doctor always called him first. One day, however, Mr LeRoy was too busy to come and sent Mr Maxwell in his place. The Doctor told Mr Maxwell exactly what to do, but the patient did not like the ether and tried to fight against it, which made Mr Maxwell quite upset. When at last the patient was sleeping quietly, the Doctor cut into her foot. As the blood spurted out, Mr Maxwell's face went white and he fell over sideways to the floor.

'For the land's sakes,' the Doctor exclaimed and looked at Mrs McCord.

She balanced her tray of instruments on the patient's stomach and ran to hold the cone of ether.

There was no time for Katie to ask what she should do. She simply grabbed Mr Maxwell by his shoulders and dragged him out into the fresh air, then ran back inside. She was afraid the Doctor would knock the tray of instruments off the patient's stomach, so she scrubbed her arms and hands with carbolic soap as she had so often seen the Doctor do, took the tray, and held it firmly beside him.

'It was strange,' she told Ndeya later. 'I watched him all the time while he took a sliver of glass from out of that woman's infected foot, and it didn't upset me at all. It was just part of the job. And after it was all over, he said he'd make a proper nurse out of me yet.'

'And he'll do it.' Ndeya seemed to think that this was already settled and not worth discussing. Whatever the Doctor said, Ndeya believed, just as he believed the words in the Bible. Never would he permit anyone to criticise the Doctor, not even Katie.

Sometimes the Doctor would be called to some homestead in the hills to treat a patient who was too sick to come to the dispensary. At such times he packed his little black suitcase and took Mrs McCord with him so that if he had to do an emergency operation she could give the anaesthetic. If for some reason she could not go, he would take Katie with him, though he never trusted her to give the ether. 'It's too great a responsibility,' he said.

On the way to a patient he was always in a hurry, no matter how many miles they had to walk. But on their return to Adams, he would sometimes pause to rest, leaning back against a rock and gazing out over the hills while Katie sat on the ground nearby, chewing at a stalk of grass. Sometimes he remained silent. At other times he spoke slowly, almost as if to himself.

'It's easy to be a Christian when you can stand on top of a mountain,' he told her once.

'But England's a Christian country and much of that land is flat.'

'I didn't say it was necessary, Katie, just that it was easy. Did you ever stop to think that all man's wisdom, all his morality, came from the mountains? For it was on a mountain top that God spoke to Moses and gave him the Ten Commandments to take to the children of Israel.'

Yet it was on a mountain top that she saw the Doctor weep.

They were returning from Enzinyathini where a young woman had already been four days in labour before the Doctor was called. He had stayed beside her for many hours and at last was able to deliver a fat and healthy boy. After he stitched her and pulled her blankets up, he crouched beside her in that heathen hut and told her that her son was born. But she was too tired to hear him. And after they had gone only a little way on their homeward path, they heard the wails of grief in the kraal behind them.

The Doctor did not pause or even turn his head. He did not wait for Katie at the top of the first hill or at the second, and she did not catch up with him until the sound of wailing was lost in the distance. Then she saw him sitting on a rock, his body outlined against the sky, his elbows on his knees and his head in his hands. At first she thought he was sleeping, but as she sat down in the grass a few feet away, he raised his head and she saw his eyes were red.

'I didn't think she'd die,' he said. 'She was young and her heart was strong.'

'It wasn't your fault, Doctor. Her husband waited too long to call you.'

He didn't reply, only turned back to rest his head in his hands as though too weary and discouraged to gaze out over the hills. The sound of his breathing was rough and uneven, and it came to her suddenly that even with all his wisdom, even here in this high place, his faith was not always easy.

She wanted so much to comfort him but she did not know the words to bring him peace. She could think of nothing except an anthem which the choir had sung at Dr Parker's church in London. She hummed the notes softly, feeling her way back into the slow melody until at last her voice came full and clear on the still air. 'I will lift up mine eyes unto the hills from whence cometh my help,' she sang. The Doctor raised up his face to listen, and for a long time after she was finished, he sat there without moving or speaking while the purple shadows grew long and the crimson streaks in the sky faded. Not until the long grass began to rustle with the first touch of the night wind did he jump to his feet, waiting only for her to lift his little black suitcase to her head before striding down into the valley.

The twilight deepened into night as they reached the mission. The Doctor put a match to the wick in the lantern when they reached the wagon tracks through the cane-fields. His steps quickened; she had to run to keep close behind him in the circle of light. At last they reached the fork in the road.

'Here, Katie,' he said, holding out the lantern. 'You'll need this. Bring it back in the morning. Good-night.'

'Good-night, Doctor.'

Katie hurried on towards Jeena's store, a little uneasy now that she was alone in the darkness. She wondered if Ndeya had put his fire right so that her food would still be hot, and if the children were still awake and waiting for her.

Before long, the Indians on the sugar estates at Illovo and from the shops in Isipingo heard about the Doctor and began coming to the dispensary. The first Indian patient was an old man with a terrible gash in his head. The Doctor had him taken immediately to the cottage hospital, and while he was waiting for Mrs McCord to come and give the anaesthetic, Katie spoke to the patient's wife. Like many Indian women she carried her money around with her in a necklace made of gold coins, each one worth twenty-one shillings.

The necklace was worth more than fifty pounds, and proudly displayed for anyone to see. She fingered it now as she told Katie how two thieves had broken into her house and attacked her in order to steal it. When she screamed and her husband tried to defend her, one of the thieves grabbed an axe and hit him on the head. Then they ran away.

It took the Doctor more than an hour to scrape out the dirt and splinters of bone from the wound, but afterwards he was whistling cheerfully and Katie knew the old man would recover. But as soon as he came out from under the anaesthetic, he got up and staggered along the path to the dispensary.

'For the land's sake,' the Doctor said, 'get back to bed.'

'No,' the old man said, 'I've got to go home now.'

'Why?'

'Because your food's unclean.'

'Then we'll send over to Jeena and have his wife cook for you.'

'Her cooking's no good. I know that Jeena. He's a beef-eater.'

'Oh,' the Doctor said. He thought for a minute and then smiled. 'Very well, your wife will have to cook for you. We'll get vegetables and fruit—'

'We left our cooking pots behind, so I have to go home now.'

'And how do you think you'll get there?'

'As I came, baas. I'll walk.'

'Then you'll die,' the Doctor said impatiently.

But the old man was very stubborn and insisted that when he grew tired he would stop to rest. He could not be kept against his will. At last Katie had to watch him going down the path, leaning heavily on his wife's shoulder while the gold coins jangled around her neck and the hem of her sari trailed through the dust.

He only lived that night. The next day his wife came to get the death certificate. Poor old thing! Her face was puffed up with weeping. Katie tried to give her a cup of tea but she would not drink.

When Katie's daughter Margaret was born, the Doctor sent word that she was to stay in bed for at least a week. But the work was growing so fast that after the fourth day she tied little Margaret to her back with a clean white sheet, and returned to the dispensary.

Patients were coming from all over Natal, many of them making their way to Durban to catch another train to Umbogintwini and from there walking the nine miles to Adams. There was no place for them to sleep at the mission, and therefore they had to find food and shelter in the surrounding hills. Those who came from Umtwalumi went to Zama's kraal because he had married a woman from there; those from Umzumbe went to Umgqibelo because they knew him from the years he had worked for the Reverend Mr Cowles; and those from around Maritzburg knew Mgidigidi's son, who was an African policeman. But the people from Zululand knew no one and so they came to Katie.

'It's worse than Johannesburg,' she whispered to Ndeya one night after they had been woken up by a man pounding on the door. 'Remember how I used to complain about your relatives? In those days I was young and knew nothing.'

In the candlelight she saw him smile. 'And now?'

'It's no use complaining. These people are sick and have nowhere else to go.'

In January and February heavy rains came. The rivers were flooded. Pools remained where no ponds had been before. Mosquitoes hatched, and the malaria became very bad. In the hospital patients were crowded so close together there was no more room for even one extra sleeping mat. Still the patients came and had to be turned away. Still others died before they could reach the mission.

The Doctor knew but he was too busy treating the living to worry about the dead, until the day a man died on the path leading up to the dispensary.

'It's madness, their walking so far,' the Doctor muttered to himself. 'We ought to move closer to the railway station.' Then, more loudly, 'Katie, how many patients do we have who come through Durban on their way here?'

'Many, Doctor.'

'How many?'

'I don't know exactly.'

He pulled out his little black ledger in which he wrote down the name of each patient, and began to count.

Several weeks later the Doctor told Katie that the dispensary was moving to Durban. 'I've found a place next to the American Board church in Durban, in Beatrice Street, not far from the railway station.'

'Already?' Katie's throat closed up and she could not speak. In spite of the talk and his many trips to Durban and the pencil marks he had drawn on his map, she had not thought he would go so soon.

'What are you going to do with her?' he asked.

'Do with whom?'

'With Margaret, when we get to Durban.'

His meaning broke over her like waves breaking on the seashore, and she felt herself tossed this way and that. She could not bring herself to think of the dreariness of living at Adams without the Doctor and their work together, nor could she imagine the emptiness of her life without Ndeya.

'Haven't you thought of this?' The Doctor stared at her in surprise.

'I didn't know you wanted to take me with you.'

'Of course I'm taking you. What could I do without my ear and my tongue?'

'But my husband? He has this store—'

'He'll make more money if he works in Durban.'

What the Doctor said was true. Empusheni was a remote place altogether.

In all the time Ndeya had run his store, he had not made enough money to pay back what he owed Pastor William Makanya. But he was ever the dreamer, still believing that things would change next month or next year. What is more, he did not like Durban. The sea air made him wheeze too much. That night when Katie asked him about moving to Durban, he shook his head.

'It's you the Doctor wants. You're his helper.'

'But how can I go without you?'

Ndeya only shrugged and frowned at the knife and piece of bamboo in his hands.

'Ndeya, didn't you hear? What are we going to do?'

'I heard.' He notched another little hole in the whistle he was making for Sagila and wrinkled his eyes as he strained to see.

'Please, Ndeya, tell me what to do.'

His hands paused in their carving, and with a deep sigh he looked at her straight. 'The Doctor needs you.'

'Then you'll come to Durban?'

'No, I have my store.'

'But how can I leave you all alone?'

'I won't be alone. Samuel must stay with me.' Now his voice had a ring of authority. 'Our children must go to the day school here at Adams. When Sagila is ready, he'll come back here also, and in time we'll send Margaret to the girls' school at Umzumbe with the Reverend Mr Cowles.'

'It will be too hard,' Katie said in despair.

But the more she hesitated, the more insistent Ndeya became. 'On Sundays and on your holidays you can come home. Durban's not so far. And twice a month I'll come to town to buy for my store. I can bring Samuel and we'll stay the night. It will be easier for us than for many.'

Perhaps he was right. If the men could not find work with the local white farmers, they had to go away to work in Durban or Johannesburg or Kimberley. Sometimes they came home once a year; sometimes they never returned. Yes, Katie thought, it would be easier for her and Ndeya. Yet she knew in her heart that Ndeya was also wrong. Once she moved to Durban the pattern of their lives would be broken. Ndeya belonged in the country, but if she left Adams to go with the Doctor, her real home would be the dispensary in Beatrice Street.

13

Durban

1904–1906

On the first day of March in 1904 the Doctor led Katie up to the door of his new dispensary in Durban. 'It's only a five-minute rickshaw ride from the railway station,' he said proudly.

Katie looked around at what he called his consulting room. After his desk and examining table were brought in, there would hardly be room enough left for the two of them and a patient as well. And the kitchen behind the consulting room was even smaller.

'Is this all?' Katie asked, trying to hide her disappointment.

'There's a shed outside for storage,' the Doctor answered. 'I'll build shelves along these walls to hold our medicines, and we'll put the paraffin stove and the carboliser on a small table over here—'

'But where will the patients sit while they wait their turn?'

'Right where they're sitting now – on that patch of sand in the middle of the road. And that's where you should be – out there telling them to come back tomorrow.'

As he spoke, Mrs McCord poked her head round the door. 'James, there's a woman out here with a child you really ought to examine—'

'I'll get your black bag. It's in the rickshaw outside,' Katie said.

'If I see one, I'll have to see them all, and I thought you wanted to get settled in the new house,' the Doctor said to Mrs McCord.

'We can't do that until Umgqibelo arrives. Everything's on the wagon.'

'Including my medicines.'

'You can go over to the chemist and get what you need for today. I'll ask Pastor Makanya to bring us a table and some benches from the church,' said Mrs McCord, who was like a Zulu woman in her love of children.

By the time the Doctor returned, Pastor Makanya had already carried one table into the consulting room and another into the kitchen. The Doctor took off his coat, rolled up his sleeves and brought out his stethoscope. Katie began calling in the patients. Mrs McCord waited in the kitchen to mix up medicines as the Doctor called out a prescription. Outside Laura Nyuswa sat in one of the three rickshaws, holding Sagila in her lap while the three

McCord children sat in another, shrieking with glee as the rickshaw men leapt high in the air to swing their seats backwards on the giant wheels.

Once the last patient left, the Doctor handed Katie sixpence and told her of a store in Grey Street where she could buy a meat pie for herself while she waited for Umgqibelo.

'We'll take Sagila,' Mrs McCord said.

After they were gone, Katie went outside to sit on the sand and warm herself in the sun. She was too tired to walk over to Grey Street, and Margaret was fussing. She untied the knots of her blanket, easing the baby around to nurse at her breast until she drifted into sleep. Then Katie rearranged her in the blanket, knitted the ends of it over her breasts and around her hips, and clambered to her feet. Her muscles felt stiff. It was so long since she had worked her fields, she was growing fat. Her old uniforms no longer buttoned properly under her apron. She would have to ask Mrs McCord to make her bigger ones.

She was hungry after her rest in the sun and wondered if there was still time to go to Grey Street for food. But she had waited too long. Already a team of sixteen oxen was turning into Beatrice Street, with Umgqibelo sitting half-asleep on the wagon.

By half past four she and Umgqibelo had unpacked everything labelled 'Dispensary' and started across the flats. The heavy sand slowed the oxen until they started up Montpelier Road to the house the Doctor had rented. On the front veranda the electric light was already turned on, and Laura Nyuswa sat jouncing Sagila up and down on her lap. As soon as the wagon came to a stop, Sagila yelled a greeting, struggled out of Laura's arms and ran to Katie. She hugged him close for a moment and then, as he clung to her skirt, she reached inside her pocket for one of the toffees she had stopped to buy with the sixpence the Doctor had given her. Yet, although Sagila held his sweetie in one hand, he would not let go of her skirt, not even when the Doctor's voice called her sharply from the back of the house.

'You be a good boy and stay with Laura,' she whispered. 'I've got to go.'

'UMame,' he began to sob.

'Just a little while,' she whispered. And then loudly, 'Yes, Doctor, I'm coming.'

The Doctor was standing on the back steps arguing with a young man by the name of Cele, whose wife was kneeling on the ground beside him. She was very big with child. Her face was shining with sweat and her lips clamped tight in the manner of heathen women, for among them a woman is not permitted to moan or cry out when her child is born lest bad luck follow it all its life. During childbirth the old mothers stand ready with their sticks to beat her if she screams. Katie could see from the way the woman looked at her that she was afraid of those sticks.

'Tell him he must take his wife to the Addington,' the Doctor told Katie hurriedly. 'Explain I have no place to care for her properly.'

But when Katie repeated the Doctor's words, the young man shook his head.

'Pastor Makanya sent him here,' she told the Doctor, 'and his wife is already in labour.'

'But I've told you, I've no place—'

Katie looked behind her at a small corrugated-iron shanty in the backyard. There were two rooms there, one for the coal and one for Katie and her children to share with Laura Nyuswa. But the coal had not yet been brought.

'The coal shed, Doctor! I can clean it quickly and you can deliver the baby there.'

'Yes,' Cele said eagerly.

The Doctor hesitated, but without waiting for him to argue further, Katie ran back to the kitchen for rags and soap and the bottle of Jeyes Fluid.

When the shed was cleaned, the woman settled on her blankets and her husband shown where to tap on her window when it was time to call the Doctor, Katie trudged slowly up the back steps into the kitchen. She was tired and very hungry, for she had eaten nothing since early morning except toffees, yet she felt very satisfied with herself. If it had not been for her, the Doctor would have sent that poor woman off to the Addington in a rickshaw, and she did not like to think of that hospital, where her baby Ethel had died.

A candle was burning in the kitchen. Umgqibelo was asleep on the floor, his blankets pulled up over his head, but a dish of stew and a pot of tea were kept hot for her on the back of the stove. She picked up the candle and a box of matches and went out on the back steps to eat her dinner. The candle flame sputtered and the flame died down. The light in an upstairs window went out. The garden was very dark, and she had to feel her way down the path to the room she was to share with Laura Nyuswa.

Once inside, she lit her candle to see how Laura had arranged their things. Two iron beds brought from Adams were set against the walls on either side of the door. Margaret slept in one and Laura snored in the other, her arms cradling Sagila. Poor child! In the flickering light Katie could see that his face was still puffed up and streaked with tears. When the Doctor had called her, she had promised to come back in just a while, but her work had kept her away.

For a long time after she blew out her candle, she stared into the darkness wondering how often other women would have to wipe away Sagila's tears. She wondered, too, about Samuel coming home after school to an empty house, and Ndeya sleeping alone. She must have been crazy to leave her husband behind and divide their children. For what? To serve this white man, this doctor, this missionary who was always too busy to preach the Word of God and did not care if a man was Christian, heathen, Muslim or Hindu?

She was just falling asleep when Cele tapped at her window. 'I think it's time,' he was saying anxiously.

The baby was a long time coming. In the end the Doctor had to use his forceps, and it was almost dawn before Katie had settled Cele's wife back on her sleeping mat with her baby girl in her arms. But there was no time to rest: Sagila was already awake and Laura Nyuswa had started the fire in the kitchen of the big house. Down at the dispensary, however, there were only eleven patients sitting on the sand. Katie was much relieved. She could leave early, she thought, rest in the afternoon, and go to bed right after her evening meal.

But Cele gave her no peace. So excited was he about the birth of his daughter that he had left his wife alone and gone to spread the news of the Doctor's skill. Before noon he arrived at the dispensary with a group of his friends who were carrying a man on a makeshift stretcher.

'Here is Dabula,' he told Katie. 'He worked in the gold mines until a big stone dropped on top of his head. When he was sent home, he went to a witchdoctor who cut into his head and scraped the bone. After that, his body began jerking and twitching and he has much pain.'

'It sounds like Jackson's epilepsy,' the Doctor muttered when Katie translated Cele's words. 'Tell him I'll have to operate. Katie, you go home and warn Mrs McCord to get things ready. I'll come as soon as I've finished with the rest of the patients.'

By the time Doctor arrived, Laura Nyuswa had moved the kitchen table to the back veranda, Mrs McCord had sterilised the instruments, and Katie had hung a sheet between Cele's wife and an empty space in the shed large enough for Dabula's sleeping mat.

When the operation was over and Cele settled beside Dabula to hold him still when he came out from under the ether, Katie went to help Laura Nyuswa scrub down the table and move it back into the kitchen. She could hear the Doctor pacing the floor of his dining-room. 'This is madness,' he was telling Mrs McCord. 'I expected to open a dispensary and slowly build up a practice here in town. But we haven't been here forty-eight hours and already we have one confinement and a surgical case in a backyard shanty. We've got to open up some sort of hospital.'

Somehow the Doctor found enough money to rent a cottage behind the American Board church. There was space in the front room for twelve patients, six women on one side of a partition and six men on the other. But there were no beds. The patients had to bring their own sleeping mats with them and relatives to prepare their food. Behind these two wards was a smaller room which became the operating theatre, beyond that a kitchen, and off to one side another small room for Katie and her two children.

'Because I'll need someone in the hospital all the time,' the Doctor told her. 'Someone who can call me on the telephone if I am suddenly needed in the night.'

Katie did not want to live there. There was no Laura Nyuswa to watch over Sagila. And Margaret would soon be walking. Worst of all, there was not enough room for Ndeya and Samuel to stay when they came to town to visit. But how could she refuse the Doctor when she knew how much he needed someone he could trust? Umgqibelo was too old and he tired easily. He might not wake up if a patient called out in the night.

'Very well, Doctor,' she said at last. 'Tomorrow, after I've cleaned the place, I'll move my things.'

On that day she turned thirty-one years old.

In the two-room dispensary, the Doctor examined the patients, then stopped to mix up their medicines for Katie to pour into little bottles. Then she wrote down the name of the medicine on gummed labels and beneath that a verse from the Bible. All that writing took time, and Katie wanted to write up each day's labels the night before. But the Doctor was afraid she would make a mistake in labelling a bottle. He needed a proper hospital, but he also needed a bigger dispensary, which he soon built on the empty land beside the American Board church. Although Katie was very excited when the new building was ready, Umgqibelo began complaining as soon as they moved in. He said the place was too big for him to clean and it was time for him to go back to his homeplace at Umsunduzi. Mrs McCord persuaded Umgqibelo to remain a little longer, and it was lucky she did, for one day Garnett Mtembu brought his wife to be examined by the Doctor.

Garnett was a thickset man with sideburns and whiskers. He had been a schoolteacher at Adams but had given up that job to take his wife back to Umtwalumi where her mother could help him care for her. 'Because she's paralysed,' he told the Doctor. 'She's helpless.'

'How long has she been this way?'

'For six months. From the day the twins were born.'

After examining her, the Doctor told Garnett that his wife might get better but she would have to stay in the hospital for a long time.

Garnett turned away and covered his face with his hands. Then, still facing the wall, he said his money was finished. 'And I no longer have any job.'

'Don't worry about money,' the Doctor told him calmly. 'Your coming here today is very lucky for me. I need a responsible man to replace Umgqibelo. I'll pay you what you used to earn as a teacher.'

'But the babies? What will I do with my babies?'

'Send them back to Umtwalumi with your wife's mother.'

'No, my wife's mother is—' He turned to Katie. 'How can I say it?'

'Old-fashioned?' Katie asked.

'Yes, she follows the old ways. She says I should have left one or both of the twins to die because they bring bad luck. I can't trust her with them.'

Katie pitied him with all his worries. 'Perhaps we can keep them here,' she suggested quickly. 'If Garnett will build a fence around one corner of the yard, then Sagila can stay with the twins and with Margaret also. If they cry, Garnett or I can see from the window.'

Garnett looked at the Doctor with sudden hope. 'If we could do this, then later I could find someone to care for them.'

'We can try it,' the Doctor said.

Katie's work was much easier after Garnett came. Because his wife was in the hospital, the Doctor decided he should be the one to live in the back room, and Katie was free to rent a room at no. 1 Umgeni Road. It was big enough for herself and the children and also for Ndeya and Samuel when they came into town to visit her.

There were other changes too. The Doctor taught Garnett how to mix his medicines and how to change the dressings on the male patients, which was a big help.

Garnett's wife, however, was very difficult. She kept calling for him because he was the only person who understood her confused speech. One day she tried to talk to Katie, who thought she wanted to see her babies and called to Garnett to bring them in. But at the sight of them his wife grew excited, rolling her eyes and frothing at the mouth.

'I think she's a little bit crazy,' Katie said sadly.

Garnett shook his head helplessly. 'Heathen book tricks,' he muttered.

Poor Garnett! He loved those twins very much. One Sunday morning he ran to Katie at her room in Umgeni Road, frightened out of his wits. The Doctor did not answer his telephone and the twins were very sick.

Katie glanced at the clock. It was half past eleven. 'The Doctor's at church in Florida Road,' she said. 'By the time I get there the service will be over and I'll bring him immediately.'

But when she returned with the Doctor, Garnett was sprawled on the floor of his little room, clutching his two dead babies in his arms.

'What happened?' the Doctor asked.

'Heathen book tricks,' Garnett kept repeating until the Doctor grew impatient.

'Katie, get me the saw.'

'Oh no, Doctor, please.'

'I'll have to do a post-mortem. I can't sign a death certificate until I know why they died. Garnett doesn't make any sense.'

Katie felt so sorry for Garnett that she could not bear to think of his horror if the Doctor cut his babies open to find out their sickness. 'It was the fever, Doctor,' she said quickly, pretending she knew and remembering the way her baby Charlotte had died in Johannesburg. 'It was that fever which comes in the night and causes convulsions. Both twins died of convulsions.'

'Heathen book tricks,' Garnett kept repeating.

The Doctor hesitated but at last he nodded his head. 'You had better call Pastor William.'

For three days Garnett was like one of those people who are deaf and dumb, never speaking or seeming to hear, not even when the Pastor preached the funeral service or when Katie went with him to the cemetery. He no longer tended his wife, and when her mother approached, he turned his face away. Although he was a Christian and much educated, Katie was sure he still believed that somehow his wife's mother had cast a spell on the twins, causing their deaths.

Three days later his wife's father came from Umtwalumi and took Garnett's wife away. In a few weeks word came that she was dead.

Only once did Garnett speak of his children again, and that was when Katie asked him if he was going to be a teacher once more. He shook his head. 'I'm staying here. It wasn't the Doctor's fault, he didn't know heathen book tricks.'

Every so often, patients came in to see the Doctor after having first been treated by an *inyanga,* or witchdoctor. They would come with virulent infections from the strange ointments rubbed into cuts in their skin, with stomach pains caused by potent medicines given them to drink, or with nervous disorders treated with the feathers and skin of a vulture or a powder made from twitching beetles. When Katie told Garnett about them, he would shake his head and mutter angrily under his breath, ' Heathen book tricks.'

These *inyangas* each had their own special skills. There were the smellers-out, who threw their bones on the ground and, from the way they fell, could detect the enemy who was causing a victim's misfortune; there were the herbalists who made their medicines out of herbs and roots and sometimes successfully treated the common diseases; and there were the sorcerers who knew about charms and the casting of spells. But all of them dealt to a greater or lesser extent in magic. For this reason they were very powerful. Even the Christians were afraid to incur their anger.

At first all the *inyangas* claimed the Doctor knew only the white man's diseases and nothing of African sicknesses. They warned people not to go to him. Consequently, too many patients came only as a last resort.

But there was one important *inyanga,* Thlambesine Ngcobo from beyond Pinetown, whose sister was a member of Pastor William Makanya's church. She told him so much about the dispensary that he grew curious. One day when he went into Durban to buy his medicines from the African market, he came to see for himself if what she said was true.

When Katie told the Doctor that an *inyanga* wanted to see him, the Doctor looked very surprised. Nevertheless, he greeted Thlambesine politely and invited him to sit down in the consulting room.

They talked for a long time, and to Katie's dismay, the Doctor showed Thlambesine some of his medicines. In return, Thlambesine brought out a piece of crocodile skin from his pouch and described how to grind it into powder and mix it with water to give anyone with a bad cough. He claimed that crushed cuttlefish was very good for sore eyes and that the dried flesh of a snake provided protection against witchcraft. He spoke of various roots and bulbs and barks from which he made special fever medicines or emetics. And he had other things at home, he said, especially one medicine which was very strong. 'I can make a fire with that one, and then I can put the fire into a bucket of water and it will not go out.'

'Hm,' the Doctor said. 'I'd like to see you make that fire.'

'I can't do it here. I've left the special medicine at home.'

'Ah! But can you make water burn?'

Thlambesine laughed. 'That is not possible.'

The Doctor looked at Katie, his eyes sparkling with amusement. 'Remember that lamp we had in the hospital at Adams, and the lumps of calcium carbide we used as fuel? We brought all that stuff with us. So run out to the storeroom and get me one of those lumps, and bring a pail of water.'

When Katie returned he dropped the lump of calcium carbide into the pail of water and waited a moment for the bubbles of gas to appear. Then with a flourish of his wrist he struck a match and held it to the surface of the water. A blue flame shot up, and then another, and another, until it looked as if the water itself was on fire.

'*Hawu!*' Thlambesine gasped. 'You must show me how you do this.'

'First you show me how you make your fire.'

'When you come to visit me – because I also have a dispensary – then I will show you.'

Thlambesine stood up, hesitated and then turned back. 'My sister tells me you have a very good worm medicine. If you give me some, I'll give you in return part of the eye of a lion. It's a very strong muti and gives strength to someone who is weak.'

'Don't give him anything,' Katie cried out in alarm. 'Who knows what he will use it for.'

The Doctor paid her no attention. 'Why do you want worm medicine? To give one of your patients?'

'No, it's for me, because I have a biting in my stomach.'

'Then you will have to get on my table and let me listen to where your stomach bites you.'

After examining him, the Doctor gave Thlambesine medicine for indigestion. 'If you're not better in two weeks, come back to see me again.'

Thlambesine came back in two weeks but not for more medicine. He came with his own children for the Doctor to examine, and later with other patients whom he himself was unable to cure. Then he came a third time. He had a big festering wound in his thigh, which the Doctor scraped and disinfected. Then he told Thlambesine to stay for a night or two in the hospital.

On that particular day Katie was not at the dispensary and she did not know that Thlambesine had been kept in the hospital. The next morning she noticed a woman with a child sitting alone at some distance from the other patients and speaking to no one. 'Who is she that sets herself apart?' she asked a man who came from the same district.

'She's Nokwazi – a smeller-out,' he whispered nervously.

Katie was surprised. Nokwazi did not look like a smeller-out. She looked like any other heathen woman in her cowhide skirt, her regulation blanket tied over one shoulder, her hair rubbed in red clay and falling in little ringlets around her face. And like any other mother, she seemed worried about her child. Nevertheless, Katie believed what she had been told. When she had a chance, she approached Nokwazi and sat down at her side. 'I don't see your throwing-bones or horn of secret medicine,' she said.

Nokwazi looked startled. 'I left them behind. I'm told *uDokotela* doesn't like such things. But how did you know?'

Katie smiled slyly. 'Tell me,' she said, 'when people come to you with their troubles, do you really know who cast a spell upon them?'

'I know,' Nokwazi answered. She seemed impressed by Katie's knowledge of her profession. 'Sometimes I throw my bones. Sometimes I know in other ways.'

'What way?'

'When I approach the evil one, my body trembles and I cannot breathe.'

'I think you're fooling me,' Katie said.

Nokwazi only smiled as though she knew some secret she would not tell. Katie stared at her uneasily, remembering that among her father's people in Soekmekaar there were certain people who did have special powers, like old Rasiaga who could turn away the lightning with his forked stick.

Before ushering her in, Katie warned the Doctor that Nokwazi was a smeller-out. He was not impressed. He just spoke to Nokwazi as he would to any other mother. After examining her daughter, he declared the child would have to stay in the hospital because he thought she was suffering from TB of the bone.

'You had better stay with her for a few days until she gets used to us,' he added.

Katie settled the child in the women's ward and brought out a blanket and headrest so that Nokwazi could sleep on the floor. But that night when Katie was sound asleep in her room in Umgeni Road there was a knock on her door. Garnett called to her to come quickly because of a commotion at the hospital. When she got there she found Garnett, red-eyed with weariness, shouting at Thlambesine to lie down and be quiet. But Thlambesine kept dancing about in spite of his wounded thigh, uttering threats and waving his arms like a fighter. At the same time, in the women's ward she could hear much moaning and cursing. Garnett yelled at Nokwazi through the partition, 'If you don't behave yourself, I'll call the Doctor to chase you away.'

'What's the matter with those two?' Katie asked.

'Heathen book tricks. First Thlambesine fights the evil spirits. Then Nokwazi gets up and jumps about like a crazy woman. They keep everyone awake. I called the Doctor but he does not answer his telephone.'

'*Hawu!*' Katie said. 'I think Nokwazi was telling me true. I think she smelled out Thlambesine and is afraid of him.' She hurried into the women's ward and grabbed Nokwazi by the shoulders.

'Stop your noise and come outside.'

'No,' Nokwazi cried, her eyes wide with terror. 'There's an evil spirit in this place. I must protect my child.'

'The Doctor does not permit any evil spirits here,' Katie said roughly and, in spite of her protests, dragged Nokwazi out the back door. As soon as they stepped into the fresh air, Nokwazi stopped her struggling.

'Now do you feel better?'

'Yes.'

'Didn't I tell you? Now come. You'll sleep in the dispensary tonight.'

As soon as she was settled in the waiting-room, Katie ran back to see Thlambesine. He too was quiet now and only wanted to sleep. When all was still, Katie walked slowly back to her room. She was trying to think how she would tell the Doctor that although Thlambesine and Nokwazi did not know each other, they had both sensed an evil presence at close quarters.

The Doctor laughed at first, but when he saw the worry in Katie's eyes and noticed that Garnett was almost asleep on his feet, his face grew solemn. 'Today Thlambesine will have to be well enough to go home,' he said. 'But before he goes, I shall have to question him about his special powers.'

He asked Thlambesine many questions, and he talked to other missionaries, to his friends in the Native Affairs Department and to some of the magistrates in the rural districts. Then, when Thlambesine came again with patients for him to see, he had more questions to ask. One day he even took Katie with him when he went out to visit what Thlambesine called his 'dispensary', although it was just a hut on the other side of the hill from his homestead.

A woman was waiting nervously when they arrived. Pointing to her, Thlambesine said she had a devil inside her head which was giving her much pain. Thereupon he brought out a stay from a white woman's corset which he had found somewhere, sharpened it and rubbed it in some powder made out of a blue stone. Then, while Katie and the Doctor watched, he cut into the woman's head to let the devil out. Katie had to squeeze her eyes shut and cover up her ears while he worked, because the woman was screaming with pain, and it took two men to hold her on the ground.

'Why didn't you stop him?' she asked the Doctor angrily on their way back to town.

'She wasn't my patient.'

'But you're a missionary. You should have helped her. Now you know how

Thlambesine operates, you should join all the other missionaries and tell the people to throw the *inyangas* away.'

The Doctor only smiled. 'When people are sick they'll try anything they think will make them better. If there's no one else to treat them, they'll cling to the *inyangas* and keep on hoping for some magic cure. That's just human nature.'

Katie felt too confused to argue. She had seen him rage with anger when some patient came in almost dead, not from the sickness in him but from the way an *inyanga* in his ignorance had cut or dosed or tried to frighten the pain devils out by magic incantations. Nevertheless, he had not scolded or interfered with Thlambesine. Instead he spoke as if he almost believed in magic cures. Katie kept puzzling over this matter until one day a heathen woman brought in her baby who had no strength to hold up his head and whose stomach was as big as a balloon filled with air.

'Before you nurse him, do you give him other food? Porridge or beans or mealies?' the Doctor asked.

The woman nodded.

'But always he vomits it up?'

'Yes, even when I chew it a long time he still vomits it up.'

'Because his stomach is too small to digest it.' The Doctor called out to Garnett to bring in a bottle of Mixture Three. 'You must give the baby a spoonful of this medicine every time you nurse him, but nothing else except the milk from your breast.'

The woman shook her head in disbelief when Katie repeated his words. *'Hawu!'* she complained. 'Do you want my child to starve?'

'UDokotela wants him to get well,' Katie said without waiting for the Doctor to speak. 'I tell you true. The muti will cure your child because the magic in it is very strong. But if you give him anything else besides the milk, the magic will be destroyed. You hear?'

'I hear,' the woman said, clutching the bottle of Mixture Three and fumbling in her purse for the sixpence the Doctor had charged her. Not until the woman left and Katie saw the Doctor staring at her with his eyebrows raised and his nostrils twitching, did she realise how quickly she had spoken without waiting for his instructions.

'There isn't any magic in my medicines, Katie,' he said softly.

'For her there is, and she will go home and tell the people that you have magic cures. Then they will come to you instead of going to an *inyanga.'*

'But I want to teach the people about disease. I don't want them calling me a magician.'

'They don't, Doctor, not exactly. They say you're very clever because you have studied long in America and England and know all about natural diseases. But they also say that you know about our African diseases as well, even those caused by evil spirits. And they ask, How can you know these things unless you've studied secretly under some famous *inyanga?*'

The Doctor's laughter rumbled under his voice. 'And where have I studied?'

Katie giggled. 'Nobody knows except perhaps Thlambesine. In Swaziland perhaps or beyond the Limpopo.'

'And you, Katie? Do you believe these things?'

She stopped her giggling and stared back at him angrily. He had no right to ask her such a question, not when he knew she was a good Christian like her mother and her grandfather and her great-grandmother with the yellowed bone showing through her hair. Not when he knew she had lived among the white people in England. Not when he knew her own sister had graduated from a university in America and even now was building a school among the heathen in Soekmekaar. Not when she had also left her husband and her eldest son alone in the country so that she could follow him in God's work. He had no right to stand there grinning as though he thought she was also spreading heathen stories.

'No. I don't believe such things.' She lifted her head and looked at him straight. 'I only tell the people what they understand.'

The Doctor knew he had made her angry with his teasing, but he was never one to apologise. Instead he came early a few days later and handed her a packet. 'Mrs McCord knows you are very lazy and don't like to write out labels for the medicines,' he said as she opened the packet and pulled out pads of coloured labels.

She gasped with pleasure. Each pad was of a different colour, and printed on the labels was the name of the medicine belonging to each – Mixture One, Mixture Two and so on up to Mixture Fourteen – and underneath, in smaller letters, a verse from the Bible. 'For God so loved the world' for Mixture One; 'Let not your heart be troubled' for Mixture Two, and so on. Now Katie would not have to bother writing the labels but had only to paste them on the bottles. The different colours would make it easy for her to avoid mistakes.

'They're beautiful,' she said. Then, pointing to the verse on one of the blue labels, she added, 'And this is the magic which makes your medicines strong. When I tell this to the heathen, they will want to know more about your magic. And because you're a Christian, they will have to come to Pastor William Makanya's church to learn it.'

The Doctor's sudden laughter rattled the bottles on the shelves in the supply room.

Soon after the Doctor opened his cottage hospital, Dr Pearson started coming to assist in the operations. Katie had first known Dr Pearson at Adams when he was district surgeon. He was a tall, thin Englishman with a big nose and a monocle, which he wore on a black ribbon round his neck and screwed into his right eye. When he learned that Katie had been a singer in England for almost three years, he began bringing her his mailed copies of *The Tatler*. Although several months out of date, she sometimes found in them pictures of people she had known, including Lord Knutsford, and one of Mrs Emmeline Pankhurst in a big black hat shaking her umbrella at a policeman. She wanted to ask Dr Pearson if he had also known these people, but she always felt too shy.

However, she did not like his friend, Dr Bray, who came with him to give the anaesthetic. Dr Bray was so short that he barely reached the Doctor's shoulder. Although he was still a young man, his hair was entirely white except for his bushy black eyebrows which almost joined together above his nose. Katie thought she smelt whisky on his breath the first time he came. When he spoke, he moved his lips around a smelly black pipe in his mouth, and she was often shocked at the words he used when he was upset or excited. She could not understand how it was that from the moment they met the Doctor and Dr Bray were like brothers.

It was Dr Bray who came to the dispensary to see the patients when the Doctor went away for a short holiday.

'But he's not a missionary,' Katie complained. 'Why doesn't Dr Pearson come?'

'He's not a missionary either.'

'No, but he's a proper Christian. Dr Bray's a drinker and a smoker and a blasphemer—'

'That's enough.' There was anger in the Doctor's voice. 'Dr Bray is a good Catholic.'

'Dr Pearson is not a Catholic,' Katie muttered stubbornly.

'No.' The Doctor's lips twitched suddenly as though he wanted to laugh. 'He's an atheist.'

'Atheist? I don't know these atheists.'

'Never mind! Just remember to call Dr Bray if anything goes wrong.'

It was a difficult few days. Dr Bray kept telling her to hurry, hurry, hurry. Sometimes he swore at Garnett. Worst of all, he looked at her as if he did not see her. She suspected he wouldn't know the difference if she stayed at home and another black woman in a blue uniform and white apron started ushering in the patients. He did not really see her until the day the Doctor and Dr Pearson were scrubbing their arms before operating on a woman with a tumour in her stomach. Mrs McCord was standing ready with her tray of instruments; Dr Bray was holding the cone of ether over the patient's nose. After the anaesthetic began to take effect, but before she was completely under, the woman began to sing.

'What's she singing?' Dr Bray asked Mrs McCord.

Mrs McCord did not answer but her face grew red with embarrassment.

Dr Bray grinned and looked over at Katie, who was standing against the wall with a broom and mop. 'What's she singing, Katie? One of your Zulu hymns?'

Katie never permitted anyone, not even a white man, to make fun of her religion. She looked straight at Dr Bray and was about to scold him when she suddenly remembered that he was a Catholic. 'Not one of my hymns,' she replied, making her voice sound very sweet. 'She's singing the "Ave Maria."'

Mrs McCord gasped. Dr Bray's mouth hung slack with astonishment. The Doctor and Dr Pearson turned around from the wash-basin to stare at her and then suddenly they both burst out laughing. Even Dr Bray chuckled. All through that long operation, while he kept his finger on the patient's pulse and listened to her breathing, he would glance up at Katie as if he knew her as a real person.

Dr Bray again took charge of the dispensary when the Doctor went off to war. This time the English were not fighting the Boers. They were trying to put down the rebellion of Bambatha, a minor Zulu chief. And all because a silly white magistrate had told Bambatha that a poll tax recently levied by the Natal government was a tax on his head.

'We've paid our hut tax and our cattle tax and our dog tax, but we'll go to war before we pay any tax on our own heads,' Bambatha replied, and called on his warriors to sharpen their spears. When a cordon of police marched to his homestead to force him to pay, Bambatha's warriors attacked in large numbers and drove the police off. Neighbouring chiefs, regarding this as a victory, joined with Bambatha to drive the white people out of their land.

Katie, like most of the educated Christian Zulus, was dismayed. How can a little chief like Bambatha do this when our great king, Cetshwayo, failed? the people around Durban asked, remembering all the troubles which had befallen them during the last Zulu war thirty years earlier. To stop Bambatha, some of the Zulus formed their own cavalry regiment, the Natal Native Horse, to fight on the side of the British. But they had no doctor to care for their wounded. Their white officers, mostly sons of missionaries, urged Dr McCord to enlist as a medical officer. At first he refused, but when he heard how cruelly the captured rebels were being treated, he changed his mind and put on a British Army uniform and went away with Dr Pearson.

While he was gone Dr Bray would stop first in the supply room to tell Katie and Garnett what news he had from the telegraph, and then he would ask what they had heard. But they knew nothing until a heathen man came to the dispensary with a piece of white bandage tied to his finger and a bullet hole in his thigh. Dr Bray did not ask him any questions. He just took out the bullet, disinfected the wound, and sent him away. Katie, however, questioned the man at length, and after he was gone she went into the consulting room. 'Did you know he was one of Bambatha's men?' she asked Dr Bray.

He pretended great surprise. 'Then we will have to report him to the authorities. He should be put in gaol while his huts are burned and his cattle confiscated.'

Katie laughed. 'How can we report him when you didn't ask his name?'

'Damn, I forgot. I'll remember next time.'

But he never questioned those men who came with strips of white bandage tied to their fingers. Dr Bray did not know their names or where they came from, but Katie knew. They all told her the same story. They had been captured at the foot of the Madlozi Mountain or at Keate's Drift and marched to a camp to wait until they could be taken to Maritzburg for trial. But in the night a white officer guarding them talked out loud to himself, walking slowly round the enclosure in which his prisoners were kept. He spoke anxiously about a hole in the fence and a path over the mountains so rugged that the soldiers did not bother to watch it, and of a cottage hospital in Beatrice Street where anyone with a piece of white bandage tied to his finger would be helped.

'Did you see that white officer? Was he missing two fingers on his right hand?'

'Yes,' they said.

'Then you've seen *uDokotela* McCordi,' Katie told them, and silently praised the Lord as she hurried inside to telephone Mrs McCord to say that the Doctor was still very much all right.

One day a man came with a festering wound in his chest. There was no white bandage on his finger and he told a different story. When he and his brothers went out to fight the government army, they were given a special medicine to protect them from the bullets, but the medicine proved useless. Before they got close enough to throw their spears, the white soldiers shot them and then rode away, leaving them to die on the battlefield.

'Then how did you escape?'

'The Indians helped me,' he said. 'They gave me water and cut out the bullet.'

Katie was surprised. 'What were the Indians doing on the battlefield?' she asked Dr Bray after the man had gone. 'They aren't fighters like the Zulus. They haven't joined with Bambatha and there isn't a Natal Indian Horse.'

'No,' Dr Bray told her, 'but there's an ambulance corps made up of the Indians who follow Mr Gandhi.'

'Who's he?'

'An Indian lawyer. He preaches non-violence. When the Indians in Johannesburg were ordered to carry passes like the African men, he urged his followers to refuse and get themselves arrested. He said the government didn't have enough jails to hold them all. He's quite a troublemaker.'

'And this Mr Gandhi is helping Bambatha?'

'No, he organised an ambulance corps to help the wounded, but most of the wounded happen to be rebels.'

'Then those Indian ambulance workers must be very brave,' Katie said, 'because who knows what the white soldiers would do if they came back to the battlefield and found them tending Bambatha's warriors.'

As she moved among the patients sitting out on the sand, she looked at the Indians with more respect. She grew curious about their Mr Gandhi. Although he was not a Christian, she thought he understood about turning the other cheek. Once someone pointed him out to her at the railway station. He was dressed in a white turban and a long cream-coloured coat which buttoned up to his neck. She was too shy to speak to him but she wrote and told Charlotte that he looked like a very nice man.

After the Doctor returned to the dispensary, she mentioned to him what Dr Bray had said, and she stopped complaining that the Indians took up too much of his time. Instead, when her work was over, she began visiting the Indian families who lived in Beatrice Street and in time came to see them as not so much different from her own people, in spite of their straight hair and strange customs. In time, Mrs Choudree, a Hindu woman who lived behind the dispensary, became her closest friend in Durban.

14

Soekmekaar

1906

Katie's sixth child, Nimrod, fussed constantly from the day he was born. The Doctor said he had the colic, 'and there's not much I can do for him. He'll outgrow it in about three months.' Sometimes Katie grew so tired from pacing the floor with Nimrod during the night that in the morning she forgot what a patient was telling her or fell asleep at the table in the supply room. Some mornings she was late, and Garnett had to call his new wife, Elizabeth, to hand out the numbers as the patients arrived.

One morning, when Katie took in his tray of tea, the Doctor told her to sit down. After staring at her thoughtfully for a moment, he suddenly asked when she had last had a holiday.

'At Christmas. I went home for three days,' she said.

'I mean a long holiday.'

'You've never given me a long holiday, Doctor.'

'Well, I'm giving you one now. I don't want to see you for a month. Go home. Sit in the sun. Sleep when you can. And no hoeing or weeding. Just rest. Here—' He reached into the cash box and drew out five pounds. 'You'll still be working for me and your job is to make yourself strong.'

'But whom will you find to help you here?'

'Don't worry about that. Elizabeth will help Garnett manage.'

To Katie's dismay, tears of relief rolled down her cheeks. It would be good to have a holiday and do nothing but gossip with her friends while she waited for Samuel and Sagila to come home from school. But as she trudged slowly back to Umgeni Road, she found herself thinking, not of the green hills of Amanzimtoti, but of the jagged koppies and monstrous cactus plants of Soekmekaar. It was the time of the first fruits, and before long the little girls, those who had not yet started to menstruate, would be dancing along the road with their baskets of vegetables, to leave them in a special place on top of the mountain where the spirits of the ancestors waited for the new harvest. Once her baby sister, Mary Ann, had danced and carried her basket. Mary Ann was no longer a child but a young woman of eighteen and ready for marriage. Katie thought, too, of Charlotte – Mrs Maxeke now – who, with her husband, had already built a school in Ramokgopa's Location. In all the years since they had been girls together in Kimberley, Katie had not seen Charlotte. And Pa? He must be lonely without Ma, who had died during the Boer War.

'It's time for me to visit my homeplace,' she told Ndeya at the end of the second week at home, 'because I do not know when the Doctor will give me another holiday.'

Nothing had changed on the long wagon journey from Pietersburg to Ramokgopa's Location. Old Rasiaga was dead but his eldest son carried a forked stick to turn away the lightning. Like his father, he cracked his long black whip over the heads of the oxen as they plodded on by way of Makapaanspoort, stopped for the night within sight of the Lutheran mission, and next day rested again at the base of Letlapa where the green streaks still showed from the vanished waterfall.

Charlotte was waiting on the dancing ground, and as soon as the wagon crested the last hill, she started running, waving her arms and shrieking a welcome. She was older now and thicker in body, but in her excitement she was shouting and jumping about like a young girl. A stranger seeing her in that moment would never have guessed that she was the first black woman in South Africa to obtain a BA degree.

'Hawu, Katie!' she called out as she neared the wagon. 'Why do you come with only this one baby? Where is your husband and your other children? Your telegram told us nothing.'

'Oh, Charlotte, you steal my eyes away, you look so beautiful.'

'Get down from the wagon and walk with me. Pa's waiting.'

Charlotte spoke with her old authority, but Katie's years at the dispensary had taught her to speak her mind. 'It's too far to walk. I'm tired since Nimrod was born. The Doctor told me to rest myself entirely.'

'Then I'll ride with you. When is Makanya coming? Ramokgopa still has land set aside for him. How soon will it take you to be rested enough to help me in my school?'

'I'm not going to help you, Charlotte. I've only come for a little holiday. Then I'll go home to Natal.'

'But this is your homeplace.'

'I'm needed in Durban.'

'I need you more. Let your Doctor find himself another servant.'

'I'm not just any servant. I'm his interpreter.'

Charlotte was not listening. 'You can take charge of the sewing classes.'

'Mary Ann should teach the sewing. As a little girl she was already very clever with her crocheting and mending.'

Charlotte's lips thinned and her voice grew bitter. 'Mary Ann's useless. I can't have her in my school.'

Before Charlotte could argue further, Katie caught her hand. 'Now, tell me about your husband, about Maxeke.'

Charlotte smiled. 'You'll like him. He's a very good Christian. After he finished at Wilberforce, he stayed in America and became ordained as a proper minister with the AME. Now he and Pa work very hard in our new church, and we have eighty-seven Christians in the village.'

'But Pa's a Presbyterian.'

'Not any more. He had a big fight with the missionary after we came and now he's AME.'

'And Ramokgopa? Is he AME also?'

'No, he's still a heathen. When we try to persuade him, he only laughs and asks how he can choose between the Lutherans and the Presbyterians and the Methodists and the Dutch Reformed and the AME. But he doesn't fight our school any more.'

'Then he's changed?'

'No, it's the young men who have changed. Some of them go to Modjadji where the Dutch Reformed have a very good boys' school. And when they come back, they want their wives to be a little bit educated also. Ramokgopa's afraid that if our girls remain ignorant, the young men will go elsewhere to find their wives. But sometimes he still makes things very difficult for me.'

'How?'

'He's very strict. He does not want the people to forget the old ways. When we first came, my husband and I, we didn't know them. Once Ramokgopa forbade all the girls to come to my school because I ate food out of my garden before he'd tasted the first pumpkin. My husband had to give him an overcoat from America before he allowed the girls to return.'

'But he did send them back?'

'Yes. He doesn't fight us as long as we're careful not to go against the ancient customs. Indeed, I try to follow them, at least those that do not go against our religion. Sometimes—' Charlotte looked away.

'Sometimes what?' Katie asked.

'Nothing.'

Katie laughed. 'Now you're afraid to tell me what you were going to say – something about pleasing Ramokgopa.'

Charlotte chewed her lips uneasily and then lifted up her chin in defiance. 'I dance with the women at feast time.'

'You dance with them?' Katie was shocked.

'Yes. The people like to see me dance. It makes them trust me. You'll see tonight, because Pa has killed an ox for you and already the men are building the fire.'

'But dancing! Ma would never let Phillip and me dance, even though she let me wear bean pods around my ankles and shine my hair with oil from amarula seeds.' Katie smiled in recollection. 'Once Pa made her very angry when he laughed at my many bracelets and told me I would make a very good heathen.'

As the wagon jolted across the river, Katie laid Nimrod on Charlotte's lap and pulled herself up to look over the edge of the wagon. Beyond the fever trees, the round huts with their pointed thatched roofs clustered together inside their courtyards just as they had in the time of the Old Man. On the other side of the meeting ground, the original church was falling into ruins but a new church towered up behind it. And further on where the hill sloped down to the Crocodile Pool, Pa's house remained as she remembered it, though no longer as neat as when Ma was alive. In front of it she saw Pa leaning on a stick, one hand shading his eyes as he watched the wagon coming. His hair was turning white and his shoulders were stooped, but though he had grown very old in the eight years since she had seen him, Katie knew him at once.

'I see you, Pa,' she screamed on the wind and, in spite of his age, he leapt up into the air when he heard her and waved his stick. He turned then, as if calling behind him, and immediately a woman in a grey-and-white striped dress appeared in the doorway.

'Is that Mary Ann?' Katie asked. 'She has grown so tall.'

'No, that's Pa's new wife.'

'He married again?' Katie looked down at her sister. 'No one told me. Why didn't you write me a letter?'

'I meant to, but I forgot.'

'Who is she?'

Charlotte's face grew sullen. 'She's related to Phillip's wife.'

'And you don't like her?'

'She's very good to Mary Ann.'

'Where's Mary Ann? I don't see her anywhere.'

'No one sees Mary Ann.'

'Why?'

'Ssh.' Charlotte looked around at the other passengers in the wagon. 'I'll tell you later.' As the wagon splashed through the river, Katie wondered uneasily why Charlotte would not speak of Mary Ann. Then suddenly Pa was peering over the wagon's edge.

'Malubisi! My little Malubisi.'

'Yes, Pa,' said Katie reaching for her suitcase.

Charlotte grabbed it first. 'You'll stay in my school. Everything is ready for you there.'

'Yes, you must stay with your senior sister,' Pa said quietly. 'It is no longer easy in my house. I have no visitors now.' The pain in his voice was like a knife at Katie's throat, preventing speech. She could only stare, bewildered, into his face. His eyes were sad like those of a man who has suffered long and knows no end to his misery. Beyond him Katie glimpsed again a flutter of grey and white, but the woman who was his new wife did not leave her veranda to come and greet her. Katie thought it very strange. But stranger still was the absence of her baby sister, Mary Ann.

Charlotte and Katie had no time to talk privately that afternoon. On the dancing ground people were already gathering round the fire. Ramokgopa was there with all his twenty-eight wives and many children, and Moihabo, grandfather's baby wife, who was properly married again with cattle in Pa's herd to prove it. Pa's brother was there, and Fika and Lithalo, and many others she remembered, and some she did not know. But for all her joy at seeing them, she fell asleep before the dancing and feasting began, and Charlotte and Moihabo between them had to guide her feet to the school and roll out her sleeping mat for her.

For three days she slept, waking only long enough to nurse Nimrod, then falling asleep again while Charlotte carried him around on her back or rocked him into silence. On the fourth day Katie felt like herself again and sat in the sun with her baby while Charlotte's two children played nearby. In the afternoon Pa came with packets of letters from her brothers. John was still in America. He had married a black woman and settled down in Chicago. He said he would never come back to Africa to be bossed around by the Boers. Phillip was a shoemaker in Johannesburg with a Zulu wife and four children. Henry was working on a farm in Blinkwater. Pa nodded with satisfaction when Katie handed back the letters. He was proud of his sons. He did not mention his new wife or Mary Ann. Charlotte did not mention them either, and talked instead of her school, until at last Katie grew tired of waiting and asked her straight what the trouble was in Pa's house.

'No trouble,' Charlotte said.

'Something is wrong,' Katie insisted. 'Is it his new wife?'

'No, she's a good woman, but—' Charlotte hesitated and then went on with a rush. 'If she was just a visitor I wouldn't mind, and I know that Ma liked Makanya. She wrote and told me that he wasn't like those other Zulus, because Christianity had softened him. But she never lost her hatred for his people.'

'You mean Pa's wife is Zulu?' Katie asked.

'Yes, she's related to Phillip's wife.'

'But if she's Christian?'

'I told you she's a good woman; but still it doesn't seem right for her to take Ma's place.' Charlotte sounded confused and hurt. Then suddenly she was again the senior sister. 'Come, the fire's low and it's time to start the porridge.'

She went down to the river for water while Katie gathered wood and built the fire. They did not talk again until the food was cooking. Then Katie asked why Pa had no visitors in his house.

'Because of Mary Ann,' Charlotte said.

'But what's wrong with Mary Ann?'

Charlotte looked with surprise at Katie. 'What's wrong? Her sickness.'

'I didn't know she was sick.'

'She's been sick for a long time. For nine years.'

'No one told me.'

'I thought you knew.'

'She was sickly that time I came to visit when Samuel was still small, but lots of people have sores. I just thought she'd get better.'

'She got worse. Pa says it was Mr Davidson's muti given at the time of the smallpox when he vaccinated everyone. He made his own muti from the sores of those who were already sick.'

'But even if she got the smallpox, it would not last so long,' Katie said.

'It's not the smallpox. It's the German pox.'

'You mean syphilis?'

'Yes. After Ma died, Pa took her to a doctor in Pietersburg who scolded her so much that she became ashamed.'

'How could she get syphilis? She was only a child, not yet nine.'

'All I know is what Pa tells me. All the time she hides in her room. Now she has no nose. Even though she ties a cloth around her face, no one wants to look at her.'

'Then I must take her to the Doctor to be cured.'

'It's no use.'

'But she can be cured. I know it. In Durban we've had patients with syphilis, and the Doctor cured them with his own muti. He makes it out of potassium and mercury.'

'She won't go.'

'Then I must persuade her.'

The next morning Katie went to Pa's house. He had already gone out and his new wife stood in the doorway, refusing to let her in.

'But I want to see Mary Ann,' Katie said.

'Leave her in peace,' the woman said, and shut the door.

Katie started back down the path but soon stepped behind some bushes. When the new wife lifted her water pot to her head and made her way towards the river, Katie ran quickly into the house and knocked on the door of the bedroom she had shared with Mary Ann so many years ago.

There was only silence.

'Mary Ann,' she called out. When there was no answer she pushed at the latch and stepped inside. Mary Ann was crouched on her sleeping mat, her crochet-hook in her hand and lace spread out around her. Her grey dress was clean and neatly mended, and a white cloth was tied around her face. Her beautiful big eyes looked up, startled.

'It's only me – Katie. I come to greet you.'

Mary Ann stared at her, eyes glistening with tears. 'You shouldn't have come.'

'Why not?'

Suddenly she jumped to her feet, dropping her crochet-hook and her lace, and ran to the corner of the room, facing the wall.

'Go away. Don't look at me.'

'Why shouldn't I look? I know you're sick. But I'm a nurse now and I've seen some very bad sickness. Why should I be afraid to see you?'

'Look then,' she cried out in wild despair, whirling around and ripping the cloth from her face.

Poor child! She looked much worse than Katie had expected. Instead of a nose she had only two small holes in the middle of her face, and about these an ugly, stinking pus oozed from scab-encrusted sores. It was only the stark anguish in her dark eyes that kept Katie from shrinking away. 'Yes, your sickness is very bad,' she said, forcing herself to speak calmly, 'but the doctor I work for in Durban can cure you.'

She spoke too quickly. The word 'doctor' frightened Mary Ann into anger and her voice rose. 'You've no right to come here, to interfere with me. Get out! Leave me alone.' She picked up a chair and raised it above her head, starting towards Katie like a crazed person.

But Pa's new wife must have returned and heard her, because she reached through the door and pulled Katie back into the dining-room, then went herself to take the chair away from Mary Ann.

'Cover your face,' she said, 'and go back to your crocheting.'

'I don't want to crochet.'

'Then rest. I'll get you food.'

'I don't want any food.' Mary Ann threw herself down on her sleeping mat, sobbing hysterically and pounding her fists on the floor while Pa's wife picked up the crochet-hook and wound the scattered lace carefully round a flat piece of wood. She looked very tired.

'You had better go now,' she told Katie.

The next day Katie returned. This time she did not try to see Mary Ann but waited on the veranda until Pa came back. She told him then that she wanted to take Mary Ann back to Durban with her to see the Doctor.

'It's no use,' he sighed.

'But it is. This doctor is not like other white doctors. He never scolds when someone is sick. Once a woman came to him with a big lump on her face which made her look very funny, and he put her to sleep and took it away, so that she now looks like a real person. Today she is married and brings her children to us when they are sick.'

'Durban's too far. Mary Ann's afraid. She won't go.'

'Then you must give her courage.' But Pa only smiled sadly and shook his head. Every day Katie went back to talk to Pa, raising her voice so that Mary Ann could hear when she spoke of Ntotisa whose leg had rotted away and had to be cut off. 'But the Doctor got her a wonderful wooden foot with an ankle that bends, and now she runs everywhere.'

On the fourth day, Mary Ann called to her softly from behind her door. 'Katie? Can this doctor also get me a wooden nose?'

'I don't know. We'll have to ask him.'

'Then write him a letter.'

'That isn't any good. He won't say unless he examines you first.'

'Oh,' she wailed, and in a moment Katie heard again the wild sobbing in her room.

'Why do you keep worrying her?' Pa's wife broke in. 'She's very difficult. Since you came, she no longer sits quietly crocheting but walks around her room crying and banging on the wall. I don't know what to do with her.'

'Then let me take her,' Katie said.

'It's no use,' Pa repeated.

'Why does everyone say it's no use? You say it. Charlotte says it. Everyone. But none of you know the Doctor. And I am telling you he can cure her. But you don't believe me. You never believe me. Only Charlotte. When Charlotte said she'd go to America, you believed, because you had faith.' Katie paused, choosing her words with great care. 'When I was a child you always used to tell me that God works in mysterious ways; now you forget your own teaching. Why else did I go to Natal? Why else did the Doctor call me to be his interpreter and then give me this long holiday so I could come to visit? Because it was God's will, and it's His will that I take her.'

'But what if she isn't cured?'

'He'll cure her. It will take a long time but he will cure her.'

Pa hesitated, frowning down at the floor and clasping and unclasping his hands.

'And he will give her a nose,' Katie added recklessly.

'Very well,' he said at last. 'If she's willing, she can go.'

Katie turned to Charlotte. 'If Ma were here, she would say Mary Ann should go.'

Charlotte stared out the window, biting her lip. Then suddenly she nodded. 'Ma would have sent her.'

'And when she's cured, she can come back here and help in your school—'

Charlotte lifted up her chin and began to laugh. 'And if she isn't cured, will you come back to take her place?'

Charlotte was a clever one, Katie thought. She was like an elephant who doesn't die of just one broken rib. If she failed to get what she wanted on one day, she worked to get it on another.

'I'd have to ask my husband. If he would agree to leave his homeplace again, then I would come.'

'You promise? And no tricks?'

'I promise, Charlotte.'

15

Durban

1906–1909

Katie and Mary Ann reached Durban early in the morning and went immediately to the dispensary. Katie took her sister round to the backyard where she would be safe from the curious eyes of other patients.

As soon as the Doctor arrived, he came out to the back steps to greet her. 'Elizabeth tells me you brought a patient all the way from Pietersburg.'

'My baby sister,' Katie replied.

Mary Ann did not object when Katie removed her clothes, but she began to fight as soon as Katie started to untie the cloth around her face. When the Doctor saw this, he told Katie she had better wait outside and call Elizabeth to take her place.

'No,' Mary Ann whispered, her dark eyes churning with fear.

'Then I'll have to take off your cloth,' Katie warned.

'Don't leave me.'

'If you fight with me, I will have to go.'

Mary Ann quietened down, clutching at Katie's hand as the Doctor examined her and afterwards reaching for the cloth even before she dressed herself.

'The syphilis is very bad,' the Doctor told Katie in English. 'It will take a long time.'

'We know that, Doctor, but she can live with me and I'll bring her every day for treatment.'

Mary Ann did not like to hear them talking in a language she did not understand. She just wanted to know when he would give her a nose.

'Not yet. Not until you are cured of your sickness,' Katie told her.

'But I want it now.'

'What's she saying?' the Doctor broke in, for Katie had answered her in Sotho.

'She wants to know when you will give her a nose.'

'She wants—Whatever gave her that idea?'

'I did,' Katie admitted reluctantly. 'I told her how you had given Ntotisa a wooden foot that bends so that she can run about. Now Mary Ann wants a wooden nose.'

'What!' The Doctor sounded angry.

'I promised you would cure her, Doctor. And she won't believe she is cured unless you give her a nose.'

'For the land's sake,' he said.

Mary Ann, alarmed by his frown and the redness of his face, cowered in her blanket. When he heard her whimper, the Doctor sat down heavily at his desk and tried to smile.

'Mary Ann,' he said gently.

She looked at him, still frightened.

'Tell her, Katie, that it will be many weeks, many months before I can cure her sickness – if I can cure it.'

'Yes,' Mary Ann said when Katie translated his words, 'but when can I get my nose?'

The Doctor's sudden laughter boomed out and then, just as suddenly, he was quiet. *'Ubekezele,'* he said in his awkward Zulu, and when she shook her head in confusion, he turned to ask Katie how to say 'Have patience' in Sotho.

'Bawa palea,' Katie said.

'Bawa palea,' he repeated, looking at Mary Ann.

She giggled at his pronunciation while Katie stared at her in astonishment. In Soekmekaar she had been sullen, hopeless, angry, but never once had Katie heard her giggle like any other young girl or seen her beautiful eyes shining like sunlight on a pond.

That same afternoon Katie found a place for them to live in Warwick Avenue. Although she still wanted to hide herself, Mary Ann found a secret place behind the coal shed at the dispensary where she sat with her crocheting on sunny days. Every few weeks, however, she would ask the Doctor when he would find her a wooden nose. Always he would tell her gently *'Bawa palea',* and she would giggle again and correct his pronunciation until in time his words were not so clumsy. She had been in Durban almost a year to the day when the Doctor called Katie into his consulting room and pushed his box of biscuits across the desk.

'I want to talk to you about Mary Ann.'

'Yes, Doctor.'

'Her sores are all cured. The syphilis is under control. If she wants, she can go home.'

'She still wants a nose, Doctor.'

'That's what I'm afraid of. There's no such thing as a wooden nose. In my books I have read about surgeons who have built one out of bone and flesh—'

'Then you can do it also,' Katie said. 'Dr Bray and Dr Pearson will help you.'

'I don't know if we can or not. I've never seen it done. None of the doctors in the medical society here have seen it done either.'

'But your books will tell you.'

'It's not that easy. Even if I tried, it would take two, maybe three, operations and much pain for Mary Ann. And many scars on her face—'

'She won't mind the scars. Among my father's people many of the young girls are tattooed, and the young boys also. If she has scars of her own, she will think them marks of beauty.'

'Nevertheless, I feel it is better for her to go home now.'

'Go back to hiding in her room and waiting for death? No, Doctor. I promised her. And you can do it. I know you can.'

'But what if we fail?'

'You won't fail,' Katie said.

God would not let him fail, she kept telling herself while she listened to him discussing his plans with Dr Bray and Dr Pearson. They sat around his desk in the dispensary, looking at the books open in front of them and then at a skull which the Doctor held in his hand as he talked.

'It may work,' Dr Pearson said.

'If we're lucky,' Dr Bray added.

Mary Ann was very calm on the morning of the operation. Afterwards Katie sat by Mary Ann's bed while she came out from the anaesthetic, ready to hold her steady if she writhed in pain. But Mary Ann did not moan or grumble. When her mind was clear, she talked only of the time when she would look like other women.

Katie did not have the courage to watch when the bandages were taken off, and Mary Ann pushed the looking-glass away. 'Not until it's all finished,' she said.

A month after the second operation, the Doctor slowly began to unwind the bandages as Mrs McCord, Dr Bray, Dr Pearson and Katie watched. Mary Ann waited until all the bandages were off, then she opened her eyes and stared into the looking-glass, slowly twisting her head this way and that. Her nose was very fine, large and rounded at the end, and a little bit flattened by the nostrils.

As Mary Ann silently admired herself, Dr Bray could not contain himself.

'Well?' he said.

'What do you think, Mary Ann?' Dr Pearson said.

Still she did not speak. Mrs McCord was biting her lips and the Doctor waited quietly, not even a muscle in his face moving.

'Why don't you say something?' Katie burst out.

As though she had not heard, Mary Ann smiled, touched her nose gently with one finger, then suddenly clasped it with her hand and squeezed, twisted and pulled it until she was satisfied that indeed this new nose was a part of her face. Only then did she look up at the Doctor.

'I am beautiful,' she said proudly. 'Now I must have a new dress to match my nose.'

'We'll go to the stores this afternoon,' Katie said.

'No. Now. For too long the Doctor has told me *"Bawa palea."* I've no more patience left to wait before I walk on the streets without a cloth on my face.'

'But I've work to do,' Katie objected.

'Then I will go alone. I am not afraid to be seen. I can find the way.'

Mary Ann seemed so sure, walking down the street looking tall and dignified that Katie forgot about her temper.

Shortly before noon there was a great commotion at the door of the dispensary. Katie ran outside to find Mary Ann struggling against two big Zulu policemen.

'What are you doing, interfering with my sister?' Katie gasped to one of the men.

'Hawu! Is she really your sister? She said she came from *uDokotela* but we didn't believe her. She's a crazy woman, I tell you; she picked up rocks this big—' (he stretched his fingers and held his hands apart) '—and threw them at a man in the street who had done nothing. When we tried to stop her, she grabbed my stick and hit me on the shoulder.'

'That man insulted me,' Mary Ann screamed.

'Stop this noise and tell me what happened,' Katie said.

'I was walking to the stores and a man insulted me. Me! Myself!'

'How?'

'He said he wanted to make love with me. But I'm a Christian girl. He had no right to speak of such things.'

'Oh, Mary Ann! He wasn't trying to insult you. That's just the way of men. You shouldn't have paid any attention.'

'But he had no right.' She began to struggle again. One of the policemen clenched his fist in a threatening gesture while the other looked to Katie for help. She thrust herself between them and took Mary Ann in her arms.

'Hush! Don't fight any more. Not while I'm here.'

At that moment the Doctor spoke, his voice full of authority. 'What's going on here?'

'It's Mary Ann, Doctor. She got herself in trouble. There was a man on the street— My sister's ignorant. Since she's been young, she's been hidden away. But now she walks so proud and beautiful, the men see her and call out. But she knows nothing about the ways of men. She thinks she has been insulted.'

The Doctor's lips twitched as though he was trying not to laugh. 'Mary Ann, hold out your arms so the handcuffs can be taken off. Now go into the waiting-room and stay there quietly.' Then he turned to the policemen. 'There's no need to report this. I'll be responsible for the girl. Katie, come into the consulting room. I have to talk to you.'

As she shut the door, he sat down behind the desk. 'Now! What are we going to do with Mary Ann.'

'I don't know, Doctor. It's no good for her to stay in town. She'll have to go back to Soekemaar.'

Katie arranged for Charlotte to come and fetch Mary Ann. She stayed for two weeks, visiting Ndeya, Samuel and Sagila.

Sometimes in the late afternoon Charlotte talked to the Doctor about America, and once he lent her some books to read while Katie was busy. One of the books was about David Livingstone, his missionary work and his explorations and how his heart was buried in Africa. But for once Charlotte was not interested in books. She wanted to sit out on the sand gossiping with the patients. 'I hear you are a very big person among these Zulus,' she told Katie before she left with Mary Ann.

'Yes,' Katie said, knowing at last that Charlotte no longer thought of her as just a junior sister but as a woman of equal importance to herself.

Katie named her seventh child Livingstone. When he grew up she wanted him to go to America and learn to become a doctor. There were already too many Zulu McCords running around on the hills of Natal, so she called him after that other missionary doctor who was buried in Westminster Abbey but whose heart remained in Africa.

Livingstone was an easy child as long as Katie carried him around on her back, but when Hamilton was born two years later, Livingstone grew very jealous. Left in the backyard with Nimrod, he kicked and screamed until Katie ran out to pick him up. The only way she could pacify him was to tie him to her back and leave Hamilton with Garnett's wife. But by the time he was three years old and Katie was expecting her ninth child, the Doctor told her firmly that she would either have to send him back to his father or have to find some woman to come during the day to care for him.

Then, Mrs Choudree, whose little girl had been cured by the Doctor, agreed to look after Livingstone. On Sundays he would push away the stew Katie made and ask for curry instead. He wanted to keep a dab of soot on his forehead to protect him from the evil eye. One night he spoke to Nimrod in Hindi. Nimrod looked at him blankly until Livingstone grew angry and raised his arm as though to strike out. Katie caught his wrist.

'Your brother doesn't understand, because you know things even I don't know. So you must teach us.' She asked him how Mrs Choudree said this or that, pretending he was a teacher and she, Sagila, Nimrod and Margaret were all his pupils. The other children soon tired of this game, but Livingstone liked being a teacher and every night he would come home with new words for Katie to learn. Before long, Katie heard those same words spoken by the Indians who came to see the Doctor, and in time she was speaking to them in their own language.

Livingstone was not Katie's only worry. Although Dr Bray and Dr

Pearson were helping to build up the missionary work, there were other doctors in Durban who were trying to tear it down. They not only wanted to interfere with the work of the dispensary, but also objected to the Doctor's new hospital on the Berea and tried to prevent him from opening it. For four years the Doctor had to fight them in the law courts. Because of all this, he often came late to the dispensary. The patients waiting on the sand would grow restless and begin to grumble while those in the cottage hospital kept calling out to ask where the Doctor had gone. Katie was often exhausted from running back and forth in her efforts to pacify them. Likewise she had no rest at home, where she was always trying to keep the peace among the children.

Ndeya had grown very thin with no wife to cook for him. She seldom saw Samuel because he no longer wanted to come to town with his father but only wanted to stay in the country with his friends. Sagila was now ready for the day school at Adams, and she would have to send him back to live with his father when the new term started. And the following year Margaret would be ready for the girls' school in Umzumbe. In the evenings she had no one to help her keep Livingstone and Nimrod apart or help her with the two youngest boys.

And then, after six years of earning nothing from his store in the country, Ndeya decided to return to Johannesburg. Some of his friends had gone back and told him there were plenty of jobs on the mines.

'We'll send Samuel to Mr Dube's boarding school at Ohlange,' he said. 'And Sagila will come back here to live with you.'

But her two rooms in Warwick Avenue were much too crowded. Margaret and Katie slept in one while Sagila, Nimrod, Livingstone, Hamilton and Clifford slept in the other. There was barely enough space for all the boys to lie down. They were constantly shoving and pushing one other. They needed a bigger place, but the only way Katie could afford this was to take Samuel out of boarding school.

While she was still wondering what to do, the Doctor came very early one day to the dispensary, his blue eyes fired with excitement and the creases of worry on his forehead smoothed away.

'Katie, how would you like to live on a farm?' he asked.

'You mean we're moving back to Adams?'

His laughter boomed out and shook the walls. 'No, but I've rented a farm in Sydenham. There are houses on it; one for you and one for Garnett.'

'How much money?' she asked him cautiously.

'It won't cost you anything.'

'How can this be?'

The Doctor laughed again. 'It's a big joke, but not on us. The court has finally given me permission to finish my new hospital, and the Town Council can't prevent me. They can only deny me proper sewerage. Just in case they try to do this, I've rented this farm where all the refuse and garbage can be buried at night. It's a big place – four acres – with all kinds of fruit trees, and plenty of room for a vegetable garden.'

'How soon can we live there?' Katie asked eagerly.

'As soon as you like.'

The feel of the earth between her fingers and the smell of growing plants had always eased Katie's heart in times of trouble or loneliness. And she was still having trouble with Livingstone. With the money she saved in rent, she was able to hire a woman to come and stay with Nimrod, Hamilton and Clifford while Sagila and Margaret were in school, but she still had to take Livingstone down to stay with Mrs Choudree during the day. And when she took him home in the afternoon, she had to keep him separate from the other children.

Sagila and Margaret were a great help to her. While she and Livingstone planted her garden, they amused the three younger children, who seemed quite content with plenty of space to play in and no one shouting at them all the time to be quiet. Livingstone too seemed happy, trailing after her as she planted the seeds of carrots, spinach, green beans, mealies and pumpkins, and digging holes for the tubers and cuttings which the Doctor gave her from his own flower garden.

Livingstone was the cleverest of all her children. In the evenings, when Hamilton and Clifford were asleep, the older children worked on their lessons and Katie began teaching Nimrod his letters and numbers. But Livingstone kept interrupting until she bought him a slate as well.

'Livingstone is younger but he knows his numbers best,' she wrote to Ndeya. 'Already he is trying to read Margaret's school books. When we send him to America, he will do very well in his studies and come back a fine doctor.'

At night when all their work was done, she would tell the children stories about their ancestors, about the grandfather in Blinkwater and the old, old woman with the yellowed bone showing in her head, and about Ndeya's father's brother, Mtambo, chief of all the Makanyas. 'You must always remember the names of those who have gone before,' she taught them. 'Because a man's spirit lives on only so long as his children and his children's children remember his name and sing his praises.' Sometimes she spoke to them of her years in London and the wondrous things she had seen, and she taught them the songs English people liked to hear and the hymns she had learned as a child in Uitenhage. And she spoke to them of their father's friend, Mbambo. 'Whenever you hear the train's whistle, then you must sing praise-songs for Mbambo. Because he saved Samuel and me during the war between the white people.'

She thought of Mbambo often on summer evenings after the children were settled on their sleeping mats and as she sat quietly looking out at the petunias, carnations, dahlias and cannas, their blossoms shining in the moonlight. Sometimes it seemed to her that she could hear his voice in the rustle of the wind among the bamboo or the boom of his laughter in the sudden thunderstorms. On that farm in Sydenham she felt his presence with her, protecting her and the children.

In March 1909 the Doctor opened his new hospital on the hill overlooking the town of Durban. He called it his Mission Nursing Home. He needed Garnett there to help with the male patients and supervise the workers, but Katie never had much to do with the new hospital. Her job was down at the dispensary. This was not easy without Garnett. The Doctor hired one man after another to take his place but none of them were satisfactory until Mpandlana persuaded the Doctor to let him come.

Katie had known Mpandlana a long time. Although he was born in Zululand, he said the dispensary was his home and he called the Doctor *uBaba*, or 'father'. As a child he had suffered much from ear infections but somehow he had heard about the Doctor, and while still very young he had walked more than a hundred miles to the dispensary. The Doctor had operated on his ears three times in the old cottage hospital, and in-between operations put him to work washing bottles and running errands.

Once he began working at the dispensary, Katie was able to spend all her time with the patients, interpreting for the Doctor, and going with him when he was called out on emergencies. Now that Livingstone was staying with Mrs Choudree and all her other children were safe on the farm, Katie had no more worries, and was looking forward to Samuel coming home for his holidays.

On the afternoon of his arrival she killed a rooster and was busy cooking a big feast. If little Clifford was already sickening, she did not notice. That night she stayed up so late listening to Samuel talk that in the morning she slept too long and had to leave the farm in a hurry to get down to the dispensary on time.

At two o'clock when the patients were almost finished, an Indian from Clairwood came to say he thought his wife was dying. The Doctor and Katie went immediately. It was almost half past five when they returned to Beatrice Street. Sagila was waiting anxiously on the steps.

'What's the matter?' Katie called out as soon as she saw him.

'Clifford's very sick and Samuel needs you.'

The Doctor knew that Samuel did not frighten easily and he was already pulling a sixpence out of his pocket. 'Sagila, run to catch the tram. Tell Samuel to bring Clifford to the hospital right away. Your mother and I will meet him there.'

It was no use for Katie to try and follow Sagila. She was too fat to run quickly and too impatient to wait for another tram. Instead, she half-walked, half-ran up that long Berea hill. The Doctor passed her, his long legs pushing hard on the pedals of his bicycle. By the time she reached the hospital he was already taking swabs of her baby's throat.

'We'll have to do a tracheotomy,' he was telling Mrs McCord.

But it was too late. Little Clifford died of diphtheria while the Doctor was still scrubbing his arms and hands. None of the other children sickened but the Doctor told Katie they would all be kept in quarantine for several weeks. Katie was not even permitted to attend the funeral. Ndeya came down from Johannesburg and it was he who buried Clifford. Afterwards he came and talked to her across the fence, but according to custom he dared not open the gate. That night he returned to his job on the mines.

Strangely, it was Livingstone who mourned the longest, sometimes waking in the night to call out Clifford's name and never quieting until Katie rocked him back to sleep. In the mornings she was too tired to cook or wash or hoe the ground. Some days she was too tired to dress herself, and only wanted to lie on her bed or sit in her rocking-chair doing nothing.

The Doctor came every few days to swab their throats, and always brought her something – a bunch of flowers from his garden, toys for the children, a bag of toffees. He tried to comfort Katie with words, but she would not be comforted. What did he know of grief? It was her child, not his, who had been sacrificed for the work. After he left she would still sit there on her porch, letting his flowers wilt in her lap and tossing his sweets aside, which the children came to pick up.

'Please, Mama, eat,' Margaret would say as she pushed a piece of toffee into Katie's mouth. 'Please, Mama, drink,' she would say again as she held out a cup of hot tea.

One night when Livingstone was crying, Katie rocked him back to sleep, then laid him on his mat. But as she turned in the dark, she stumbled and fell, hitting her face against the jagged edge of a tin can left on the floor. Margaret heard her fall, ran in from their bedroom and lit a candle.

'Please, Mama,' she whispered, 'you've cut your cheek. Let me wash out the blood with disinfectant.'

The next morning Margaret washed her face again, and in the afternoon when the Doctor came to swab their throats, she ran out to meet him at the gate. They spoke together for a moment and then walked back to the porch.

'Katie, you've got to pull yourself together. Look how thin Margaret is from tending the other children and waiting on you as well. She's only a child. If you don't look out, she'll be sick from weariness,' the Doctor said.

For a moment Katie was altogether confused. It was not the Doctor's voice she heard but another voice from another time when another child had died.

'She tells me you've cut your cheek. Here, let me see.' The Doctor leaned down and lifted Katie's chin up. She stared up at him, bewildered and stupid. At last, like one of his patients slowly coming out from under the ether, she saw the tired lines around his mouth. It came to her then that he too, in his own way, had mourned the death of Clifford. Yet how could he have known when he took her off to see the Indian woman that he was also taking her away from her child's need?

Katie's lips moved thickly, 'I'm all right, Doctor.'

He thought she was speaking of the cut on her cheek. 'Yes, it should heal quickly. There's no infection, thanks to Margaret.'

'She's a good girl, Doctor. Don't worry about her any more. I'll see she gets some rest.'

He gripped her shoulder. 'And you too, Katie. We miss you at the dispensary, Mpandlana and I. We're just waiting for the quarantine to be lifted so you can come back to boss us around.'

16
Johannesburg
1909–1910

One Thursday morning about six months after Clifford's death, the Doctor did not reach the dispensary until almost half past twelve. He brushed past Katie without a greeting. He spent less time questioning the patients and hurried his examinations. Not once did he take his three minutes or stop for a cup of tea. Katie knew something must be wrong. When at last he motioned her to a chair and sat down behind his desk, he turned away to stare out of the window so that she could not see his face.

'Something is troubling you?' she asked tentatively.

'My father is dying,' he said abruptly.

'*Wo bandla,*' Katie said softly, sharing his sorrow.

'Mrs McCord and I are leaving for America next week with the children. I'm closing up the hospital and the dispensary.'

'Closing up the work?' Katie could not believe what she heard.

He turned back to look at her and she saw that his eyelids were red. 'Only for a year, Katie. Then I'll be back. But I want you to pass the word among the patients tomorrow. And tell Pastor Makanya to announce it in church on Sunday.'

'Yes, Doctor.'

'And now I must talk to Mpandlana.'

While she waited in the supply room, she thought about the other medical missionary at Adams, the one before the Doctor. He went back to America for one year but never returned. She thought of her brother John, who had gone to America and was still living in Chicago, and of Pastor Makanya's son who had gone to America and died in the snow. A year was a long time and America was far away.

Even on the last day, it was hard to believe the Doctor was really going. He arrived as usual at nine o'clock, put on his long white coat and began to examine the patients. When the last one was gone, he called to Mpandlana to help him pack. By the end of the afternoon, the bookcase hanging on the wall beside his desk was empty. The black notebook which usually lay open on top of his desk was put away. Even his framed certificates had been taken off the walls. Only boxes remained, all labelled, tied up and stacked in a corner. The dispensary was as neat and as tidy as a coffin.

For the last time he called Katie into his consulting room and handed her ten pounds. 'This should tide you over until you find another job.'

'I don't want another job, Doctor.'

'But I haven't the money to pay you while I'm gone, and you have to eat.'

'My husband will feed me. He makes good money on the mines in Johannesburg.'

'Then perhaps you'll find a good job up there. Here,' he pulled an envelope out of his coat pocket, 'I've written a reference for you to show.'

Katie took the money but left the envelope on the desk. 'I don't want to show it. I work only for you, Doctor, not for anyone else.'

He grinned suddenly. 'Take the reference anyway, just in case, and be sure to let Reverend Taylor know where you are so I can write and tell you when to open up the dispensary again. I'll leave the key with Mr Taylor.'

'Yes, Doctor.'

His heavy footsteps followed her into the supply room where he held out his hand to Mpandlana. 'You'll remember all I've taught you?'

'I'll remember, *uBaba*.'

'Then stay well.'

'Go –, go –,' Mpandlana cleared his throat. 'Go well.'

Then he reached for Katie's hand and held it for a moment. She felt the smooth skin of his scarred knuckles. 'You will come back, Doctor?'

'Of course.'

'Do you promise me?'

'Have I ever told you any lies?'

'No, Doctor.' She felt ashamed for doubting him, because he was not like those who went away and did not come back. 'I'll be waiting for you all the time.'

'Then stay well, Katie.'

'Go well, Doctor.'

He grabbed the handlebars of his bicycle, jumped on the saddle, and with one last wave of his arm, he pushed his feet down on the pedals and was gone from her sight.

Ndeya was waiting at Park Station when Katie and the children arrived in Johannesburg. In their excitement at seeing him, the children gave Katie no chance to greet her husband. She and Ndeya just smiled at each other, knowing that for a whole year they would be together.

Out on the streets, Katie marvelled at the changes in the city. Electric trams had taken the place of the horse-drawn buses; the main streets were tarred; four- and five-storey buildings rose up in the centre of the town. Most startling of all was the presence of Chinese people everywhere, some dressed in plain blue smocks, others in rich brocades, but all of them with pigtails down their backs and talking a strange language in high-pitched voices.

'Who are these people? Where did they come from?' she asked Ndeya.

'From China. After the Boer War the government brought them to work in the mines, but they're all being sent back, because the war is long over.'

There were also changes on the mines. Large compounds to house the workers had been built, some for single men and some for those who wanted their families with them. Ndeya felt very lucky because the superintendent in his compound had assigned him a place in the married quarters.

Katie did not feel so lucky. They had only one small room about twelve feet square. After Ndeya moved in his furniture – a narrow bed, one table with a paraffin stove on top and two chairs – there was hardly enough room for them all to crowd inside. There was no space in the room for her to curtain off a corner where she and Margaret could wash themselves and dress in privacy. 'Even in the heathen kraals there are separate huts for boys and girls,' she complained. 'We need two rooms.'

'We're lucky to have any place at all,' Ndeya said.

In the morning she grew even more discouraged. The building was old and infested with bedbugs. No matter how hard she scrubbed with Jeyes Fluid, the bedbugs came up from beneath the floor and out of the walls. Moreover, in spite of all the people living in the compounds, there was only one tap for water in the middle of the yard; all day long, even in the rain, there was a long queue of children and women waiting with their buckets. Then, too, Ndeya had forgotten to tell her there was no school in the compound. Katie did not like to have Sagila walking alone on the streets outside. At the end of the first week she sent him back to Pastor Makanya with a letter and five of the ten pounds the Doctor had given her. As soon as the new term started, he was to go to boarding school with Samuel.

While Hamilton napped, Katie tried to teach Margaret, Nimrod and Livingstone, but they were distracted when they heard other children playing in the bare, dusty yard. Katie did not blame them. She, too, needed to escape from the tiny room and would sit outside with her neighbours until a rising wind, gritted with mine dust and fouled by the stench from the public lavatories, drove them indoors. During the first rains, water dripped through the roof, forming puddles on the floor.

'You must tell the superintendent to fix the roof,' Katie said in despair.

'We can put a bucket to catch the drips,' Ndeya replied. 'If I ask to have it fixed, the superintendent will say there's no money.'

'No money! With all this gold under the ground? If the mine-owners want us to live in compounds, they should build us a place where we can live properly.'

But Ndeya was afraid to complain. Katie had to go herself.

The superintendent was a white man with a potato face and eyes as brown and as flat as the bedbugs which came out of their walls at night. He glared up at her from behind his table, his neck growing red and his eyes squeezing into slits of anger when she complained about the leaking roof. 'If you don't like it here, then go somewhere else. There are plenty of others waiting to take your place. Now get out.' When he stood up and lunged across the table, Katie backed away quickly. She felt defeated, helpless.

The mine compound was bad enough in the summer, but in winter the cold wind blew through the window and under the door. The paraffin stove gave out no warmth. The children began coughing and Katie herself was sick. Her bones ached and her right arm swelled to twice its normal size. At last she went to see the mine doctor. He told her she had rheumatism, rubbed her arm with antiphlogistine and tied it up in splints. Then he said she should go home, stay in bed and stop eating sugar. But how could she stay in bed with all those bedbugs? How could she go on living in a place that was not even fit for animals?

One morning when she woke up, her whole right side was paralysed. Ndeya called her brother Phillip, who had returned to Johannesburg after the war. Phillip came immediately, and he and Ndeya lifted up her bed and carried her all the way to Germiston to the house of her cousin David from Soekmekaar. David's wife was very kind. She kept Katie in bed, looked after her children and never grumbled about the extra work. But kind as she was, David's wife knew nothing about caring for the sick. Katie developed painful bed sores on her back and thighs. Yet she did not want to go to the government hospital because she had heard that conditions there were worse than at the Addington in Durban. Lying there in her bed, unable to move her body, she felt more and more desperate. What was the use of living if she could not care for her children or go back to the dispensary when the Doctor returned?

One night she dreamed about the old cottage hospital in Beatrice Street. She was running to find the tray of instruments to take to the Doctor in the operating room, but when she got there she saw that the patient on the operating table was herself. And in her dream the Doctor was holding out a bowl of *amasi*, and she was reaching out for the thickened curds of soured milk when she woke up.

For the first time in weeks she felt hungry. As soon as she heard David's wife moving around in the kitchen, she called out and asked for a bowl of *amasi*. For several weeks she refused to eat anything else. When Ndeya brought her a bag of toffees to cheer her up, she gave them all to the children. 'That mine doctor told me not to eat any sugar,' she reminded him and asked him to bring plenty of milk instead so that David's wife could make *amasi*. She began to feel better. The swelling in her arm gradually went down and she was able to move her shoulder and then her arm. For days she practised lifting her arms and bending her elbows. Slowly her strength returned and she was able to sit up and lean over to rub the muscles in her leg. As she learned to move again, her bed sores disappeared. One day she swung her legs over the edge of the bed and, with the help of David's wife, stood up for a few moments. Each day she could stand a little longer. Two weeks later when Ndeya came to visit, she was able to take a few steps by leaning on his shoulder. At last, with a strong stick in each hand, she was able to walk by herself.

Yet it almost seemed that as her own strength returned, little Hamilton weakened. He was too tired to play. Red spots appeared on his body. With the last of the money the Doctor had given her, Katie hired a rickshaw and took him to a doctor in Germiston, and then to another, and another. But none of their medicines cured him. At last, when she was strong enough to stand without her sticks, she heard of a doctor in Vereeniging whose medicines were known to be very strong. She took Hamilton there on the train. But it was already too late. He died of typhus in Vereeniging.

She wept when she buried Hamilton there among strangers. He was so little, so very much alone. But she had to leave him and return to her other children because she was afraid they too might sicken.

The city was a bad place for children. Charlotte, Ethel, Clifford, and now Hamilton had all died in the city. 'Who knows what will happen to Margaret, Livingstone and Nimrod if we stay in Johannesburg?' Katie asked Ndeya. 'I think we should go back to Adams and wait there until the Doctor returns.' Ndeya agreed. He, too, was afraid for the children. Moreover, with the money he had saved, he was ready to start a harness and shoemaking store across the road from Jeena's.

Katie reached Adams almost exactly one year after the Doctor had left for America. Much had happened in that time. She had known sickness and pain and the death of another child. But she had not forgotten her promise. She was still waiting to open up the dispensary for the Doctor.

17

Durban

1910–1917

Katie waited alone in the dispensary on the day the Doctor returned from America, knowing that after he had walked once around the new hospital he would hurry down to Beatrice Street. At about four o'clock she heard a distant clatter like hailstones on an iron roof. In her alarm she ran out to the front steps and looked up at the sky. There were no clouds. The clattering grew louder, became a roar. Suddenly the Doctor swerved round the corner of Cross Street on his new motorcycle. He jumped off, leapt up the steps and grabbed her hand.

'I knew you'd be here,' he said.

As she looked up into his face, the year of his absence dropped away. He was still the same except for a touch of grey in his black moustache – a great mountain of a man with blue eyes and earth-shaking laughter. They stood there, not knowing what to say, while in the road the people who lived in the neighbourhood gathered to call out his name and ask him questions.

'Hey,' he shouted out suddenly to three young boys who were stroking the shining metal of his motorcycle, 'don't fool around with that machine.' And then to Katie, 'Go on inside. I'll be with you in a minute.'

But it took him a long time to make his way through the crowd and wheel his motorcycle to the backyard. Katie already had a pot of tea ready when he came through the supply room and sat down behind his desk. 'It's good to be home again,' he said.

'Yes, Doctor.' Her voice was muffled by the happiness that filled her chest at hearing him call the dispensary 'home'. She thought briefly of the Old Man who had slaughtered an ox when Pa returned to Soekmekaar. She thought of Pa, who had also slaughtered an ox when she took Nimrod to visit him and Charlotte. She wished she had an ox. But all she had to celebrate the Doctor's return was a tin of Baumann's Biscuits which she had bought for him with her own money.

'It's in the bottom drawer of your desk,' she said shyly.

He reached down and brought out the tin. 'Thank you. This is better than any feast.' Katie smiled happily.

In a few weeks it seemed as if the Doctor had never been away. The patients returned to sit out in the sun or crowded into the waiting-room to escape from the rain. Mpandlana returned and found a man to help with the cleaning. Occasionally Dr Bray or Dr Pearson dropped in to visit the Doctor, and every few weeks Thlambesine appeared from beyond Pinetown with those of his patients he could not cure.

But there was one big difference in their work: that motorcycle! It was easier now for the Doctor to drive out into the country to see some patient too sick to walk or be carried to the railway station. But Katie hated it. The Doctor always drove very fast, laughing into the wind as though exhilarated by the speed and power of his machine, never noticing that Katie winced every time he jounced over a pothole or moved her lips in prayer as he raced around a curve. Often when they reached their destination he could do nothing but settle the patient in the sidecar and drive back slowly and carefully to avoid any bumps. But Katie, perched on the pillion behind him with her arms around his waist, choked on the dust from the country roads and felt her muscles grow stiff from clamping her knees against the sides of the engine. Once she suggested he take one of the nurses from the hospital instead, but he just shook his head.

'They're too young and excitable. If this is an emergency, I'll need you with me.'

It was on one of those trips that Katie came to know Mr John Dube. She had seen him many times, a tall, imposing man who sometimes came to visit the Doctor at the dispensary, not as a patient but as a friend. Mr Dube, like Charlotte, had gone to America for his education. Both he and the Doctor had attended Oberlin College in Ohio, although at different times, and they often talked about it. When Mr Dube returned to Natal, he built an Industrial School at Ohlange, where Samuel and Sagila were both studying. He also started publishing a Zulu newspaper, *Ilanga lase Natal*, or the 'Natal Sun'.

On the day when the Doctor went out to Inanda mission station to vaccinate the girls in the boarding school, he took Katie as far as Ohlange to visit Samuel and Sagila. On the way back he stopped to vaccinate the boys in the Industrial School. While he was busy, Mr Dube talked to Katie about the Natives Land Act, a new law that took away freehold land from blacks outside the native reserves.

'Now that the Boers and the English have joined in one government, more and more laws will be passed against us. And we will have to protest against them – not as Zulus or Tsongas or Basotho or Xhosa, but as one people.'

'How can we do that?' Katie burst out. 'Even in our churches the people cannot agree, but break away into this congregation or that.'

'That's a problem,' Mr Dube replied, 'but some of us, not only from Natal but from the Cape and the Orange Free State as well, are coming together to form one organisation to fight against this Land Act. And you must help us.'

'How can I do that?'

'By reading my newspaper out loud to the patients who come to the dispensary,' he said.

It seemed very strange that John Dube, with all his learning and his newspaper and his deep thoughts about the government, needed her help. As soon as she read in *Ilanga* about the formation of the South African Native National Congress (later re-named the African National Congress) with John Dube as its first president, she moved among the patients in the early mornings to talk about the need for all people of all tribes to come together to work against unjust laws.

Then the Great War started in Europe and spilled over into Africa. Once again the Doctor joined the army. Every morning, as soon as he had finished at the dispensary, he went with Dr Bray and Dr Pearson to treat the wounded soldiers brought in on the ships from South West Africa and East Africa. After that, he still had his own work in the hospital.

Fewer and fewer patients were coming into town now. The Zulus in Natal remembered that other war when the white people had fought against each other. No one wanted to travel except those young men who were fooled by the army recruiters into going to France with the Native Labour Battalion. Katie was glad Ndeya never listened to the recruiters. He said he would not work for the army again until he was given the medals and extra pay he had been promised when he drove the ammunition cart for General Buller. But he heard that because of the war the pay was very good in Johannesburg. So he brought Margaret and Nimrod to Durban to live with Katie and Livingstone, and went back to work on the mines.

Although Katie still remained in the dispensary during the afternoon in case some patient came late, she was free to run next door to meetings in the American Board church, knowing that Mpandlana would call her if she was needed. She read John Dube's newspaper, talked with ministers and teachers about the Congress, and worked once more for the Temperance Movement. On her way home, she would stop and visit Mrs McCord, who once again was growing big with child.

She prayed constantly that Mrs McCord would have a son. It was good for young women to have daughters to please their husbands, but older women needed sons to take care of them in their old age. And she and Mrs McCord were growing old. They were both over forty!

Durban

1954

Katie picks up her microphone, hesitates, puts it down. She looks at me uneasily, hesitates again, and then lifts her chin defiantly.

'I was very disappointed when you were born. When I went up to the hospital to commiserate with Mrs McCord, I could not think what to say. I just blurted out, "All of us women are very sorry about this girl." Your mother asked me why, and I told her how we'd prayed she'd have a son.'

'But Auntie, that wasn't fair. I couldn't help—'

Katie laughs. 'Don't worry. Your mother wasn't sorry. She said she already had two sons to look after her when she was old, and she wanted a namesake. You were going to be christened Margaret, after her, because you were born almost on her birthday. But the Doctor always called you Peggy to avoid confusion.' *Katie laughs.* 'So then I said it didn't matter what they called you, because among our people your home-name would always be Ntombikanina – Girl of her Mother – since your mother was old, yet rejoiced at having a daughter.'

'But what about you? Did you still feel disappointed?'

She looks at me in surprise. 'How could that be? I named you.' *Now she laughs again until the rolls of flesh under her chin quiver and her eyes water.* 'But you were not as easy as my own children. Always into mischief! Once you buried John up to his neck in the sand and started preaching a funeral service over him. When I ran out to rescue him you complained bitterly. "I'm playing Pastor Makanya," you said. Another time you gathered up a lot of frogs and let them loose in the supply room. They leapt up on the tables and into the cupboards, and Mpandlana had a job catching them. He gave you a big scolding.'

'I thought Mpandlana was an old crosspatch.'

'You made much extra work for him.'

'Didn't he complain to my father?'

'No. I would not permit it. The Doctor was working too hard and I did not want to worry him.'

18

Durban

1917–1930

After America declared war on Germany in 1917, the Doctor told Katie and Mpandlana that he was closing up the work again and going back to the United States to join the American army.

'It's no good for you to do that,' Katie said.

Mpandlana thought only about the work. 'After you win the war, will you come back?'

'Of course.'

Mpandlana said he would find a job until the Doctor returned, and Katie went to join her husband in Johannesburg once more.

In lonely times each hour can be a month of waiting. Yet in the end the long years vanish into nothingness. It was difficult for Katie to recall the few years she spent in Johannesburg. She remembered the birth of her youngest son, John; the trouble she had with Nimrod running off to be a caddy on the golf course when he should have been in school; the praise-songs in honour of the seven hundred African men of the Labour Battalion who were drowned when the battleship *Mendi* was sunk by the Germans during the war; and her long talks with Charlotte, who moved to Johannesburg with her husband after the war and was working in the probation department of the Johannesburg courts. Most of all, she remembered the sound of Ndeya's coughing through those long cold winters, and her fear that he, like so many of her friends, would die in the influenza epidemic of 1918.

Yet, when the Doctor's letter came, all this seemed like the life of some other woman in some other time. She read his letter a second time, then realised it had been written months before. He must already be in Durban! She packed up her things, swung little John up on her hip, called Livingstone out of school and left on the train that same afternoon.

When she reached the dispensary early the next morning, Mpandlana dropped his measuring cups and greeted her with a big grin. 'Where have you been, Auntie? *UBaba* has been very much upset because you didn't come.'

'Just yesterday I got his letter.'

Mpandlana paid no attention. He was too busy babbling some nonsense about a motor car.

'*Hawu,* Mpandlana! Don't talk so fast.'

'But I'm telling you about the Doctor's motor car. It's the first Buick in South Africa – a big green one with little windows that button on the sides.'

Katie wasn't interested in motor cars. 'Tell me about the Doctor.'

Mpandlana hesitated. 'He's well, Auntie. You'll see.'

'And Mrs McCord?'

'She's well also.'

'And Dr Bray?'

Mpandlana shook his head. 'No more Dr Bray. He died of the 'flu.'

'*Wo bandla!*' Yet even as she grieved for that good man, she kept watching the road, only half-listening as Mpandlana chattered on.

Promptly at nine o'clock, the big green Buick turned the corner into Beatrice Street. Katie stood on the front steps, wiping her hands down the sides of her dress and trying to breathe in enough air to quieten the pounding in her chest. At last the car stopped almost in front of her, the door opened and the Doctor stepped heavily onto the sidewalk.

For one brief moment her heart almost stopped beating.

This big man coming up the steps towards her was a stranger with a white moustache and white streaks in his black hair, a stranger whose massive shoulders drooped and whose step was slow. Not until he reached for her hand and she felt again the strength of that skin-roughened thumb and those two fingers with the silky smoothness of the scars did she know the Doctor.

'Katie! At last! I was beginning to think you'd forgotten us.'

'Your letter only came yesterday. You shouldn't have sent it to Adams. You should have sent it to Mr Taylor, because he knew where I was.'

'Well, you're here now. That's all that matters.'

She laughed foolishly to hide her uneasiness with this old man. Perhaps he was still mourning his lost friend, she thought, and she grieved again for Dr Bray. 'Ah, Doctor, I'm sorry.'

'You've heard?'

'Mpandlana told me.'

He nodded, motioning her to follow him into the consulting room. As she started after him, she heard a clatter of high heels and a young white girl called out, 'Sorry I'm a bit late. I missed the tram.'

'Who's that?' Katie asked Mpandlana as she passed through the supply room.

'She's Miss Ball, *uBaba*'s secretary. She looks after the cash box and writes his letters and—' But Katie was already at the door of the consulting room, asking if she should call in the first patient.

The Doctor sat behind his desk, tipping his chair back against the wall.

'Not yet. We must talk first. How's the family?'

'All well. Ndeya's still working in Johannesburg. Nimrod's at Ohlange with Samuel and Sagila. He didn't like his school in Johannesburg so I sent him to the Catholic mission at Mariannhill. But he wanted to burn all my candles on holy days, and when he came home with a rosary I decided he should be with John Dube. Margaret's at the girls' school at Umzumbe. John's here with me. Just now he's with Mrs Choudree until I find a place for us to live.'

'And Livingstone?'

'Ah, Livingstone! He's also at Ohlange. John Dube says he's the cleverest of all my sons. I want him to go to America and learn how to be a doctor, because his name is Livingstone.'

'That may not be necessary. I'm planning to train doctors here.'

'Then he must learn from you. Now tell me about Bobby. When's he going to finish his medical school and come out here to help us?'

'Bobby won't be coming. He's not interested in medicine. Instead I'm bringing out another doctor – Dr Alan Taylor. He'll come next year.'

'Oh.' Katie fell silent. Bobby had always been her favourite of all the McCord children. It didn't seem right that he should stay in America when his father needed his help. But as she was thinking of Bobby, the Doctor spoke of his other son, William, and of Mrs McCord and baby Peggy.

'And Laura?' Katie asked.

The Doctor turned quickly to look out the window but not before she'd seen such sudden anguish on his face that she knew without his telling her that Laura was dead.

'Wo bandla,' she mourned.

He nodded, his head still turned away. After a moment he added in a voice so low she could hardly hear: 'And Jesse also. Of appendicitis.'

'Oh, no. Not Jesse too.' Katie stood there, helpless and silent, knowing no words in any language to ease the Doctor's suffering while he sat with his head turned away and his great body drooping like a plant which has gone without water for a long time. It seemed strange to her that this man, whose cleverness had saved many of her own people from pain and death, was no more able to save his own daughters than he'd been able to save her little Clifford those many years ago. She wanted to weep then for Clifford and Charlotte and Ethel and Hamilton, and also for Laura and Jesse. Yet when she needed her tears, they did not come and there was nothing to wash away the heaviness of her heart.

At last the Doctor pulled out a handkerchief to blow his nose. Then he glanced at Katie, his mouth firm under the white moustache.

'You had better call in the first patient.'

'Yes, Doctor.'

The Doctor was no longer the man she had known before. He was gentler. He smiled more often, and though he still told his little jokes, the sudden boom of his laughter was gone. And Katie, who had always known his thoughts without the telling of them, was sometimes confused by his silence.

Mrs McCord, too, was different. She worked very hard over the years that followed – raising money to build more wards for the hospital, visiting women in jail, planning new churches where they were needed, and travelling around the country to organise African girls into troops of Wayfarers, a branch of the Girl Guides. But always in the midst of her laughter and even in her moments of impatience, there still remained a shadow of grief behind her deep-set eyes. Although Katie never heard her speak again the names of her lost daughters, the knowledge of Jesse and Laura was there between them, like the blood of a common ancestor, for Katie, too, was a mother who had seen her children die.

Dr Alan Taylor arrived from America to help the Doctor in 1922. He was shorter than the Doctor and had no hair on top of his head. His face was round and pink, and he was full of jokes and quick to laugh – a soft rippling laughter very different from the Doctor's sudden boom. Mpandlana liked him immediately but Katie, disappointed still because Bobby McCord had not come, found much about this new doctor to displease her. He brought out instruments she had never seen before and then scolded when she did not know their names. Worst of all, he tried to make friends with the Europeans who had fought against the hospital in the early days, and she did not think this right. She was shocked when the Doctor announced that Dr Taylor would be taking charge in Beatrice Street.

'In charge? Here?' she asked.

'Yes. Our work has grown so big that I can't be here and up at the hospital as well.'

'But you've always said that we'd grow old together in this place.'

'In our work,' he corrected her.

The months passed, and Katie grew more used to Dr Taylor's ways. Then, a year later, Dr Morledge came out from America. The Doctor told Katie that it was important for him to understand the special ways in which the people spoke about diseases, and therefore he was keeping Dr Taylor up at the hospital and sending Dr Morledge down to Beatrice Street.

It was easy for Katie to get used to Dr Morledge. She liked him immediately. He reminded her of Dr Pearson because he was tall and thin and very serious. It was he who started giving her regular holidays and hired a woman to help with the laundry.

Still, with these two young doctors, it was never the same as the old days with just the Doctor, Mpandlana and Katie together, like a family with no secrets between them. She seldom saw the Doctor now.

After the Great War, Ndeya lost his job in Johannesburg. Once again he set up his harness-making store and opened their old house across the road from

Jeena's store. He took Margaret and John back to Adams with him. Margaret was now ready for the mission's teacher-training college and John for day school.

For the first time since she had come to Durban, Katie was without any of her children. To ease the loneliness of living by herself, she moved into the Native Women's Hostel, a boarding-house run by the Native Affairs Department. Life was much easier for her there. All her meals were prepared, and during the day her possessions were safe. The European matron, Mrs Bailey, was very friendly because she knew the Doctor. She treated Katie with respect and often called on her for advice whenever there was trouble at the hostel.

It was there that Katie came to know a group of younger, educated women. One of them, Violet Makanya, was related to Ndeya, and Katie had known her since she was a child. Violet was a slender girl with a lively, intelligent face. Like Charlotte, she too had gone to America to finish her education and had then come back to teach in the girls' school at Inanda mission. Now she was a social worker among the young people of Durban and organising secretary for the Purity League. She was friendly with all the American Board missionaries and moved with easy confidence among the Europeans who worked with Africans.

Her friend, Bertha Mkize, a big clumsy girl with a broad forehead and a loud raucous laugh, was altogether different. She spent her time reading newspapers – the *Natal Mercury, Ilanga lase Natal* or the African National Congress paper, *Abantu-Batho* – and then discussing what she had read to anyone who would listen. One night Bertha began talking about an American Negro called Marcus Garvey, who cursed the white people and said that Africa should be kept for the Africans and all whites should be chased away.

Katie was shocked. 'How's he going to do this? Dingane tried it. Cetshwayo tried it. Even Bambatha tried it. But they failed. So why does this foreigner think he can do what our own chiefs failed to do?'

'Because he knows what he knows,' Bertha said.

'He knows nothing,' Katie retorted.

Violet also knew of Marcus Garvey. 'Some of his ideas are good,' she told Katie, 'but some of the things he wants to do are a little bit crazy.'

'Bertha doesn't think so.'

'Oh Auntie, you know Bertha. She's too impatient.'

That was the trouble with Bertha. She wanted to change everything at once. She said it wasn't fair for black mineworkers in Johannesburg to lose their jobs when white soldiers came back from the war and paraded around the streets with banners calling for a 'White South Africa'. She said it wasn't fair for the Zulus who had gone to France with the Labour Battalion to be given none of the things they had been promised by the army recruiters.

Katie knew what she said was true. Thousands of Zulus like Ndeya had lost their jobs on the mines and were sent back home to look for work but could find none. There was also discontent among the men who had been to France and had grown used to being treated like real people. But back in their own country they were called 'boy' and ordered about like animals. Yet Katie did not believe that the laws could be changed as easily as Bertha seemed to think. Nevertheless, she listened to Bertha and Violet and their friends, and because she listened they thought her old and wise – she was over fifty then – and before long they started coming to her with all their problems. Bertha in particular used to come for advice. She was a very good teacher yet was often in trouble with the school inspectors from the Education Department.

In time Bertha, who for all her talk was very shy in front of white people, began speaking out more boldly. She grumbled about the rules at the hostel until Mrs Bailey called her cheeky; she sneered at John Dube for being a *hamba kahle* person. 'All those people in the African National Congress are too slow in fighting against the laws that hold us down. They just want to wait a bit in order to win the favour of the Europeans.'

'Yes,' Katie told her. 'John Dube doesn't rush about like a wild bull, frightening everyone. He looks for the right path, one that may be a long way round but will in time take him safely home.'

Bertha tossed her head. 'In time! I don't want to wait for your "in time," Auntie. I want to see our men gather to burn their passes and—'

'Do you want to see them beaten up and arrested? Stop talking this way, Bertha. I don't want to hear you say such things.'

One night Bertha came home after everyone else had gone to bed. From upstairs Katie could hear pounding on the front door, and then Mrs Bailey's angry voice. Immediately she went down to find out the trouble.

'You know the rules,' Mrs Bailey was telling Bertha. 'The door gets locked at half past ten. If you're late you have to remain outside.'

'That's not fair,' Bertha shouted. 'I pay my money every month—'

'*Thula,*' Katie told her sharply. Then to Mrs Bailey, 'Please, Matron, I'll see to it that she isn't late again.'

'Very well,' Mrs Bailey said. 'But I'll hold you responsible for her.'

Bertha was still angry when Katie took her upstairs. 'Why should Matron tell us when to come back. We're grown women—'

'Then you should act like a grown woman. What were you doing, running about on the streets until eleven o'clock at night? What would your mother and father say if I told them you were out so late?'

'I wasn't running about. I was at a meeting of the ICU.'

'What's this ICU? I don't know it,' Katie said.

'The Industrial and Commercial Workers' Union. There are branches in Cape Town, Port Elizabeth and Pretoria, and now Mr Champion is starting one here.'

'But you're a teacher, not a commercial worker.'

'That doesn't matter. Anyone can join. Women as well as men. I've joined,

Violet's joined. Many others. You must join also. Soon we'll have thousands
of workers, so many that the white people will have to listen to Mr
Champion. He's going to get our wages raised, abolish the pass system, get
our land back—'

'I don't know about this ICU,' Katie said slowly. 'But I do know about
Champion. When he was on the mines in Johannesburg, he worked with my
sister Charlotte on committees and things like that. But I don't think he
can—'

'But he can, Auntie. You should come to our meetings and listen to what
he says.'

'Perhaps when I am not too tired,' Katie said. She did not think much
more about the ICU until Champion came to the dispensary to ask the
Doctor for some medicine to help his indigestion.

He was a ponderous, slow-moving man with a pleasant smile. When he
heard that Katie was Charlotte's sister, his face lit up with friendliness. 'I
knew Charlotte Maxeke very well when I was in Johannesburg,' he said. 'We
used to help each other on the Joint Council. Perhaps you and I can help
each other as well. You know I've started a branch of the ICU?'

'I know. My friends have asked me to join, but I don't have the time.'

'It doesn't matter if you can't come to our meetings. It will be enough for
you to join and pay your dues. Then we will know you are with us.'

'But I am not altogether sure,' Katie said. 'I have heard some of your members say they want to chase all the white people out of Africa.'

Champion laughed. 'Mrs Makanya, you know that's impossible. I may be
an extremist but not that much of an extremist.'

'But what will you do with your ICU?'

'Help the workers. If a man loses his job or isn't properly paid, then I go to
his employer and try to put things right. In this way we will get the Europeans
to pay our people better wages. When the people understand this, then everyone will want to join us, and we'll be strong enough to fight against the pass
system.'

Katie did not believe that he could do all these things, but his promise to
fight against the pass system convinced her that she should pay her dues and
join the ICU. The pass system was a heavy burden on the backs of the people.
It was just as bad as in Johannesburg before the Boer War. A man had to have
a pass in order to look for work, another when he found a job, another when
he wanted to travel, and still another when he wanted to be out on the streets
after dark. A man had to have a pass for anything he wished to do, and in
order to get it, he had to wait in line at the pass office, sometimes for a whole
day. And every month he had to have it renewed. Even those men like Ndeya
or Dube who had been exempted by the government from having to carry a
pass could be stopped at any time and asked to show their exemption papers.
'So what good does it do to be exempted?' Katie had once asked Ndeya. 'You

still have to carry special papers.'

At that time the women did not have to carry passes. But soon rumours started to circulate that the Durban Town Council was going to pass a law requiring women to have passes too.

'Are you going to carry a pass?' Violet Makanya asked Katie one night while they were eating their dinner at the hostel.

'No,' Katie said. 'I'll refuse. I always have. Because this isn't the first time. Long ago, before the Great War, we were told to buy our passes. But this was one matter on which all of us women agreed. Christian and heathen, educated and ignorant, we all refused. And because we were many, the police could not arrest us all. Therefore the government forgot about that nonsense. So now if they try to make us carry those silly slips of paper, I'll just refuse again.'

Violet looked around at her friends among the younger, educated women who were also living at the hostel. 'You see? I told you Auntie would refuse.'

'This time you'll be arrested,' Bertha interrupted. 'There are more jails now. Big ones!'

Katie shook her head. 'Not big enough to hold all of us who live here in town. If these rumours are true, then we have to protest. We should start making our plans now and spread the word in the churches, the market, the streets, the shops along Grey Street—'

'And at our ICU meetings,' Violet interrupted eagerly.

'Yes,' Katie said. 'Everywhere. And when the Town Council has its next meeting, all of us women will come together and march down to the Town Hall—'

'Will you lead this march, Auntie?' Bertha's words were more of a challenge than a question.

'Yes,' Katie said quietly. 'If you want me to, I will lead it.'

Katie thought the Doctor would be pleased when she walked up the steep Berea hill to talk with him and Mrs McCord about her plans. She did not think he would object. But when she told him she was going to lead the protest march, he shook his head. 'For the land's sakes, Katie! You'll only get tossed in jail.'

'But there are many of us. The jails aren't big enough.'

'That's just the point. It's the leaders who'll be arrested. And your first duty is to the dispensary. How can you help Dr Morledge if you're in prison?'

'But I've promised Violet and Bertha and all the others.'

'Then you'll have to unpromise them.'

Katie looked at him in dismay. She could not disappoint those girls but neither could she disobey the Doctor.

'How can I do that? Everyone's expecting me. If I'm not there to lead them, some of the women will think I am too frightened, and that will make them frightened as well.'

The Doctor creased his forehead and opened his lips as though to forbid her again, but before he spoke Mrs McCord broke in. 'James, I think a peaceful protest march is an excellent idea.' And to Katie, her grey eyes flashing with determination, 'And the police wouldn't dare arrest a white woman for walking down the street. So I'll march beside you.'

Thus it was that Mrs McCord and Katie together led hundreds of women to the Town Hall in a march of defiance. The policemen rode on their horses, but when they saw Mrs McCord they did not arrest anyone. And in the Town Council all the talk about passes for women was forgotten.

Violet and Bertha thought Katie was very clever to bring Mrs McCord with her to keep them from being arrested.

'That's because I am a *hamba kahle* person,' Katie told Bertha. 'If Mrs McCord wasn't my friend and willing to help us, we'd all be sitting in jail tonight. Sometimes it's good to have European friends.'

Bertha shook her head. 'You yourself have told me that the people at Umsunduzi call Mrs McCord "Daughter of a Chief" and the Doctor "Brother in Law." So how can you say they are Europeans? It's only their skin that is white. Their hearts are black.'

Katie laughed at Bertha's cleverness in throwing her own words back at her. Bertha never liked to admit to any mistakes; but she was an intelligent young woman. Katie was confident that after the success of their march, Bertha would throw away the ideas of Marcus Garvey and become more of a *hamba kahle* person.

But she was mistaken. Once again Bertha returned to the hostel very late one night. Katie heard her banging on the door and rushed down to let her in before Mrs Bailey woke up with all the shouting.

Katie was very angry. 'Do you want to get me into trouble? I promised Mrs Bailey that you would not be late again. So the next time I see Mr Champion, I'll tell him you're still a child and have to be told when it's time to come home.'

'I'll come home when I'm ready,' Bertha said. 'Matron has no right to lock the doors against us.'

'She has every right. She's the boss of this hostel, and if you want to stay here, you have to obey her rules.'

Bertha was still sulking the next day. It was Violet who came and thanked Katie for keeping her friend out of trouble. And it was Violet who told her that Mr Kadalie, the President of all the many branches of the ICU, was coming down from Johannesburg to address members on Saturday afternoon. The time had come, Katie decided, for her to go to one of the meetings and hear for herself what Mr Champion and Mr Kadalie had to say.

It was after one o'clock by the time she closed the door of the dispensary, and close to two when she reached the meeting place. There were thousands of people milling around as she pushed her way through the crowd looking for Violet or Bertha or some other familiar face. Suddenly a roar of applause

sounded from the other end of the field, and everyone began to push forward
and stretch their necks to see Kadalie and Champion as they climbed up on a
wooden platform. Katie was not wearing her spectacles and could not get
close enough to see them clearly, but she could hear every word they spoke.
And she did not like what she heard.

'Even if the angel Gabriel comes down from heaven and tells me not to
walk on the sidewalk, I won't obey him. I'll kick him out of my way and walk
where I want to walk,' Kadalie shouted in English. Being a foreigner from
Nyasaland, he did not know the Zulu language and Champion had to translate for him.

Katie could not believe her ears. She never permitted anyone to speak
against her religion, and no man, white or black, had any right to say he
would kick an angel of God. She looked at Champion, waiting for him to
deny those words, but he only repeated them and then waited for Kadalie to
continue with his heathen talk. Yet while she stood there stupidly, disbeliev-
ing, the thousands of Zulus around her went mad with excitement. They
yelled and waved their arms and surged forward again until she thought she
must surely be squashed by all the bodies pressing against her from every
side. The wild eyes, heavy breathing, hot smell of oil and sweat sickened her:
she felt in her blood the terror of her old, old ancestor in the Cape warning
against the Zulus.

Katie turned around in a panic, pushed, shoved, scratched and fought her
way back through that crowd until at last she was free. Her dress was torn,
her headscarf untied, and one of her shoes was lost, yet she had no thought of
her appearance as she stumbled back to the hostel. She could not understand
this madness. How could these people listen to someone who said he would
kick an angel of God? How could Champion, who was friend to Charlotte,
repeat those words? How could Bertha and Violet listen to him? But they had
listened.

Bertha returned to the hostel first, her eyes triumphant. 'You came,
Auntie? You heard him?'

'I heard. I don't like your Kadalie. I won't have anything to do with a man
who thinks he can kick an angel of God. I'm not a member of your ICU any
more. I've torn up my ticket.'

'Oh, Auntie, you didn't!'

'I did. And I don't want to hear any more about this heathen. Not from
you or anyone else.'

Bertha's face blazed with fury. 'You're a coward. You're crawling like a
worm before the Europeans—'

'No one makes me crawl, Bertha. And I tell you this: I am what I am
because of the Doctor. So why should I listen when your Kadalie says he'll
drive a man like the Doctor onto the mailboat and send him away to
England? Why should I dam the river up until the waters flood over the

banks and make a big mess everywhere?'

'You talk like a clever woman but you're a fool. When the American Negroes come to help us, I myself will point you out.'

'Ha! Those Negroes aren't coming,' Katie said. 'They're not mad like you people in the ICU. Ask Violet. She knows.'

Violet tried to soothe Katie's anger. Even though she had heard Kadalie speak those words, she thought Katie was making a big fuss about nothing. 'He didn't exactly mean all those things, Auntie,' she said. 'He was just making a speech.'

'A wicked speech. If he didn't mean what he said, then he's telling lies.'

'Come, Violet. Leave the old fool alone,' Bertha said.

Katie had loved Bertha like her own daughter. She had loved Violet also. Now both girls had turned against her, and grief lay heavy in her stomach. But it was useless to try and reason with them. They thought of nothing but the ICU.

Violet continued with her social work but she broke with the missionaries of the American Board and discarded her European name. From that time on she used her home-name of Sibusisiwe Makanya.

Bertha gave up her teaching and hired a stall in the African market where she made dresses for sale. Katie heard from other women in the hostel that Bertha was earning more in this way than she had ever made as a teacher. But she was giving it all to Champion. All the members of the ICU were giving what they had to Champion. They even took their savings out of the post office for him to start some enterprise. Katie tried to warn them that they'd never see their money again, but they shouted *thula* at her and no longer sat to gossip with her in the evenings.

Bertha would not speak to her at all. But she spoke to all Katie's friends and told them that Katie was a no-good coward. She even talked to the Indians and they, too, began to look at Katie with suspicion. One of the Indian shopkeepers who had come many times to the dispensary over the years would no longer sell her anything. He told her bluntly that he would have nothing to do with someone who was an enemy of Champion.

Even at the dispensary some of the patients who worked in town looked at her with mistrust. It didn't matter that she had worked among them all those many years. It didn't matter that she was married to a Zulu and had borne him many children. Because of the ICU, these people were throwing her away.

In the middle of all these troubles, Samuel was married to Josephine Mkize, a nurse at Adams. Dr Morledge gave Katie four days off to attend the wedding. While she was gone there was a big to-do at the hostel. Some of the ICU members came home very late, and when Mrs Bailey refused to let them in, one of them broke a window and another hit Mrs Bailey on the shoulder. The police arrived and took the assailants off to jail. For some reason Bertha and Violet were not among them, but the next day they told everyone the fight was Mrs Bailey's fault and they promised that Mr Champion would soon get the women out of jail.

Champion did try very hard to help them. He even came to see Katie at the dispensary and asked if she would be a witness on their side. When she reminded him that she had been at Adams, he asked if she would testify that they were only fighting for their rights.

'What rights?' Katie asked. 'Mrs Bailey locked the doors at half past ten as she always does. Those women had no right to be roaming around at twelve o'clock or one o'clock at night. What would you think of a woman like myself coming home so late? You'd ask, What was she doing out on the streets so late?'

'Mrs Makanya, if you won't help us, you'll be sorry.'

After he went away, Katie felt uneasy. Champion was an important man; if he was against her she would find enemies wherever she went. However, he had no influence to get those women discharged. They were each fined two pounds and told that at the end of the month they would be kicked out of the hostel.

On the morning they were to leave, a hostel resident woke Katie up. 'Come and see,' she said. 'Those girls are going to Canaan. They're leaving Egypt for the land of milk and honey.' Katie was glad to see them go. Now, she thought, she would not have to bother her head about their politics.

Katie had not had time to talk to the Doctor about her troubles with Bertha and Violet. He was too busy planning his medical school. The first time she went up to the hospital after hearing Kadalie speak, the Doctor was away in Cape Town. The second time he was visiting the Principal of the South African Native College at Fort Hare. The third time he seemed very tired and discouraged, because he had had to give up his plan for training doctors when the government decided instead to send some of the best students at Fort Hare to a medical school in England. Dr Morledge announced he would go back to America. And the Doctor appointed Dr Taylor as superintendent at the hospital and came back himself to take charge at the dispensary. With all these changes taking place, she forgot about the ICU.

One morning, however, Bertha stopped at the dispensary on her way to the African market and warned Katie to be more careful in what she said about the ICU. 'You're making some of our members very angry,' she said.

'I'll say what I like,' Katie told her sharply. 'Anyway, I'm too busy with my Temperance Union to worry about this nonsense of the ICU.'

But a few days later her friend Mrs Mtetwa was badly frightened. Like Katie, she was short and round and very black. While she was waiting at her tram stop, a very fierce young man came running towards her with a stick raised in his hand as if to strike her.

'Mrs Makanya!' he called out.

'I'm not Mrs Makanya,' she told him. 'I'm Mrs Mtetwa.'

'Oh,' he said, eyeing her uncertainly. But he watched until he saw her catch the tram to Musgrave Road.

'If I hadn't told him who I was, I think he would have killed me,' Mrs Mtetwa told Katie that evening.

For several weeks Katie was very careful about walking to and from the dispensary when the streets were crowded. And in the afternoons when her work was finished, she returned immediately to the hostel and did not venture out again. But when she did not see the fierce young man anywhere, she began to wonder if Mrs Mtetwa had just imagined him. And she was growing tired of remaining in the hostel every evening and never seeing anyone but Mrs Bailey and the other boarders. One night she decided to attend a meeting of the Joint Council, a group of Europeans and Zulu leaders who met together once a month to discuss the grievances of black people. She knew the Doctor would be there with his motor car and take her back to the hostel.

Dr Taylor was also present that night, as well as Mr Evans from the Native Affairs Department, John Dube, his brother Charles, Mrs Sililo and her husband, and many others. Even Champion was there. During the meeting one of the workmen at the hospital came with a note calling the Doctor back to the Berea. He and Dr Taylor left immediately. Katie felt nervous without them, especially when Charles Dube stopped her at the door and told her to wait inside while he called a rickshaw. 'It's not safe for you to be out on the streets by yourself,' he said. He stayed close beside her until she climbed into the rickshaw. The rickshaw man started running, his long legs gaining speed and the little carriage swaying up and down. The night air felt cool on her face. She saw no one on the streets and felt very much relieved as she leaned back against the comfortable padded leather. She seldom spent money on a rickshaw; with her nervousness almost gone, she thought how pleasant it would be to have someone carry her like this everywhere she wanted to go. Like a young girl dreaming, she stared up at the sky, remembering the pale starlight on the hills at Amanzimtoti and longing foolishly for the old days when the Doctor was still at Adams and she never had to worry about the ICU.

Then, as the rickshaw crossed the bridge from Alice Street into Grey Street, she heard a sudden shout. Three dark figures jumped out into the road and shouted 'Stop'. The carriage dipped as the rickshaw man paused in his running. She leaned forward and screamed at him to run, run for his life.

'Stop!' one of the three figures called out.

'No, no! Go fast. Faster. They'll kill me if you stop,' she yelled.

The rickshaw man leapt forward again, swerving to one side so that the carriage tipped up on one of the big wheels. Katie threw her weight on the other side and the second wheel dropped back onto the road to take them safely across the bridge, past the men who were still yelling and running after them. But no one can run as fast as a good rickshaw man, and in a few minutes the shouts behind them faded away and only the pounding footsteps of the rickshaw man echoed from the ground.

In front of the hostel she stepped down and took out her purse to ask how much she owed. The rickshaw man was still gasping for breath while the sweat glistened on his face and oozed out from under his arms to stain his beaded shirt.

'I think ... one and sixpence?' he said at last, his words a question, because in distance he had not brought her far.

Katie handed him half a crown. It was all the money she had. When he fumbled for change, she shook her head. 'If I had more, I would give it. Because tonight you saved my life.'

'Did they really want to kill you?'

'Yes.'

'Hawu!' He shook his head in bewilderment, and because he was a good man, he waited until she was safely up the steps and through the door.

In the morning while she was dressing, she wondered how it was that Charles Dube had known she was in danger. Had someone warned him at the meeting of the Joint Council? Champion perhaps, because he himself was helpless and no longer able to control the hotheads? Or was Champion to blame? Katie did not know. But she could feel again the hot touch of her hatred of the ICU.

She was thoroughly frightened now and never went anywhere except to the dispensary and to meetings of her Temperance Union, for in spite of all her troubles she did not want to stop trying to educate people about the evils of drink.

Yet the ICU was spreading. Even Mpandlana could not help listening to their talk, and in time he too began to grow restless. One day he told Katie the Doctor should raise their wages.

'How can he do that?' she asked indignantly. 'If he pays us more he won't have enough left over to buy medicines, and without medicines to mix, you'll be out of a job.'

'He can get more money from America.'

'You're a stupid fool, Mpandlana. The Doctor educated you out of his own pocket. He paid for the lemonade and cakes at your wedding and gave you a big money present besides. And when your children were sick that time, he got in his motor car and went all the way to see them and didn't charge you one penny. And so I tell you – just be grateful that he pays you anything at all.'

For a time Mpandlana did not speak again of wanting more money. But he was young and he could not shut himself away from the talk of his friends. At last he was tempted by a Zulu herbalist who offered him fifteen pounds a month.

'It's so much money, Auntie,' he said. 'In my whole life I've never held fifteen pounds in my hands at one time.'

'Yes, it's much money. But this fountain is shooting up too fast. Pretty soon it will run dry. And after that, where will you be?'

'It won't run dry, Auntie. You'll see. This herbalist has a proper licence and he's very clever.'

'I don't want to hear about him. You're going to find yourself in big trouble if you go there. What do you know about native muti? Nothing! All you know is what the Doctor's taught you. So why does this herbalist offer you a job? Because he wants to steal the Doctor's prescriptions and do what he's not allowed to.'

Nevertheless, the money was too big a temptation. At last Mpandlana told the Doctor that unless his pay was raised, he would give in his notice and go to work for the herbalist. When he came out of the Doctor's office, his body was trembling and he told Katie he hadn't known the Doctor could be so angry. 'His eyes burned until I thought I was shrivelling up. And he did not speak. Just paid me off and told me to clear out. Today!'

Katie felt very sad as she watched him pick up his things from around the supply room – a few books, a pocket-knife the Doctor had given him one Christmas long ago, and the newspaper he had bought that morning. Then he stood for a moment gazing around at the bottles, powders and measures arranged neatly on his shelves, gazing as if he had never seen the room before and would never see it again. At last he turned quickly and started towards the Doctor's office. But halfway there he stopped, looked at the closed door for a long moment, and then turned back, his face dulled with grief.

'Stay well, Auntie.'

'Go well, Mpandlana.'

After he was gone it seemed a long time before the Doctor called Katie to bring him his tea. He was slumped back in his chair, his eyes bleak with disappointment. 'Did Mpandlana tell you? He's going to work for a – a –' (he hesitated as though he could not bring himself to say it) '—a herbalist.'

'He told me, Doctor.'

'For a herbalist, Katie! If he was going to work for another doctor, I could have been proud and wished him well and he would still have been my son. But a herbalist! A quack! Worse than your heathen *inyangas*, because they're licensed by the government. All these years I've been fighting them, and now Mpandlana—' He stopped and swallowed but could not go on.

'Only because of the money, Doctor. He'd never have left you except for this nonsense of the ICU and their talk, talk, talk about raising wages.'

'But a herbalist!' There was pain in the Doctor's voice but anger also. And Katie wanted to weep for them both, for this old white man who was feeling betrayed and that young black man who was already regretting his foolishness.

After Mpandlana left, Edward Jali was put in charge of the medicines. In his free time he was always too busy with his cricket and his soccer to bother his head about politics. He paid no attention to the rumours about Marcus Garvey sending a boatload of American Negroes to help the factory workers call a big strike.

As she moved among the patients at the dispensary, Katie laughed at such foolishness and tried to tell the people that this was altogether impossible. But one morning Thandekile Mgobhozi came running up to Katie as she turned into Beatrice Street.

'Auntie,' she cried out in great excitement, 'you know Doonside?'

'Yes, I know it.'

'Well, the Negroes are there. They came in airplanes last night. They dropped out of the sky with parachutes and all their belongings. And all night they worked, and this morning their houses are already built.'

'Hawu! What kind of miracle is this? I don't believe it. Who told you such a story?'

'The word's been passed. Today we're all on strike. No one's going to work until more money is promised. And the Negroes have come to help us.'

'Thandekile, you're crazy in the head. There aren't any Negroes in Doonside or airplanes or houses built in the night. You people are just greedy for war but don't want to fight yourselves. So you think these Negroes have come to fight and die for you instead.'

Nevertheless, the strike was called. Workers stayed away from the factories and stores and gathered to march around Leopold Street, down Grey Street, and into the ICU hall in Prince Edward Street, laughing, shouting, dancing and making a great noise. Some white men lost their tempers and tried to storm the hall but the members of the ICU fought back; then other Africans and whites joined in. As word of their battle was spread, the dockworkers stopped working to march up from the Point docks. When they arrived, the police opened fire. Six Zulus and two white men were killed in the fighting.

The strike brought misery. When the strikers wanted to go back to work, they found their jobs were already taken. Champion, however, kept telling them that if they would do as he said, he would soon put everything right. At his urging many men refused to pay their poll tax. Within a few weeks they were rounded up; and when people ran out to watch them being marched off to jail, the police threw teargas into the crowds.

At last the Zulus realised that the ICU was not going to send the whites away on their mailboats or wipe out the pass system or give back the freehold land. Those who had turned over all their money to Champion went looking for him. But their money was lost, and Champion, fearing their anger, hid himself in the house of a Native Commissioner before the courts sent him into exile for three years.

Durban
1954

This morning as I drive down to the hostel to pick Katie up and take her back to my apartment, I wonder if I should tell her that yesterday I interviewed Mr Champion.

I found him in his office, a stolid, heavy-set man with a slow ponderous manner. His grizzled hair was almost the same shade as his grey business suit, and a gold watch-chain hung loosely across his chest. As soon as I introduced myself as Dr McCord's daughter, he clapped his hands and bowed slightly in a traditional gesture of respect and then ushered me to a chair beside his desk. When I was seated, I asked him if he remembered Katie.

'I remember Mrs Makanya very well,' he told me. 'She helped me when I was raising money to feed the poor.'

'She helped you? But I was under the impression you were enemies.'

'No, no! We worked together on the Joint Council and things like that.'

'But when you were running the ICU here in Natal—'

'That was a long time ago.'

'—some of your followers tried to kill her. That's what she told me.'

He shook his head. 'It's true that some of our members were angry because she spoke out against us. But I was too busy to worry about such things. We had twenty thousand members here in Natal and more were signing up every day. I could not know them all. That was the trouble.' He slumped back in his chair with an expression of helplessness. 'The Communist Party sent down their agitators from Johannesburg to join with us and urge the workers to strike, to burn their passes and refuse to pay their poll taxes. When the police came, those agitators disappeared, and so the magistrate blamed me for all the rioting and violence. Did you know that in 1930 I was banished from Durban for three years?'

'Yes,' I said.

Champion was silent for a moment, his expression pained. 'While I was gone, there was much quarrelling among our members, and when I returned the ICU was almost finished. There were less than three hundred members left of all those thousands. The money from the membership dues was gone.

Nobody could find any work and people were starving. So I set up a soup kitchen.' He went on to list his efforts to help his people during the world-wide Depression of the thirties, and spoke proudly of his election to the Natives Representative Council and his years as President of the Natal branch of the ANC during the forties. He did not mention Katie again. By the time I left, I knew a great deal about Champion but very little about his relationship with Katie.

Now as I pull up in front of the hostel, I find Katie waiting impatiently on the sidewalk. As soon as she seats herself in the car, I admit that I have talked to Mr Champion.

'Did he tell you that we were friends?' She seemed amused. 'When the government let him come back, he was no longer running too fast. We were able to walk together.'

19

Durban

1930–1939

It was the time of the Great Depression. Bad times had come to South Africa. No one was asking for a rise now. Stores were shut up. Factories closed down. Even the rich whites were losing their jobs and could not pay their servants or even give them food. The people were starving.

'What we should do', Katie told her friend Mrs Sililo, 'is to form one organisation to help our women and children. In Johannesburg my sister Charlotte has started the Bantu Women's League. She says it is easier to persuade the white people to give to her League than to have them hand out money to this group or that. We need a League here in Durban also.'

Mrs Sililo agreed. Together they invited everyone they knew to a meeting; and after much discussion, the Bantu Women's Society was formed.

In such troubled times everyone had to work together. Katie even became friendly with Mr Champion when he returned to Durban in 1933. He came one afternoon to the dispensary and waited very politely until Katie was free before asking if she was still angry with him.

'No,' she said.

'Then will you help me? I've reorganised my ICU. It's no longer any use to ask for better wages. Our people are lucky to find any work at all. It's more important for us all to work together. So we must burn away the dead grass between us and let the new shoots grow.'

'Yes,' Katie said.

'Then will you ask the Doctor to see me?'

'Are you sick?'

'No. I want him to give a donation for our soup kitchen. I am starting this place where those who have no money can come to eat.'

Instead of giving money, the Doctor ordered a bag of mealies and a bag of beans to be delivered to Champion every week. Katie stopped just once at the soup kitchen, and when she saw the good work Champion was doing, she no longer spoke out against his new ICU. She had other worries.

With so many men losing their jobs and no longer able to send any money to the wives they had left in the country, women were coming into town in the hope of finding some way to earn enough to feed their children. In order to discourage them, the Town Council was once again talking about passes for women. And once again the women banded together to protest. But this time they were joined by members of the African National Congress, by ministers of different churches, by schoolteachers, and other educated men.

Katie felt very nervous walking at the front of the long column of protestors, just a few feet behind John Dube, Pastor Mtimkulu, Alfred Matibela and Champion, all of whom made long speeches when they entered the Council Chambers. But she felt even more nervous when Champion suddenly turned around and asked Katie to speak for the women. She hesitated. Some of the younger women were more educated than she, and perhaps they knew as many long words as the men. But Mrs Sililo pushed her forward.

'In English, you always say "Ladies first,"' Katie began, and then paused, looking around at the white people sitting on the Town Council. 'But today I see that for us it is like the old days when we ladies had to follow the men according to Zulu custom. Nevertheless, I am speaking now. And what I want to know is this: Do you want to keep us in the old days forever? More than thirty years ago, when we women wanted to come into town to buy from the stores, we had to get permits before entering. Sometimes the policemen kept us waiting so long we had to come back the next day. At last we refused to go there. But the store owners in town still wanted us to buy from them, and so the government forgot about giving out permits. Now I ask you, Why are you taking us back to those days? Do you make women from overseas carry passes? No! Do you make Indian women carry passes? No! Then why do you want to make us carry passes when it was our ancestors who lived in this land?'

After the meeting was over, Katie returned to the dispensary. The Doctor was waiting for her with a grin on his face. Someone on the Town Council had telephoned him to say that Katie had made an excellent speech. It was a long time before there was any more talk of passes for women.

Although times were hard, those were happy years for Katie. To her surprise she found herself being treated with deference by younger women in the Bantu Women's Society, and at meetings of the Joint Council important leaders asked her opinion. Her children were doing well. Samuel was working in the print shop at Adams mission station. Sagila was a carpenter, and Margaret was a schoolteacher, both living in Johannesburg. Nimrod was going to England to record songs for the gramophone. Her youngest son, John, was still in boarding school at Ohlange and doing very well. And Livingstone had almost finished his studies at the agricultural college. Already, he told Katie, he had been offered two jobs as an agricultural demonstrator, one in Nyasaland and one at Mapumulo in Natal.

'An agricultural demonstrator? I thought he wanted to study medicine,' said the Doctor.

'No,' Katie replied. 'That was me. I wanted him to be a doctor, like you. Like that David Livingstone you told me about. But it was no use. He doesn't like sick people. They make him nervous.'

'Then this is the best job for him,' the Doctor said.

Katie nodded. 'He likes planting seeds and watching things grow. Even when he was a child and giving me all that trouble, I could always trust him to work my garden. He will do very well at Mapumulo.'

But Livingstone never finished his schooling. Two weeks before his final examinations, a telegram came to the dispensary.

Katie looked up at the Doctor in despair. 'There must be some mistake. How can Livingstone be mentally ill? Mr Dube has always said he was the cleverest of all my sons.'

'You had better go and see.' The Doctor reached into his pocket and brought out five pounds. 'Get your ticket for the next train.'

At the agricultural school the Principal told her that Livingstone had tried to run away. After his teachers brought him back, he refused to eat or speak to anyone, and when they tried to force him, he grew so violent that it had taken three men to hold him still. Now they had him locked up in a little room with only one small window high up on the wall.

When Katie saw him, he looked no different than before. He was very quiet and polite, but as soon as the Principal left them alone, he came up close and whispered in her ear.

'Ma! The people here are trying to poison me.'

Katie tried to reassure him by forcing a laugh. 'Now why would they do that? Come, Livingstone, stop playing your tricks and tell me your troubles.'

'I'm telling you, Ma.' His grip tightened on her wrists until his fingernails were digging into her skin. 'The people here want to kill me because when the government puts me in charge, they know I'll give them all the sack.'

'Yes,' Katie whispered back, thoroughly frightened now by the wild look in his eyes and the twitching of a muscle in his cheek. To pacify him, she pretended that she, too, felt threatened by the people at the school. 'Yes, we had better run away to Durban and find refuge with the Doctor.'

By the time they reached the dispensary, he seemed like his old self, greeting Edward as his friend and boasting happily to the Doctor about his many important jobs. Once or twice while he was talking, the Doctor glanced at Katie. Very slightly, so that Livingstone would not notice, she kept shaking her head to let the Doctor know that all these important jobs did not exist except in his imagination.

'All this is very interesting,' the Doctor said at last. 'I would like you to explain all this to a friend of mine.'

'But I have to take Ma home.'

'Mr Smith will come soon, before she's ready to go.'

'Yes, Livingstone,' Katie said firmly. 'I have work to do first, and Edward needs your help today. Out in the shed there are empty bottles which need to be washed.'

As soon as Mr Smith arrived, the Doctor called Livingstone into the consulting room. They talked for a long time while Katie sat in the supply room, her fingers twisting her apron, her thoughts going back over all the troubles she had had with Livingstone when he was little. At last the Doctor brought him out, gave him more bottles to wash, and beckoned for Katie to come in and talk with Mr Smith.

Mr Smith was a specialist in mental diseases. But he did not look special: he seemed like any white man, too ordinary to remember. 'Sit down, Katie,' he said. 'I've examined your son. He's had what we call a nervous breakdown. Perhaps he's been working too hard. What he needs now is plenty of rest and quiet. No excitement of any kind. Nothing to worry him. His condition is a little like what you call—' He hesitated and looked at the Doctor.

'Like *ufufunyane*,' the Doctor murmured.

'But he isn't a girl!' Katie had to laugh.

'I didn't say that's what it is,' the Doctor muttered. 'I said it's *like* that. A form of hysteria.'

'Why don't you put ammonia under his nose? That's what we do with the young girls.'

Mr Smith just smiled. 'Ammonia won't help Livingstone; only time and rest. Take him back to Adams. Don't press him. Just let him do whatever he wants to. In a few months he should be all right.'

'But what if he wants to do something crazy?'

'Then let him do it – unless he'd hurt himself or someone else. In that case, try and distract him. The important thing is this: he's not like other boys, so don't argue with him. Don't make him angry. Just keep him contented.'

After the Doctor walked outside with Mr Smith, Katie remained behind in the consulting room. She needed time to think, and it was very quiet in there with the door shut. Yet that familiar room in which she had spent so many hours of her life was suddenly like a foreign country, and the strange words spoken about her son some foreign language she could not understand. Her son, her cleverest son, was not like other boys! He was crazy in the head! She slumped down, resting her head against the back of the chair, feeling a great weakness in her body. When the Doctor returned she had no strength to open her eyes. She only sensed his presence, heard him opening the door to tell Edward to make a pot of tea. Then he pulled out his tin of biscuits from his bottom drawer.

'I don't want any biscuits, Doctor.'

'You had better eat a couple, and drink some tea. You'll need all your energy because this is a bad time, Katie.'

'Very bad, Doctor.'

'Don't give up hope. Mr Smith thinks that Livingstone might get better.'

'Yes. If I'm with him I can keep him quiet and contented because he trusts me. But what's going to happen when I leave?'

'Then stay at home for a month. It's almost time for your holiday. I'll get one of the nurses from the hospital to come down to help, and Edward and I will manage here.'

'Thank you, Doctor.'

Livingstone was very quiet on the way back to Adams, and he went to bed after greeting his father on their arrival. When Ndeya asked questions, Katie shook her head until she was sure that Livingstone was sleeping soundly. Only then did she speak of the telegram.

'The Doctor and Mr Smith think he might get better if he has plenty of rest and quiet. But we mustn't make him angry or excited.'

'He looks all right to me,' Ndeya said.

'He's not all right, Ndeya. Look at my wrists. They're still sore where he grabbed me so hard. And that letter he wrote about his important jobs! There aren't any jobs for him. They are just in his imagination.'

'But he can't be really crazy. The Doctor said he'll be all right.'

'The Doctor said he *might*. He did not say he *would*.'

Katie felt very discouraged. Ndeya had not seen him when his eyes were wild or heard his talk about the people who were trying to poison him. Ndeya did not like to worry. He just kept telling Katie that soon Livingstone would get better.

Indeed, for the first few days he did seem more like his old self. He ate hungrily of whatever Katie cooked, helped her around the house, chopped wood, fetched her water from the river, and after doing all this would come to her and say, 'Ma, is there something more you want, or can I go down the road to visit Jaja's people?'

However, on Sunday, which was the first day Ndeya did not go to work in his harness store, Livingstone would not eat. 'The food is poisoned, Ma,' he said. 'That man', he pointed to his father, 'wants to kill me with poison.'

'Nonsense,' Katie replied. 'That man is your father, who loves you.'

'No, he's not my father. Don't let him fool you, Ma.'

His eyes stared wildly and his cheek was twitching. Katie could see he was growing very excited, and so to soothe him, she cooked a fresh pot of rice and vegetables and roasted a few extra strips of meat in the fire while he watched. Then, as he ate, she sat down with the dish of food he had pushed away.

A few days later he began to complain about Theresa, Ndeya's older sister, who was living with them. 'She'll try to kill us, Ma, because she wants your nice house and all your clothes.'

There was no reasoning with him. Katie tried everything she could think of during that month she was home with Livingstone. She saw to it that Ndeya and Theresa did everything he wished, yet each day he came to tell her about some new person who was trying to poison him. It was obvious that he was getting worse.

On the third Sunday she took him to the church of the faith healers. She felt very uncomfortable, because the Doctor had no time for faith healers. He had often told her that God helps those who help themselves, and when people are sick they need medicine, not prayers. However, an old woman she knew had told her how she had been cured of a nervous tic in her cheek when she went to that church. If the Doctor could not cure him, Katie hoped the faith healers could.

But Livingstone grew restless during the service. 'I don't like them,' he told her. 'They make too much noise with their dancing and chanting. They'll make me worse than I am.'

She had only one more week at home before she had to go back to the dispensary. She kept praying for some miracle. One night, as she was dozing off, she thought she saw one of the Zanzibari men from the Bluff in Durban coming for Livingstone. So vivid was the image that she was startled into sudden wakefulness. She had not thought of the Zanzibaris for many years, and had never seen them, but she had heard about them from Mrs Choudree and some of her other Indian friends. The Christian Indians were afraid of them, not because they were Muslims but because they were said to practise black magic. The educated Hindus laughed at them and called them charlatans. But there were some like Mrs Choudree who believed they had special powers. Katie lay in the darkness pondering her vision of that Zanzibari man. In her state of half-sleep she could not but wonder if God was showing her a way to help Livingstone. Although she did not believe in magic, she did know that there were people with mysterious powers, like Thlambesine Ngcobo and Nokwazi. She knew then what she must do.

In the morning she took Livingstone with her on the train to Durban and from there to the Bluff where the Zanzibari lived. A woman on the road directed her to the house of a wise man, and holding firmly to Livingstone's arm, she entered a small courtyard. The man was tall and thin. He looked more like an Arab than an Indian. He did not ask any questions. He just looked at Livingstone and said there was an evil spirit in his head. Then he put his hand in his pocket, brought out some scissors, and without any warning cut off a locket of Livingstone's hair. This he tied with a piece of string and attached to a bush which was growing next to the road outside the courtyard, all the time muttering something unintelligible.

'Now your son is cured,' he told Katie. 'His evil spirit lives in that hair and will jump on some other person who passes by the bush.'

Livingstone was fingering the bald spot on his head where his hair had been cut. His cheek was twitching. Katie pulled out her purse and gave the Zanzibari the ten shillings he demanded, and hurried Livingstone away.

'He was only tricking you,' Livingstone told her on their journey home.

'No one can cure me. I know I'm sick. I got this way at school because I was poisoned. But I'm not so bad when I stay with you.'

'Oh Livingstone!' Katie said helplessly, 'I wish I could look after you all the time. But you know I can't. I have my work at the dispensary and I have to earn.'

'Then take me to Durban with you.'

'I can't. I haven't any proper place for you to stay. And all the people in town? They'll only make you nervous.'

'Not if we go back to Sydenham. I was always happy on the farm.'

'But we can't go back. The Doctor had to give it up. There isn't any place in Durban where you can be quiet. You'll have to stay with your father.'

'But I've told you: he'll poison me. Is that what you want?' He slid away from her, leaving a space between them as though he no longer trusted her.

'Of course not,' she said. 'Haven't I always been on your side?'

He said nothing, just stared at her suspiciously until the train stopped at Amanzimtoti. He followed her onto the platform, keeping several steps behind her as she started up the long road to Adams. He did not catch up with her until she called back over her shoulder: 'Come. When we get home, we'll go out on the hills and search for *amakhowe*. You can pick them yourself and I will cook them for your supper tonight.'

'Yes, we'll look for *amakhowe*.' Livingstone had always liked those big mushrooms that grow wild on the hills, and at the thought of picking them, he grew calm again.

All night Katie worried about Livingstone. She had tried very hard to keep him contented. But in spite of all her care, she knew he was getting worse. In her heart she was sure he needed more than just rest and quiet. He needed medicine. But neither the Doctor nor Mr Smith had any medicine to cure his madness. No European doctors had such a medicine, but perhaps— No! She would not think about the heathen *inyangas*. She had seen too many patients come to the Doctor with terrible wounds and infections resulting from an *inyanga*'s treatment, and too often she had heard the Doctor rage against their ignorance and superstition. Yet many believed that the *inyangas* had magic potions. Even her own grandfather in Soekmekaar had lived much longer than others of his age group because he had drunk of just such a medicine made from the blood of a leopard.

All the following day and the next she could not put aside the thought of heathen medicine. Perhaps the *inyangas* could heal Livingstone. Yet the very thought frightened her. Each night she asked the Lord to cure Livingstone, and each morning she woke up hoping to see some improvement. But she was always disappointed. She grew more and more frantic.

On the Saturday before she had to return to the dispensary, she decided to take Livingstone to an *inyanga* who lived beyond Umbumbulu. She did not tell Ndeya where she was going. He would have been shocked and angry because she was going against the Doctor. She did not tell Samuel or Josephine for fear they would think that she, too, had gone mad, nor did she even tell Livingstone lest he be frightened and refuse to go.

They left very early in the morning and did not rest until they came to Violet Makanya's house. She gave them tea and bread, but when she asked where they were going Katie did not answer.

One mile beyond Violet's house, Katie stopped at the homestead of a man she knew and bought a goat for five shillings to show her good faith when she came to the *inyanga*. They were still some distance from his place when one of his messengers appeared and stopped them on the road.

'Go back,' he warned. 'You're not wanted here.'

He began shaking his fist. Katie caught quickly at Livingstone's arm as she saw the muscle in his cheek begin to twitch and his eyes grow wild.

'We're going.' She clutched Livingstone's other arm and tried to pull him with her, but he half-crouched on the road, his muscles bulging under her fingers until the messenger stepped backwards, then suddenly turned and ran away. Only then did Livingstone's body ease.

'Come, my son,' Katie whispered softly. 'We've no business mixing ourselves up with these heathen.'

He straightened himself but still stood there watching as the messenger disappeared over the next hill. 'You mustn't bring me here again, Ma.'

'No, my son.'

'This is a bad place. He's a bad man.'

'Yes.'

He started walking quickly back the way they had come. Katie let him go. She was too old to hurry so fast although she, too, was very afraid. She had been foolish – wicked – to go against the Doctor's teaching and seek out that *inyanga*. But how had the *inyanga* known they were coming? How did he know to send his messenger to stop them? How did he know, without being told, that Livingstone was mad? Or was he only afraid of Katie because he knew she worked for the Doctor?

On Monday she packed her clothes. She did not want to leave Livingstone behind, but what could she do? If she found a place to rent where they could live together, she would still have to leave him during the day; and who knew what mischief he might cause without her? No, it was better for him to stay in the country where people knew him.

During the next few months he was a great worry for her. Many times he ran away from home, so that in the afternoons, when Katie left the dispensary, she never knew if she would find him waiting for her on the street. Once in the middle of the night he came banging on the door of the hostel: there was nothing she could do but take him to the dispensary and stay with him there until first light.

'How did you get here?' she asked him while they huddled together under some blankets in the waiting-room.

'I walked.'

'You walked eighteen miles through the night? How could you do that? How could you get through the sugar-cane fields at Isipingo in the darkness?'

'It's easy, Ma. No one can do me harm. Not even the wizards, because I'm not alone. I have six horse-powers in me and I'm strong enough to knock them down.'

'Then if no one can harm you, why don't you stay at home?'

'Because I don't like that old woman who lives in your house. She treats me like a madman, and I'm not mad. It's just that all these people are jealous and poison my food to make me like this.'

'But Livingstone, you can't keep running into town. There are too many rogues here. This time I'll take you home. But you mustn't come again, you hear?'

He did not like her scolding. Once he realised that she would not keep him in Durban, he began to set himself apart from her. When she went home on Saturdays she would find him missing. Although Ndeya did everything he knew to please him, Livingstone would slip out of the house. He was never afraid of the dark, knowing himself to be strong because of those six horse-powers in him, and indeed his madness was like an engine driving him long distances. Sometimes he went to Umbumbulu to visit Violet, or else he hid himself in the bush. At last she brought him back to the Doctor and Mr Smith, and they told her she would have to send him to the insane asylum in Pietermaritzburg.

Livingstone stayed there for several months, at the end of which time the superintendent of the asylum told Katie he was well again. And it was true that when she went to fetch him, he seemed very happy to see her and acted like his old self.

'My sickness is finished, Ma. Now I can go home and plant a big garden and use fertiliser the way I was taught at school. Then I'll sell my mealies and cabbages and other vegetables, and when I have enough money I'll buy a big motor car and drive into town to visit you.'

All the way home he talked of this wonderful garden which would make him rich. When they reached Adams, he greeted his father with much affection. He even joked with Theresa as if he no longer feared her. As soon as Katie could buy him seeds, he ploughed and hoed the field beside their house. Some weeks later when she went home to visit, he took her outside and showed her proudly how the little shoots were sprouting out of the earth.

But long before harvest time, he tired of his garden. 'It's no use, Ma. I work hard in the day, but that old woman is very jealous. In the night she runs around gathering up worms and caterpillars, and in the morning I find them eating up all my plants.'

'Oh no, you're mistaken,' Katie said. 'In a garden there are always worms and caterpillars. Don't you remember how I used to send you children out to pick them off my green beans when you were little, and when you filled up your box I would give you a ha'penny to buy some sweets?'

But Livingstone would not listen. He grew more and more difficult. One afternoon Ndeya telephoned from the office of the teacher-training college at the mission and told the Doctor to send Katie home. Livingstone had taken her new clock and thrown it on the floor, then piled his clothes about it and set them all on fire.

'No,' she cried out in desperation. 'No, I don't believe it. Not again!'

Ndeya and Theresa were both waiting for her on the front veranda as she walked across the fields past the drooping vegetables which Livingstone had planted. They did not speak when she reached them, just led her into the kitchen and pointed to the charred marks on the hard dung floor.

'It must have been an accident,' Katie said. 'Where is he now?'

'I don't know,' Theresa said through tight lips.

Katie ran outside, calling his name. She ran to the river, to Jeena's store, to Samuel's house, and when at last she started down the new road to the mission, he jumped out from behind a pile of rocks. For one brief moment Katie closed her eyes and thanked the Lord for keeping him safe, then realised he was talking quickly and with much excitement.

'She's making big trouble for me.'

'Who's making trouble?'

'That old woman. I told you she was jealous. Now she hides poison in my clothes to make me sick.'

'No, you just made a little mistake. She isn't trying to harm you. If you'll just come home—'

He drew back. The muscle in his cheek began to twitch. 'You're on her side.'

'Oh no, my son! I'm not on her side. I only want to help you. If you're frightened of her, then we can go to Josephine's.'

'Josephine?' He hesitated, although he had never before been frightened of his brother's wife. Katie remained very still, just waiting. At last the wildness left his eyes. When they reached Samuel's house, Josephine sent her children over to Theresa so that they would not disturb Livingstone. Then, when she asked him to help her make tea, Katie went over to the mission and telephoned the Doctor.

'It's Livingstone,' she said.

'How did you find him?' he asked.

At the sound of the Doctor's voice she began to sob. 'He's worse than he ever was. It's just lucky he didn't burn himself to death, and the house as well. And now I'm very afraid. Who knows what he will take it into his head to do next?'

'Then stay with him, Katie. Don't let him out of your sight. It's too late now for me to do anything. You and your husband and Samuel, all of you, must take turns watching him all through the night. I'll arrange to have him taken back to the asylum first thing in the morning.'

That night after they had eaten, Samuel, Ndeya, Josephine and Katie were sitting at table in the kitchen when Livingstone got up to put another stick on the fire. Suddenly and without any warning, he whirled around and clubbed Samuel on the forehead with all his strength. Samuel lost his temper, jumped up with the blood pouring down his face and went for his brother. But Livingstone leapt out of the way and threw himself at Katie's feet.

'Don't let him kill me, Ma,' he pleaded.

'I'm not going to kill you,' Samuel shouted. 'I'm only going to give you a big thrashing. I'll teach you not to hit me.'

'Stop it, Samuel,' Katie yelled. She looked down at Livingstone and very gently asked why he had tried to fight.

'I don't know,' he whimpered.

'Poor child,' she murmured, stroking his face as though he were still little. 'I think you must be very tired. Come. Let's go to bed.'

He went with her obediently, and she lay beside him all through the night, never sleeping but always quick to lay her arm across his chest and whisper soft and loving words whenever he stirred. Ndeya and Samuel took turns guarding the doorway. Early the next morning men from the asylum came to take him away.

Livingstone did not want to go with them. When they came into the house he started to yell and fight. But they were strong, and with Samuel's help they strapped a canvas sheet around his body so that he couldn't move and tied him down on a stretcher. As they carried him outside, Katie leaned forward and tried to pat his cheek. But he jerked his head away. When the men tilted the stretcher to push it into their ambulance, he looked at her for the last time. She felt as though she herself were dying when she saw the fear, anger and childish confusion mixed up in his eyes.

Katie went to visit him just once in Pietermaritzburg. He was kept all alone in a room like a prison cell so that he could not hurt other patients. When he heard Katie speaking to him through a little window in the door, his cheek began to twitch and he shouted out angrily to the men in charge that she was not his mother. The nurses at the asylum told her not to return until he improved. But Livingstone got worse instead of better, and finally he was transferred to an asylum in Bloemfontein for the incurably insane, hundreds of miles away.

Every few months Katie wrote to the European superintendent of the asylum to ask if there was anything she could send her son – a bag of toffees, perhaps, or a new shirt. But the answer was always the same. She realised then that there was no longer anything she could do for Livingstone.

After her trouble with Livingstone, Katie felt very old and discouraged.

Indeed, she was old. It was almost forty years since she had started working for the Doctor, and he too was growing old. Yet strangely, to her he seemed no different from when he'd returned from America after the Great War.

Therefore, on the day in 1939 when she read that England was going to fight another war, she asked the Doctor when he and Dr Pearson would put on their uniforms and leave for duty as they had done at the start of the last war.

He laughed. 'I've grown too fat for that uniform. Anyway, I'm too old for the army now.'

'I'm glad. Because then you stayed in America too long.'

'But Katie,' he hesitated, no longer smiling, 'pretty soon I'll have to retire. I'll be seventy next April, and all the missionaries have to retire when they're seventy. I've been planning to talk to you about this. Dr Taylor will put someone else in charge of the dispensary, and I don't know if you want to go on working—'

'I only work for you, Doctor, not for anyone else.'

'Then you'll retire also?'

'Yes, Doctor.'

It was strange to think of retiring, of not coming to the dispensary. On the hot sunny days when her rheumatism did not trouble her too much, Katie did not think she could live without all the excitement of 86 Beatrice Street, without the hum of different languages spoken all at once, the shouts of the rickshaw men and the honking of the motor cars, without the mingled smells of flowers, petrol, garlic, fish and body sweat blown around by the sea breezes, without the vivid colours of the Indian women in their saris and the bright patterns of African beadwork. Yet, at other times when the rain crowded the patients onto the benches in the waiting-room and the pain in her knees grew tiresome, she dreamed of a small country dispensary where she would work with the Doctor in the mornings and plant her garden in the afternoons.

On Christmas Eve he brought presents for all the workers at the dispensary. For Katie he had a bag of toffees, a tin of Baumann's Biscuits, and two large photographs, one of himself and one of Mrs McCord. 'So you won't forget us,' he said. This talk of forgetting puzzled her. As she travelled out to Adams and during the Christmas service in the mission church, and afterwards when she showed her friends his photograph hanging on her wall, she kept wondering what he had meant. Had she complained too much about the rheumatism in her knees? Did he think she would leave him and come back here to Adams when their work in the dispensary was finished?

On the first day after the Christmas holiday she waited uneasily for the sound of his motor car, and as soon as he arrived she followed him into his consulting room.

'Please, Doctor, where are we going to have our new dispensary after we retire?'

'What are you talking about?' he asked her as he put on his long white coat.

'Don't you remember? You've always said that when you retired, we'd find a place in the country where the people would need us, to have a small dispensary?'

'Oh.' He sat down behind his desk, not smiling. 'That was a long time ago. When we are young we don't know what it's like to grow old. Now you and I know. Neither one of us has as much energy any more. It's time for us to sit back and enjoy our children and our grandchildren.'

'But our people still need you. You're not too old to doctor them.'

He smiled sadly. 'The Bible says a man's too old when he reaches threescore years and ten.'

'But not you. You're still strong. You're still the best doctor.'

'That's the way I want to be remembered.'

'But what will I do?'

'You'll go back to Adams to live with Ndeya. When it's warm you will work in your garden, and when it's cold you'll sit by the fire and tell stories to your grandchildren. And you will be happy there. Do you hear me, Katie?'

'I hear you, Doctor.'

'Then you had better start calling in the patients.'

That last day was the same as all the other days of their many years together. She passed around the bread and tea, waited for the Doctor's car to come at nine o'clock and, as soon as he had changed into his long white coat and picked up his stethoscope, she called in the first of the patients. The day was no different from all the others. Late in the afternoon the Doctor called out for her to bring his tea into the consulting room. 'With two cups,' he said.

When she brought in the tea tray and laid it on his desk, he motioned her into the chair across from him and opened up his tin of biscuits. 'There aren't many left, so we might as well finish them off,' he said.

'Thank you, Doctor.' Not knowing what else to say, she rolled the sweetened crumbs around on her tongue.

'Well, Katie, we've come to the end of a long road.'

'Yes, Doctor.'

'You've made my work easy.' He hesitated for a moment and cleared his throat. 'We've been through much together, you and I.' He paused again, finding it difficult to speak, and again cleared his throat. 'You've sacrificed much for the sake of our work. I want you to know I've always been grateful.' He paused again, but in that moment there was no need for words between them. Katie could read his thoughts and knew that he loved her as he loved all the people and loved Africa and that he did not want to go away.

'I, too, am grateful,' she said.

'Now it's time for each of us to have a long, long holiday.'

'Yes.'

'If you ever need anything after I'm gone, anything at all, go to Dr Taylor.'

'Yes, Doctor.'

Katie knew now that everything was finished. How could she live when he was gone? In front of her his face blurred until the wrinkles disappeared and he seemed like a young man again and his laughter was shaking the earth.

She felt the rush of movement, his hands grasping her shoulders. 'Steady there. Good! Now put your head down on your knees.'

The floor steadied under her feet.

'Drink this.'

He was holding her cup of tea to her mouth. Even with plenty of sugar it tasted very strong but she had to swallow quickly because he was tipping the cup against her lips. At last she pushed it away.

'I'm all right now, Doctor.'

He stepped back and half-leaned, half-sat on his desk. 'For a moment you startled me. I thought you were going to faint.' He chuckled softly. 'Like that first day you came to work, remember?'

'I remember. I was very frightened that day.'

'But still you came back. That took courage.'

Her tears came then. 'But now I've no more courage,' she sobbed. 'I'm very frightened. Because I never thought you'd leave us. I thought we'd bury you here.'

He tried to make her laugh. 'I'm not ready to be buried yet.'

'You know what I mean.'

'Yes, I do know. But Katie, a man needs to go back to his homeplace.'

She nodded silently, remembering Mbambo, who left her to go back to Umgeni when he was dying.

'Oh, Doctor, will you ever come back?' He did not speak, only looked down at her, unable to find any words. But because he was a true man and had never lied to her, he shook his head.

The silence between them was long. Then he stepped forward and reached out that right hand, the one with the two fingers missing, and very lightly touched Katie's face. His words were low and between them alone. 'Who can see into the future? But one thing I think you know already. My heart will be here always.'

'Here? In Africa? You mean like David Livingstone?'

'You remember that too?'

'You gave my sister Charlotte a book once about David Livingstone. She left it with me and I have it still.'

Miss Ball's voice jarred at them through the door. 'It's the hospital, Doctor. They want you on the phone.'

'All right, I'm coming.' He dropped his hand from Katie's face. 'This isn't goodbye. I'll see you again, many times, before I actually leave.'

'Yes, Doctor.'

But it was goodbye. She saw him again only at the parties and receptions in his honour during the month before his ship sailed.

20

Adams

1939–1954

Katie and Ndeya had five good years together after she retired. He, too, had grown old and almost blind, but he was still the same, a quiet, thoughtful man with a quick smile and a kindly word for everyone. He still gathered his friends around him to joke and sometimes argue, and their house was always full of people in the early evening and after church on Sunday. After everyone left, they would sit quietly together in front of the fire while he carved whistles for Samuel's children and Katie read to him from the Bible or sewed a dress for one of her granddaughters.

In time, as the Doctor promised, Katie grew content at Adams.

Then Ndeya sickened. He complained of pains in his stomach. Katie wanted to take him to the hospital to see Dr Taylor but Ndeya was stubborn. He said he knew what his sickness was, because he could feel the worms crawling around inside him and all he needed was an old muti which the herbalists used to make from a plant called *intambo*. Ndeya said he could have made that muti himself except that the plants were no longer easy to find. But he had heard that a white man at Hillcrest made pills from the same muti, and mailed them on order.

The pills arrived by post on a Friday. Ndeya got up very early on Saturday morning, and swallowed them all. About ten o'clock he went outside. He was gone a long time. At last Katie went to look for him and found him lying in the pathway, too weak to walk back to the house. She called for Josephine, Samuel's wife, and between them they carried Ndeya back to his bed and made him plenty of hot tea.

Josephine, who was a proper nurse and worked in the clinic on the mission, felt his forehead and took his pulse. She sighed with relief. 'For a little while I thought he was dying. Why did you let him take all those pills, Ma? You know better.'

'Even if I'd known what he was doing, I could not stop him,' Katie told her. 'He's old enough to know what's good and what's bad.'

'He's old enough, but about such things he knows nothing. The next time he sends for medicine, you had better steal it away and throw it outside.'

Ndeya stopped complaining about the pains in his stomach but he never quite regained his strength, and as time passed he grew very frail. Then he began to get confused. Sometimes he started off to the store to buy mealie-meal and came back with a pound of sugar instead. One Sunday on the way to church he turned in the wrong direction and looked puzzled when Katie asked if he was going to church with her or to visit his friend, Ngcamu, who lived at Stony Hill. Yet in between these moments of forgetfulness, his thoughts could be very clear. Katie found this confusing, too, because she could not tell by looking at him whether he would wander off and forget where he was or remain safely at home. One morning while she was still sleeping he got up very quietly. When she woke up, it was to the sound of loud voices. Ngcamu was in the kitchen with Ndeya, who was standing there wearing only his white shirt and tie.

'What are you doing in here without your trousers?' Katie asked.

'I don't know.'

'I found him three miles down the road without any blanket,' Ngcamu said. 'He told me he wanted to go to town to get some money from the bank.'

'You wanted to go to the bank without your trousers?' Katie said.

'I forgot,' Ndeya mumbled.

Katie led him into the bedroom and held out his trousers, but Ndeya did not want them. He wanted to sleep because he had been up for so long. When Katie leaned over his bed to pull the blankets up around his shoulders, he caught her hand. 'I know I'm sometimes foolish, Mother of Samuel, but I can't help it. I get all mixed up.'

'Don't worry,' Katie said. 'I will look after you.'

He still kept holding her hand until she sat down on the edge of the bed. He smiled and closed his eyes, then suddenly opened them wide and looked straight at her. 'Do you remember? When we were married you promised you'd never leave me until death?'

'Yes, I remember.'

'You won't go away from me?'

'No, I'll never leave you, Ndeya.'

As his moments of confusion came more often, he began to object if Katie left him with anyone but Ngcamu, whom he had known all his life. Ngcamu came down almost every day from Stony Hill, and he and Ndeya would sit on the veranda, two old men together, talking of the days when they were young. Katie used to marvel at the way Ndeya spoke of every little detail of his child-hood as though the events of sixty or seventy years ago were clearer in his thoughts than anything which happened that day or the previous one. As he grew weaker, he thought more and more often of the children. He was quite content with Samuel, who came over every day to see how he was, and with John, who travelled from Durban once a month. But he worried constantly about Margaret, Sagila and Nimrod, who were all living in Johannesburg. At last he told Katie to send for them because he wanted to see them before he died.

Sagila came first and stayed for two weeks. He mended the roof, fixed the broken furniture and hired some oxen to plough Katie's field. When these things were done, he went to his father and said it was time for him to go back to his job.

'Yes,' Ndeya said. 'Now that I've seen you, I won't try to keep you here. But you mustn't forget your homeplace. That's the trouble with young people nowadays. They go away and forget their families. And so I'm telling you, Adams is your homeplace.'

'Yes, Father,' Sagila said.

'Then go well, my son.'

Nimrod came later but only for a day and a night. He was travelling with his choir and could not leave his singers alone in Durban for very long. He brought his father a hat and coat and a new shirt and tie, and for Katie a silk dress to wear to church. After Nimrod left, Ndeya kept asking for Margaret.

'She'll come soon,' Katie said to pacify him, although she knew that Margaret could not leave her teaching until the school holidays. Moreover, Margaret had many children – four who were still very young and living at home, and older ones who were at school at Adams.

'I want to see Margaret,' Ndeya kept insisting.

'Then when you're better, we'll take your money out of the bank and go to visit her. Perhaps we'll go also to Soekmekaar—'

'I'm not going to get any better, Mother of Samuel.'

In those last weeks he knew his life was coming to an end. Some of the time he talked nonsense, then suddenly for a few minutes he looked straight at Katie and spoke with intelligence. Each morning she would dress him in his new coat and hat and the shirt and tie which Nimrod had brought him and lead him out to his chair on the veranda to wait for Ngcamu. But the last time Ngcamu came to visit him, Ndeya grew excited and ordered him away because, he said, he would not allow any heathen in his house.

'After all these years he doesn't know me,' Ngcamu told Katie, turning his face away to hide the tears falling down his face.

Later that same afternoon, Ndeya jerked around in his chair and called out suddenly, 'Katie.'

'I'm right here beside you,' she said softly, caught up for a moment in the wonder of hearing him speak her name. He had not called her Katie since the day Samuel was born.

'Don't leave me, Katie, because death is beginning.'

'No, you mustn't say that.'

He smiled at her in the gentle way he had. 'I know what I know. Look at the sun. It's rising in the wrong place.'

'It's almost night, my husband. Tomorrow it will rise again over the hills and we can watch it together.'

'I don't know if I will see the sun again. Because I can hear my father calling. My mother also.'

'Then they are cruel. Why should they take you away from me?'

'You have the children. You can go and live with them.'

'And leave this house you built for me? No, Ndeya, I'll stay here.' But she did not think he heard her, for his eyes dulled again and he began muttering some nonsense to himself. After she put him to bed, she sat beside him through the night, listening to his breathing and jumping up to cover him each time he tossed off his blankets. Towards morning he told her he felt cold. 'Then I'll keep you warm,' she said, and eased herself into his bed to lie close beside him. His skin was as dry as a leaf withering in the dust, and his arms and legs seemed brittle like the twigs of a dying tree. Just before first light he stirred, opened his eyes and cringed back from her.

'Who are you?'

'I'm your wife.'

'No.' He tried to sit up. 'No, you're not my wife. And I have no business lying in bed with a woman who's not my wife.'

'But I am. I'm Mother of Samuel.'

'No, you're not my wife at all. You're just some dirty old woman who's come to be her servant.' His voice trembled with anger. Katie slipped out of the bed, and at once he settled back against the pillow. 'That's better. Now you can call my wife. Her name is Katie. She's a singer and she comes from the Transvaal and she's beautiful like a bird when it soars up into the heavens. And I need her now. So go away, old woman, and call my wife.'

'Very well,' Katie said, wondering how to bring herself back to him in the way he had known her long ago.

'Hurry. I want my wife.'

She pulled on her dress and stumbled into the kitchen. As she started the fire, he called again. When she ran back to him, he was smiling happily and reaching out his hand to the wall.

'What is it, Ndeya?'

'Ah, Mother of Samuel!' He turned, knowing her at last. 'Just look at those children. Those four who went away: little Charlotte, Ethel, Clifford, Hamilton. They're calling me. See them standing there?'

'Oh, Ndeya,' Katie sobbed.

'Don't cry, Mother of Sam—' But those last words were lost in the sudden wheezing in his throat as he turned his head to the wall.

Katie fell to her knees beside his bed and tried to clutch him back to life, but he was gone. Her husband, who had waited so patiently over the years for her to come back to live with him forever, had gone away at last and left her to her loneliness.

In 1950 word came from America that the Doctor had died. Her long period of waiting was almost over.

She went down to the cemetery on the mission station, and some distance from where the Reverend Mr and Mrs Cowles were buried, she dug a trench. It was hard work and took her several days. She did not ask for help. This was her job, and she had never wanted anyone to interfere with her work for the Doctor. When the trench was almost three feet deep, she lined the bottom with stones and covered these with six inches of ash from her fireplace, then shovelled back some of the dirt and transplanted her dahlia bulbs, which were already beginning to sprout. Early the next morning she went down to the river to gather up clumps of ferns. In the afternoon she went out into her garden and dug up the wild amaryllis bulbs she had found in the hills during her years of waiting, and in the evening she divided her clumps of Barberton daisies. The Doctor had always loved his garden.

The plants she set out in the cemetery bloomed and died and bloomed again, and she was still waiting.

At last, two and a half years after the Doctor's death, Dr Taylor stopped on his way to the mission to tell her that Mrs McCord was coming back to Durban for the opening of a new wing to the hospital. 'And you must be there also,' he said. 'I'll arrange for Mr Christofersen to bring you.'

On the day of the ceremony Katie was too impatient to wait for a ride into town with the missionaries. Soon after first light she went over to the local store to wait for a taxi. In Durban she caught a tram from the railway station to Overport, then walked the rest of the way to Dr Taylor's house. She sat patiently there on the back veranda until Mrs McCord came and reached out for both of her hands.

'I see you,' she said, her smile wiping away the years which were etched into her face and her eyes bright as a young girl's. 'Are you well? And your children?'

'We're all well,' Katie began, but she had no time to answer properly because the hospital workers rushed over at that moment to crowd around Mrs McCord and escort her to the chairs set up on the lawn. Mrs McCord whispered something to Dr Taylor, who nodded, paused, beckoned to Katie and seated them both together in the front row.

Many people gave speeches. As Dr Taylor introduced them, Katie often recalled the names but did not always recognise the faces. Those she had known had grown older, and like many old people they talked for a long time. Her attention wandered.

After everyone had said what they wanted to say, Dr Taylor opened the door of the new wing of the hospital and led the way towards the new operating theatre. He began to point out the plaques above various rooms honouring those people who had given money for the building. Katie listened carefully, not reading the names because it was no longer easy for her to see from a distance, even with her spectacles.

'And here—'

Dr Taylor paused and looked at Katie. She became aware that all the people standing around were nudging each other and staring at her as if expecting her to say something. She looked at Dr Taylor in confusion, and while she was trying to think what to say, he went on speaking. At first his words made no sense:

'—is the Katie Makanya room.'

Katie thought she must have heard him wrong. How could there be a Katie Makanya room right next to his new operating theatre? She had had no money to give for the new building. She was only an old woman living out in the country with little strength left. She peered through her spectacles at the plaque above the door and saw her name in big letters.

A Katie Makanya room! Her heart thumped in her chest until she thought everyone must hear it, but suddenly all the people around, whites, Zulus, Indians, were speaking and shaking her hand. She could hardly hear what they said. She could only think of the honour that Dr Taylor had paid her. Even afterwards when someone pushed a paper cup of lemonade into her hand and later when a grey fog closed down about her and she was being carried on a stretcher into the women's ward of the old familiar hospital, she could think of nothing else.

In the morning she felt quite all right. When Dr Taylor made his rounds, she told him that as soon as she saw Mrs McCord again, she would be ready to go home. But he only laughed and shook his head. He said her heart was weakened by all the excitement of the ceremony, and he wanted her to stay in the hospital to be sure she was properly rested.

'But my children—'

'Don't worry. I've already sent word to Samuel.'

'But the baby! You know I've taken my granddaughter's baby – Gugu's baby – to raise. And also Fikile, who's only six.'

'I've told you not to fret. Josephine will look after them.'

Nevertheless, Katie could not help worrying. Gugu's baby was at an age when she was getting into everything, and Josephine did not have time to watch her every minute. But she did as Dr Taylor said, rested in the hospital bed and took her medicine without complaint. Every morning Mrs McCord stopped by to see how she was, but she never stayed for long, and with all the other patients listening, Katie did not like to ask about the Doctor.

One day Mrs McCord said that she was going to visit some friends upcountry but that when she came back she would spend several days with Mrs Christofersen at Adams. 'I will see you there,' she added.

Once she was gone, Katie felt very foolish, wasting her time by doing nothing. As soon as Dr Taylor said she could sit up, she sent one of the nurses down to the sewing room to bring back mending for her to do. After she was allowed to get up and walk around for an hour or two in the morning, she dressed herself and went down to the front veranda to preach to the out-patients. When Dr Taylor found her there, he decided she could go home.

Katie waited impatiently for Mrs McCord to visit the missionaries at Adams. At last she came, and Katie walked over to drink tea with her in Mrs Christofersen's house. Katie wanted to know at once how long Mrs McCord was staying.

'I'll decide when Peggy comes. She will be here for a year while her hus-band works at the university.'

'Ntombikanina is coming?' Katie gasped. 'She didn't write and tell me.'

'Perhaps she wanted to surprise you.'

Mrs Christofersen came out from her kitchen with the tea tray and sat down next to Mrs McCord. In her presence Katie felt too shy to ask any ques-tions about the Doctor. Instead she spoke of the people she and Mrs McCord had known together. Laura Nyuswa had been married and widowed and was now running a little grocery store at Umtwalumi. She didn't know what had happened to Garnett, but she had been told that Mpandlana had died during the war. Mr Champion was still in Durban.

'Do you ever see Bertha Mkize?' Mrs McCord asked suddenly.

Katie smiled affectionately. 'She used to stop and see me whenever she came to Umbumbulu to visit Violet.'

'Wasn't she in some kind of trouble?' Mrs Christofersen asked.

'Yes. In 1948 when this new government came into power, they brought up the matter of passes for women. Bertha led a protest march.'

'Remember when you and I marched together against those passes?' Mrs McCord said.

'I remember. But times were easier then. These days the government is very harsh. Bertha was banned for three years. But now she is still carrying on our work. And she is very brave. During the Zulu–Indian riots of 1949 she hid Mrs Choudree in her own house along with some other Indian women and kept them safe. It was a very bad time. Many people were killed.'

'Dr Taylor told me about those riots,' Mrs McCord murmured.

'Our people went mad,' Katie said. 'But you can't really blame them. It was a trick of this new government. They sent out their spies to stir up trouble. Chief Luthuli and Manilal Gandhi had a big job working together to calm everything down.'

Mrs Christofersen interrupted to ask if Mrs McCord remembered Albert Luthuli. 'He used to teach here at Adams. Now he's President of the African National Congress.'

'Yes,' Katie said bitterly. 'And this new government doesn't like the Congress. So they've banned Luthuli. All our educated people, all our Christian leaders, are being shut away by the government. I don't know what's going to happen. I hear the young people talking, and they are growing very restless and impatient.'

'You mustn't lose faith,' Mrs McCord said.

Katie sighed. 'Faith is not enough. The Doctor used to say that God helps those who help themselves. This is what I teach my grandchildren, but I do not know what kind of help they will find when they want to rebel.'

The shadows were growing long. Mrs Christofersen picked up her tray and went into the kitchen; her rattling of pans signalled that it was time for Katie to leave.

'Please,' Katie said when at last she was alone with Mrs McCord, 'I must go soon or else the little ones will be hungry, but first I wanted to know—'

'What little ones?'

'The two girls I'm raising. The older one, Fikile, has just started school. Her father was related to my husband, but he died last year and his wife has too many children to feed. So I've taken Fikile. She's only six but she's a big help in caring for the baby, Margaret's daughter's child.'

'But Katie, aren't you too old to raise a child?'

'No, I can still look after her very well. Moreover—' (she hesitated, but then without thinking how to say it, she blurted out in a rush of words) '—I'm still strong enough to look after the Doctor's grave.'

'What do you mean?' Mrs McCord was staring at her as though she were talking nonsense.

'Didn't you bring back his heart?'

'I don't know what you're talking about.'

'I thought you'd bring back his ashes. When he left he told me his heart would be here always.'

'Oh, Katie.' Mrs McCord started to smile in spite of the glint of tears in her grey eyes. 'He only meant he'd love—'

'He meant his heart would be buried here.' Katie spoke out very loudly to hide her uneasiness. 'Like David Livingstone.'

'You don't understand—'

'I understand very well. The Doctor told me. And the Doctor never told me any lies.'

But Mrs McCord was shaking her head. 'He wasn't telling any lies; but this was just his way of saying he would always love this place the best.' She frowned in thought. 'It's like if we say *lokho kwamqeda inhliziyo*, we don't mean "that takes the heart out of him," we're just saying "he's discouraged." It's what we call an idiom. You know this. You always knew it when you worked for him. You never made a mistake.'

'No. I never made a mistake, and I'm not making one now.' But Katie's thoughts were crumpling up, and suddenly she was no longer so sure. She just felt very tired, too tired to argue, and all she wanted was to sit alone in her rocking-chair and look out over the hills. As though from a long distance, she heard Mrs McCord telling her to come tomorrow for another visit. She slowly pulled herself out of her chair, reached down for her walking-stick, and began to push it along the floor of the veranda to find the steps.

Beyond Mrs Christofersen's garden the road was wide and smooth, and Katie could move more quickly. There had been no road through the tangled bush and grass on this part of the mission when she had first come to work for the Doctor. Everything was different now, with the motor cars and the younger missionaries always in a hurry and new houses blocking off the old short-cuts. Even the original dispensary was different now, with its bright curtains hanging at the windows and a teacher living there and planting rose bushes in the back where the patients used to sit and wait on the grass. The paths Katie knew were overgrown, and it took her a long time to follow the wide road past the Principal's house, the dormitories, the big student dining-room, the classroom buildings and on down towards the river. The footbridge over that still pool under the trees had washed away, and no one had bothered to repair it because of the new road across the river and up past Jeena's store. But it was no longer Jeena's store. It belonged to Mohammed now.

The hill looked very long and steep. Halfway up, Katie had to stop and rest on an outcrop of rock. Sitting there, she looked back over the mission and beyond to the mountains purpling against the sky. 'It's easy to be a Christian when you can stand on top of a mountain,' the Doctor had told her once. But she could no longer walk as far as the mountains, and nothing was easy any more.

During the last few years she had missed Charlotte, who had died in Johannesburg soon after her retirement. And all the old missionaries were gone. Most of the people who had lived on these hills when she was young were also gone, and those few who were left were old, like her, and no longer able to do anything but sit at home. She felt weary. For the first time since her husband died, she felt the tears splashing down on her cheeks as she thought of the Doctor, whose life was finished now, and that mad clown, Mbambo, who'd promised her long ago that even after death he would run and run until he found her. The Doctor, Mbambo, Ndeya – all gone. And she had nothing left except the little ones at home. It was time for their dinner and they would be frightened if she stayed away too long . . .

Now already she was passing Jeena's store, and her two little girls were waiting on the veranda.

'*We* Fikile,' she shouted. '*We—*' She almost said 'Gugu' but no, it's the baby's mother who's Gugu. Strange that in this moment she could not think of her baby's name. She was trying to remember it as she pushed her walking-stick ahead of her to make sure she did not stumble. It was hard for her to see the rocks which might be lying in the path, for already the mountains were eating up the sun. But she could see her hand very clearly, her fingers hooked over the knob of her stick, her knuckles crooked with rheumatism, and the skin of her wrist as black and wrinkled as a dried prune.

'*We* Fikile,' she shouted again as the older child ran forward and skidded to a stop with the little one close behind, clinging to her dress and stretching her head around to peer at Katie out of her wide eyes.

'What's the matter, child?' Katie laughs. 'Why are you suddenly so shy? Do you think I'm a witch?'

'No, Granny,' Fikile answers for her.

'Let her speak for herself,' Katie says, glancing down at her great-grand-daughter. 'Don't be frightened, little one. I'm not a witch. I'm just your old, old ancestor, and tonight, after we've eaten, I'll tell you a story . . .'

California

1993

It is forty years since I last saw Katie. I drove out to Adams two days before I returned to America and found her waiting for me on the veranda of the little house Ndeya had built for her when she was young. The first question she asked was whether I had started writing her book.

'Not yet, Auntie,' I said. 'I've just finished transcribing all those tapes. But as soon as I'm settled in California—'

'How long will it take?' she asked with a flash of her old impatience.

'I don't know.'

Her shoulders drooped but only for a moment before she straightened up and started talking with determined cheerfulness about her children and her grandchildren. I've wondered since if she recognised the significance of her swollen ankles and shortness of breath, because six months later she was dead of congestive heart failure. After a large memorial service at the hospital and a smaller funeral in the church, she was buried in the mission cemetery among the dahlias and lilies she had once planted in memory of the Doctor.

Breinigsville, PA USA
11 July 2010
241528BV00003B/24/A